INVENTORY
OF
MARYLAND
BIBLE RECORDS

VOLUME ONE

Prepared Under the Supervision of
Robert W. Barnes
Chairman, Bible Survey Committee
Genealogical Council of Maryland

HERITAGE BOOKS
2012

HERITAGE BOOKS

AN IMPRINT OF HERITAGE BOOKS, INC.

Books, CDs, and more—Worldwide

For our listing of thousands of titles see our website
at
www.HeritageBooks.com

Published 2012 by
HERITAGE BOOKS, INC.
Publishing Division
100 Railroad Ave. #104
Westminster, Maryland 21157

Other Heritage Books by the author:

Inventory of Maryland Bible Records, Volume 1

Directory of Maryland Burial Grounds

Directory of Maryland Church Records
Edna A. Kanely, under the auspices of the
Genealogical Council of Maryland

International Standard Book Numbers
Paperbound: 978-0-940907-12-6
Clothbound: 978-0-7884-9170-2

TABLE OF CONTENTS

iii

PREFACE

The Genealogical Council of Maryland was established in 1976 as a coord-
inating mechanism for the various organizations in Maryland which had an interest in genealogy. In the Spring of 1982, the Council, noting an interest in
Bible records within the member groups, appointed a Bible Survey Committee to
promote the collection of Bible records and to make them accessible.

This book is the first publication resulting from the state-wide work of
the Bible Survey Committee. Hopefully the publication of the current volume
will encourage continued effort. In this respect, the Committee has already
collected several hundred additional records for inclusion in the next volume.

The Council is grateful for the many persons, both within the member
societies and in the general public, who have contributed to this project,
which is being accomplished entirely by volunteers. It would be impossible to
name each person. However, special thanks are due Mr. Robert W. Barnes who,
despite his full-time employment as an educator and his active practice in
genealogy, finds time to do considerable pro bono work for genealogical societies. His devotion in promoting the Bible project, his managing the collection
process and his personal research have been essential to the project.

S. E. Clements
Chairman, Genealogical Council of Maryland

v

INTRODUCTION

This Volume I contains information on about 2700 Bible records that were located in the first phase of the Bible Survey Project. It consists of two main sections: the Bibles and the Surnames section.

Only essential data is recorded in the Bibles section. The Bible is listed under the name of the principal family or families contained in the record. The date of publication, if known, or in some cases the date the Bible was inscribed as being given given to an individual; the year of the earliest birth; the year of the earliest marriage; the other surnames in the record; any places of residence mentioned; and, finally, the location of the records are given.

The Surnames section is an alphabetical index of the surnames in given in the records. Note that this index does not include the title family name of the various records.

The reader should be aware that there are several possible sources of error in this work. The source document might not be accurate. A comparsion of the Bible publication date and the earliest dates recorded therein shows that many dates were entered years after the early events. While some of the records are the Bibles themselves or photocopies of the Bibles, many of the records are transcriptions, made by unidentifed persons at unknown times. Some might even be transcriptions of transcriptions, and others might have been intentionally edited for a variety of reasons. Finally the preparation process involved abstraction, then in many cases, transcription onto uniform forms, followed by entry into a computer. Thus there are several potential sources of inaccuracy and omission in the Inventory.

As outlined above, this first Inventory of Maryland Bible Records is the result of the planning and work of many people. Initially a few member societies appointed Bible records committees who inventoried Bible records already held by the Society, and who arranged for Bible Copying Days when members and the public were encouraged to bring the Bibles to be copied.

During the last few years, many societies have participated in the project, and some have extended the original scope of the project. The Harford County and the Howard County Genealogical Societies have published volumes of Bible Records. The Prince George's County and the Upper Shore Genealogical Societies have published many Bible records in their periodicals. Both the Prince George's and the Carroll County Societies have published surname indices to the Bibles they hold. The Upper Shore Genealogical Society, at its first Bible Copying Day made photocopies of 120 Bibles. One member of the Baltimore County group attends estate auctions looking for Bibles to copy or purchase. She not only transcribes the records, but does additional research in census, tombstone, and vital records to fill out family group sheets, which accompany the Bible records to the Society's files. To date, some 400 additional records have been inventoried for inclusion in Volume II. The success of this ongoing project is due entirely to the volunteer work of many members of the societies.

Lastly, the data for this Volume was entered into a computer, edited, and indexed by S. Eugene Clements.

Robert W. Barnes

ABBREVIATIONS

Maryland Counties

AA	Ann Arundel	How.	Howard
Balto.	Baltimore	Mont.	Montgomery
(Balto.	City indicates city)	PG	Prince George's
Caro.	Caroline	QA	Queen Mary's
Chas.	Charles	St.M.	Saint Mary's
Carr.	Carroll	Som.	Somerset
Calv.	Calvert	Talb.	Talbot
Dor.	Dorchester	Wash.	Washington
Fred.	Frederick	Wico.	Wicomico
Harf.	Harford	Worc.	Worcester

ABBREVIATIONS USED IN DATA NOTES

pd	Publication date of Bible
ins	Inscribed date Used if pd not known, but Bible was inscribed as gift or otherwise dated
eb	Earliest birth
em	Earliest marriage
rb	Records begin
rs	Record span.
res	Residence of family where noted on report.
on	Other surnames in the record.
dep	Depository of the record.
pub	Publication containing record.

ABBREVIATIONS FOR DEPOSITORIES

AAGS - Anne Arundel Genealogical Society

AAHS - Anne Arundel Historical Society

BCGS - Baltimore County Genealogical Society

BCHS - Baltimore County Historical Society

CCGS - Carroll County Genealogical Society

CLDS - Family History Branch Library, Columbia, MD.
(Church of the Latter Day Saints)

DAR - Daughters of the American Revolution Library, Washington, DC.

DSA - Delaware State Archives, Dover, Delaware

FCHS - Frederick County Historical Society, Frederick, MD.

GPL - George Peabody Library of Johns Hopkins University, Baltimore, MD.

HCGS - Harford County Genealogical Society

HOGS - Howard County Genealogical Society

MdHr - Gift Collection of the Maryland State Archives.

MdSAR - Maryland Society of the Sons of the American Revolution.
(Applications for membership)

MHS - Maryland Historical Society, Baltimore, MD.
MHS/FCA indicates Filing Case A at MHS.

MSA - Maryland State Archives, Annapolis, MD.
The accession number is given in parenthesis.

MCHS - Montgomery County Historical Society

NGS - National Genealogical Society, Arlington, VA.
Bible records collection as given in Schreiner-Yantis,
"Genealogy and Local History Books in Print" 4th ed.
vol. II pgs. 1666-1684.

PGCGS - Prince George's County Genealogical Society.

PSL - Pennsylvania State Library, Harrisburg, PA.

SMGS - St. Mary's County Genealogical Society.

WaCFL - Washington County Free Library

WaCHS - Washington County Historical Society

WCFL - Wicomico County Free Library

ABBREVIATIONS FOR PUBLICATIONS

Ardery I - Mrs. William B. Ardery: "Kentucky Records" (Baltimore: Genealogical Publishing Co., 1981) reprint.

Ardery II - Mrs. William B. Ardery: "Kentucky (Court and other) Records"
(Baltimore: Genealogical Publishing Co., 1984) reprint, vol.II.

Austin - Jeannette H. Austin: "Georgia Bible Records" (Baltimore:
Genealogical Publishing Co., 1985).

Burnett - not identified

BMGS - "Bulletin of the Maryland Genealogical Society."

BMORS - "Bulletin of the Maryland Original Research Society of Baltimore."
(Genealogical Publishing Co., 1973) reprint, three parts in one.

BRP I - "Bible Records of Pennsylvania" (Pennsylvania State Chairman
Genealogical Records), Pennsylvania State Library, Harrisburg.

ABBREVIATIONS FOR PUBLICATIONS, continued

CC - "Chesapeake Cousins" Upper Shore Genealogical Society. Copies at MHS.

CH - "Calvert Historian" (The Calvert Historical Society). Copies at MHS.

CMF - Anna Cartlidge: "Miscellaneous Families" 3 vols. typescript at BCGS.

DAR Mag. -"Daughters of the American Revolution Magazine"

DCGM - "Dorchester County Genealogical Magazine" Copies at MHS.

DBR - "Delaware Bible Records" 12 vols. Delaware State Archives.

DOBR - Nellie M. Marshall: "Bible Records of Dorchester County, Maryland, 1612-1969" (Cambridge: Dorchester County Historical Society, 1971). Copies at DAR.

Fort - "Mid-South Bible Records," (First Assumption Chapter, DAR, 1973) Copy in the Library of Congress.

GKF - "Genealogies of Kentucky Families" (Baltimore: Genealogical Publishing Co.) 3 vols. reprint.

GPF/B - "Genealogies of Pennsylvania Families from the Pennsylvania Magazine of History and Biography." (Baltimore: Genealogical Publishing Co.) One volume.

GPF/PGM - "Genealogies of Pennsylvania Families from the Pennsylvania Genealogical Magazine" (Baltimore: Genealogical Publishing Co.) Three volumes.

HBFR - "Harford County Bible and Family Records" copied by the Gov. William Paca Chapter, DAR; typescript at MHS.

HCMR - "Howard County Maryland Records" volume 5, Howard County Genealogical Society.

KBG1 - "Bible and Gravestone Records of Kent County, Maryland" collected and indexed by London Bridge Chapter, DAR; 1933; Copies at MHS, DAR.

KBG2 - 1934 issue of KBG1 above. Copies at MHS, DAR.

KBR - "Family Bible Records of Kent County, Maryland;" collected and indexed by London Bridge Chapter, DAR; 1937; typescripts at MHS, DAR.

KBT - "Bible and Tombstone Records, Kent County, Maryland;" collected and indexed by the London Bridge Chapter, DAR; Copies at MHS, DAR.

Lester - Memory Aldridge Lestory, "Old Southern Bible Records;" (Baltimore, MD.: Genealogical Publishing Co., 1974.)

Lu - Helen Mason Lu and Gwen Blomquiest Neumann, "Revolutionary War Period: Bible, Family, and Marriage Records, Gleaned from Pension Applications" 5 vols. 1980-1983. Copies at MHS, Library of Congress.

MBR - "Miscellaneous Bible Records"; (source unknown); 2 vols. at the Baltimore County Genealogical Society.

ABBREVIATIONS FOR PUBLICATIONS, continued

McAdams - Mrs. Harry K. McAdams "Kentucky Pioneer and Court Records"; (Baltimore, MD. Genealogical Publishing Co., 1981)

MDG - Maryland and Delaware Genealogist

MGB - Maryland Genealogical Bulletin, (Hayes)   Copy at MHS.

MdGRC - Maryland Genealogical Records Committee, NSDAR. at the DAR Library, Washington, D.C.

MG - "Maryland Genealogies" 2 vols. (Baltimore, MD.; Genealogical Publishing Company, 1980)

MMAF - "Michael, Mitchell, and Allied Families of Harford County", typescript at BCGS.

MMG - Maryland Magazine of Genealogies: 5 vols.

NGSQ - National Genealogical Society Quarterly.

NEHGR - New England Historical and Genealogical Register

OBR - Cooch's Bridge Chapter, DAR "Old Bible Records with Charts and Genealogical Sketches"; (typescript, 1941-44) at MSA.

O'Brien - Margaret O'Brien, "Calvert County, Maryland Family Records 1670-1929"

OSR - "Ohio Source Records from the Ohio Genealogical Quarterly" (Baltimore, MD.: Genealogical Publishing Co. 1986)

SCHM - South Carolina Historical Magazine. Copies at GPL.

VSL - Guide to Bible Records in the Virginia State Library. Richmond, Va.

WMG - Western Maryland Genealogy, ed. by Donna Valley Russell.   Copies at MHS, GPL.

Wright I - Dora Lee Wright, "Index of Bible Records in the National Archives, Washington, D.C. " in MDG 7-4:71.

Wright II - Dora Lee Wright, "Bible Records in the National Archives" NGSQ 55-2:149-f.

Yingling - Mrs. William F. Yingling,"Bible Records" book in DAR Library, copies of individual records in BCGS vertical file.

BIBLES

(Abbreviations are given on pages ix-xii)

A001 John ABBOT Bible; rs 1775-1820; res Georgetown, DC.;
     dep VSL (acc. #29937).
A002 ABBOTT Bible; pd 1634; eb 1689; pub BMORS 2:84.
A003 ABBOTT Bible; eb 1754; em 1770; on RUFFNER; pub MBR 1:5.
A004 ABBOTT-COMAN Bible; pd 1847; eb 1844; em 1867; on SUTER, HAMILTON,
     OSGOOD, COMAN; dep MHS/FCA.
A005 Edward ADAMS Bible; pd 1781; eb 1732; em 1756; on BOWNESS, MASON, CANNON;
     res Dor. Co., MD; pub DAR Mag. 66-10:673; dep MHS/FCA.
A006 Edward ADAMS Bible; em 1735; res Dor. Co., MD; pub MGB 7:1.
A007 ADAMS Family Record; eb 1756; on WILLIS; pub DAR (in MdGRC 13:111).
A008 ADAMS Bible; eb 1757; em 1787; res DE; pub MGB 6:27,37.
A009 Rev. Eli ADAMS Bible; eb 1785; em 1838; on BEEKS; res Snow Hill, MD;
     dep MHS/FCA.
A010 ADAMS Bible; eb 1790; em 1837; on FLOWERS, AARON, TALL; res Dor. Co., MD;
     pub DOBR,7.
A011 ADAMS-CARVER Bible; eb 1792; em 1847; on CARVER;
     pub DAR Mag. Nov. 1960 p.660.
A012 ADAMS-EDGELL-TWIFORD Bible; eb 1797; em 1820; on CRANOR, EDGEN, EDGELL,
     TURFORD, TWIFORD; dep MHS/FCA.
A013 ADAMS Bible; eb 1850; em 1848; on MILBOURNE, MARTEN, WHITE, GUY;
     dep BCGS (from DAR).
A014 Orrin H. ADAMS Bible; pd 1860; eb 1844; dep BCGS.
A015 ADAMS Family Record; eb 1871; em 1870; on WILSON, HACKETT, LANKFORD,
     VICKERS, DAVIS; res Dor. Co., MD; pub DOBR,27.
A016 ADAMS Bible; pd 1872; dep BCGS (deaths only).
A017 Rev. Henry ADDISON Bible; pd 1723; eb 1703; em 1701; on TASKER, SMITH,
     DULANY, MURDOCK, CALLIS; pub BMGS 17-3:127; 20-4:338.
A018 Rev. Henry ADDISON Prayer Book; eb 1754; em 1751; on DULANY, KNIGHT,
     MURDOCK, CALLIS; pub BMGS 20-4:337.
A019 A. ADDISON Bible; pd 1838; eb 1803; em 1831; on THOMPSON, WEST, INGLE,
     CALLIS; res Leesburg, VA; Balto., MD; Wash., DC; pub BMGS 17-3:129;
     20-4:340.
A020 ADKINS-BROWN Bible; pd 1824; eb 1770; em 1822; on HAZELLWOOD, PETTY,
     ERWIN; dep MHS/FCA.
A021 ADY Bible; eb 1743; em 1804; on YARLEY, ROBISON, PRESTON, WOLSON;
     pub BMGS 20-3:237; dep BCGS.
A022 ADY Bible; rb 1743; on AYERS, ROBISON, YARLEY; res Harf. Co., MD;
     dep HCGS.
A023 ADY Bible; pd 1769; eb 1771; em 1770; on McATEE, STANDIFORD, LIWES,
     PRESTON, WILSON; dep BCGS.
A024 ADY Bible; pd 1759; rb 180(?); em 1770; on McATEE, STANDIFORD, BUCKLEY,
     CAIN; res Balto., MD; pub BMGS 20-3:239.
A025 ADY Bible; rb 1770; on McATEE, PRESTON, STANDIFORD, WILSON; res Harf.
     Co., MD; dep HCGS.
A026 ADY Bible; pd 1840; eb 1803; em 1814; pub BMGS 20-3:238; dep BCGS.
A027 AILES Bible; rb 1771; on PHILLIPS; res Chester Co., PA; dep HCGS.
A028 AIREY Bible; pd 1844; eb 1791; em 1837; on CARROLL, CLINE, RHODES,
     WALTERS, HYLTON, McKENLEY, GEIST, KAPLAN; res Balto., MD; VA; CA;
     dep MHS/FCA.
A029 AISQUITH-KLOMAN Bible; pd 1778; eb 1804; on NELSON, HELM, KLOMAN;
     res Perryman, MD; Warrenton & Fauquier Co. VA;
     dep MHS/FCA.

1

INVENTORY OF MARYLAND BIBLE RECORDS

A030 ALBAUGH Bible; rs 1777-1899; on SPURRIER, MILLER; res Fred. & Carr. Cos.,
MD; dep MSA (G-863:1).
A031 ALBRIGHT Bible; eb 1839; em 1886; on ROWE, KONE, BOGGS, PRICHETT,
HOFFMAN, WHITTINGTON; dep MHS/FCA (Hoffman Family Records).
A032 ALCOCK Bible; eb 1690; on SAVAGE; res St. Clement Dane's Parish, London,
Eng.; dep MHS/FCA.
A033 John P. ALDRIDGE Bible; eb 1802; em 1832; on GILL, ROBINSON; res Mont.
Co., MD; KY; pub Lester,4.
A034 John Simpson ALDRIDGE Bible; eb 1761; em 1783; on LAKIN, LAYTON;
res Fred. Co., MD; IN; pub Lester,4.
A035 ALEXANDER Bible; eb 1756; em 1790; on SHREVES, STROTHER; pub MBR 1:4.
A036 ALEXANDER-LAWSON Bible; pd 1744; eb 1766; on SMITH, LAWSON; dep MHS/FCA.
A037 ALLER Bible; eb 1783; on ALER; dep MHS/FCA.
A038 Patrick ALLISON Bible; pd 1802; eb 1792; em 1787; on BROWN, BUCHANAN,
BRUNE, MORRISON, RIXDELL, TIFFANY, DOBBIN; res Balto., MD;
dep MHS/FCA.
A039 ALLNUTT Bible; eb 1835; em 1833; on BLAKE, WILLIAMS, ROBERTSON;
dep MHS/FCA.
A040 ALRICKS Bible; pd 1858; eb 1837; em 1859; on PEGRAM, STEELE, GARY,
FOSTER; dep MHS/FCA.
A041 ALTER Bible; pd 1710; on GROFF; res Balto. Co., MD; dep CCGS.
A042 ALVORD Bible; pd 1856; eb 1819; em 1788; on POTTS, CHESTER, WAIT, CHAPIN,
WOLFONBARGER, PATTERSON, on McCORMICK, EARLY; res IN;
dep LDS Columbia, MD.
A043 AMMERMAN Bible; eb 1822; em 1841; on KINSLOWE; dep BCGS.
A044 O. H. AMOS Bible; eb 1792; on LEE, CALDWELL; res Harf. Co., MD;
pub CMF 1:87.
A045 ANDERSON-WARFIELD Bible; eb 1727; em 1811; on DUVALL, LOWNDES, WOODWARD,
GRIFFITH, MEEK, WARFIELD; dep MHS/FCA.
A046 ANDERSON-PARSLY Record; on PARSLEY; pub BMGS 16-1:38.
A047 ANDERSON Bible; eb 1773; em 1812; on WOODWARD, DISNEY, MOLER;
res Davidsonville, AA Co., MD; dep MHS/FCA.
A048 ANDERSON Bible; eb 1775; em 1812; rs 1775-1941; on DISNEY, DULANY,
WOODWARD; res AA. Co., MD; Moles, OH;
dep MHS/FCA; dep MSA (G-236:53 with D-150).
A049 James ANDERSON Bible; eb 1776; em 1774; on BOYD; res MD & York Co., PA;
pub GPF/B, 839.
A050 Mrs. Saulsbury Thomas ANDREW Bible; eb 1835; em 1861; on STANTON;
dep MHS/FCA.
A051 ANDREW Bible; rb 1819; on KEEN, MILLER, FORWOOD, FISHER, TALBOTT, WILLIS,
JACKSON, GEORGE; res Harf. Co., MD; dep HCGS.
A052 ANDREWS Bible; eb 1842; em 1840; on PRITCHETT; res Dor. Co., MD;
pub DOBR,7.
A053 ANDREWS-MEDFORD Bible; eb 1711; em 1734; on PARKER, ORREL, MEDFORD,
THOMAS, WILLIS, ELLIOTT, CARROLL, JEFFERSON, FLETCHER, SIMMONS;
res Dor. Co., MD; pub DOBR,8.
A054 ANDREWS Scrap book; eb 1744; em 1844; on STEVENS, MEDFORD, CORKRAN,
BONNER, CARROLL, WRIGHT, PARVIN; dep MHS/FCA.
A055 ANES Bible; pd 1791; eb 1753; on HASELTINE, BARNES, PEABODY, EATON,
BAYLEY; res NH; MA; VT; pub HCMR 5:72.
A056 ANTHONY Bible; rs 1797-1807; res Talb. Co., MD; dep MSA (G-564:19).
A057 APPLE Bible; pd 1813; eb 1780; em 1815; on HAUSE; res York Co., PA;
pub BMGS 19-2:124.
A058 APPLEGARTH Bible; eb 1877; em 1873; on BENNETT, ROBBINS; res Dor. Co.,
MD; pub DCGM 1-3:6.

BIBLES

A059 APPLEGARTH Bible; eb 1874; em 1872; on HUBBARD, SPEDDEN, PHILLIPS, MOORE,
      EVANS, COLLINS, SMITH, BACON; res Dor. Co., MD; pub DCGM 2-5:11.
A060 APPLEWHITE Bible; eb 1760; em 1784; on MOORE, JONES;
      pub MBR 1:3 (in BCGS).
A061 ARCHER Bible; pd 1799; eb 1777; em 1802; on STUMP; dep MHS/FCA.
A062 ARDINGER Bible; eb 1813; em 1835; res Williamsport, MD;
      pub DAR Mag. Dec. 1960 p.711.
A063 ARDINGER Bible; pd 1815; eb 1835; em 1852; dep BCGS.
A064 ARDINGER Bible; pd 1867; eb 1840; em 1839; on STEINMENTS, SMITH, GARRISH;
      res Hagerstown, MD; dep BCGS.
A065 ARDINGER Bible; pd 1870; em 1902; on GARRISH, ZELLER, HUMMER, ROTH, WOOD;
      res Wash. Co., MD; VA; PA; dep BCGS.
A066 John ARMACOST Family Record; eb 1789; em 1811; dep BCGS.
A067 Rezin ARMACOST Bible; eb 1830; em 1854; dep MHS/FCA.
A068 ARMACOST Bible; pd 1848; eb 1852; em 1850; on TRACEY, BURGOYNE, EBAUGH;
      dep BCGS; dep MHS/FCA.
A069 Samuel ARMOR Bible; pd 1914; eb 1766; em 1788; on GUY, SENTMAN, BROWN,
      BENNETT, SEIDENSTRICKER, SCOLEY, ADRIAN; res Hagerstown, MD;
      Springfield, IL; dep MHS/FCA.
A070 ARNOLD Bible; eb 1806; on HARSHMAN, YOUNG, SIEGLER, WHIPP, FINK,
      MILLER; res Burkittsville, MD; pub MGB 14:8.
A071 ARNOLD Bible; pd 1877; eb 1880; em 1879; on FLATER, GREEN, SHAMER, GRAY,
      LOCKARD, HARTZEL, POOL, HILLSINGER; res Carr. Co., MD; dep CCGS.
A072 ARTHUR-COLE Bible; pd 1876; eb 1858; em 1873; on COLE; dep MHS/FCA.
A073 ARTHUR Bible; eb 1883; em 1882; on WAREHIME, PRICE, RINEHART, MYERS,
      GRABILL; res Waynesboro, PA; pub DAR (in Yingling).
A074 ASBURY Bible; eb 1761; em 1780; on THORNTON, CLAIRE, MURDEN, LYNE,
      NEWSON, ROGERS, DANIELS, WATTS, ROBERTSON, RANDLE, WEST;
      dep MBR 1:1 (in BCGS).
A075 William ASHLEY Bible; eb 1785; em 1781; res MD; SC; pub LU 1:92.
A076 ASHLEY-ELBURN Bible; eb 1810; em 1860; on De FORD, ELBURN, SMITH;
      pub BTR (in MHS); pub DAR (in MdGRC 12:104).
A077 ATHEY Bible; eb 1813; em 1810; on JAMES; res Marietta, OH;
      pub CMF 1:70 (in BCGS).
A078 David ATKINSON Bible; eb 1794; em 1822; on JONES, WATERS; res Harf. Co.,
      MD; dep MHS/FCA.
A079 George ATKINSON Bible; eb 1776; em 1787; on RUSSUM, WOLLFORD, STANFORD,
      DASHIELL; res Som. Co., MD; dep MHS/FCA.
A080 William F. ATKINSON Bible; pd 1855; dep MHS/FCA (no family records).
A081 ATKINSON Bible; eb 1822; em 1847; pub MDG 22-4:107.
A082 ATLEE Bible; eb 1767; em 1861; on JONES, STANSBURY, SLINGLUFF, DOWNEY,
      WORTHINGTON, SWOPE; dep MHS/FCA.
A083 ATWELL Bible; eb 1814; res Balto., MD; dep MHS/FCA.
A084 AUGHINBAUGH Bible; pd 1825; eb 1799; em 1828; on HUBLEY, TAYLOR, LACHMAN,
      BRICKER, STORK, LAWRENCE; res Cumberland Co., PA; IN; IL;
      pub DAR (in MdGRC 33:83).
A085 AUGHINBAUGH Bible; pd 1881; eb 1840; em 1870; on WERNER, GILLEN,
      McCAUSLAND, THOMPSON, LARGART, GREENAWALT; res PA;
      pub DAR (in MdGRC).
A086 AULD Bible; pd 1634; eb 1668; em 1689; on RUE, SHERWOOD, HADDAWAY,
      COOPER, CARROLL, WRIGHTSON, PEPPER; dep MSA (G-125, G-142).
A087 AULD Bible; pd 1850; eb 1767; em 1793; on WILSON, ANTHONY, SEARS,
      HAMBLETON, HARPER, THOMPSON; res Balto., MD; dep MHS/FCA.
A088 AULD Record; eb 1767; em 1784; on WILTBANK, CATMAN, RIDGEWAY, HARMAN,
      COOPER, HARRISON; res Talb. Co., MD; dep MHS/FCA.
A089 AULD Bible; eb 1828; em 1860; on CLARK; dep MHS/FCA.

3

INVENTORY OF MARYLAND BIBLE RECORDS

A090 AULD Bible; rs 1828-1880; dep MSA (G-518:2).
A091 AVESSER Bible; pd 1872; eb 1848; em 1872; res Balto., MD; dep MHS/FCA.
A092 AYDELOTT Bible; eb 1740; em 1770; pub GPF/PGM, 818.

B001 BABYLON Bible; pd 1873; eb 1883; on HOOVER, KOONTZ, SMITH, LERNARD,
     BRILHART; res Carr. Co., MD; dep CCGS.
B002 BACHER Bible; eb 1890; em 1877; on KAHLER, ASKEW, SCHLIER, LeFEVRE;
     res Balto. MD; Phila. PA; dep MSA (G-493).
B003 BADEN Bible; eb 1900; em 1895; on ROBERTSON; dep MHS/FCA.
B004 BADEN Bible; pd 1852; em 1829; on GREENWELL, WEBB, WISE, WILLIAMS, BLAKE,
     ROBERTSON, ALLNUT, LOWE, OWENS, THOMPSON; res Calv. & Talb. Cos.,
     MD; dep MHS/FCA.
B005 BADEN Bible; pd 1834; eb 1805; em 1829; on GREENWALL, THOMPSON; res Calv.
     Co., MD; dep MHS/FCA.
B006 BAER Bible; pd 1843; eb 1825; em 1824; on RIDGELY, STEWART, LUCUS, BROWN,
     FESSLER, PRICE, CHERRY, HOBBS; dep MHS/FCA (may have been extracted
     from two Bibles).
B007 David BAGGARLY Bible; eb 1761; em 1782; on BELT, McKEE; res PG Co., MD;
     TN; pub LU 2:26.
B008 Abraham BAGGS Bible; pd 1801; eb 1767; em 1800; on ROE, MILBOURN; pub DAR
     (in MdGRC 35:89).
B009 BAGGS Bible; rs 1767-1886; res QA & Caro. Cos., MD;
     dep MSA (G-223:42 with D-150).
B010 BAGGS-ROE Bible; eb 1767; em 1800; on MILBOURN, KEIRN, ROE; res QA Co.,
     MD; dep MHS/FCA.
B011 BAGGS-STARKEY Bible; pd 1804; eb 1769; em 1796; on PRICE, BLUNT, STARKEY;
     dep MHS/FCA.
B012 Abraham BAILE Bible; dep MHS/FCA.
B013 Isaac C. BAILE Bible; eb 1819; em 1811; on HAINES, SMITH, CASSELL, NAILL,
     DEVILBISS, SNADER, NICODEMUS, EBY, REPP, GILBERT; dep BCGS.
B014 BAIL Bible; eb 1844; em 1842; on CASSELL, OSLER; dep BCGS.
B015 BAILEY Bible; eb 1796; em 1825; on ATKINS; pub DAR (in MdGRC 13:161).
B016 BAIN Bible; pd 1752; eb 1799; res Balto. Co., MD; pub NGSQ 59-1:33.
B017 BAIRD Bible; eb 1764; em 1794; on NISBIT; res Zanesville, OH;
     pub MGB 15:6.
B018 William BAKER Bible; pd 1769; eb 1752; em 1780; on BURNESTON; res Fred.
     Co., MD; VA; dep MHS/FCA.
B019 BAKER Bible; eb 1810; em 1837; on CAREINS, GREENLAND, MILLS, BRUCE,
     GILBERT, WELLS, MONROE; dep BCGS.
B020 BAKER Bible; pd 1831; eb 1816; res Cecil Co., MD; dep MHS/FCA;
     dep MSA (G-205).
B021 BAKER Bible; pd 1834; eb 1797; em 1820; on HEATH, BAXTER, TOMLENSON,
     BOYLEN, HUFF, McDANIEL; pub MGB 16:41; 21:26.
B022 BAKER Bible; pd 1877; eb 1803; res Worc. Co., MD; pub NGSQ 65-2:134.
B023 BAKER-RICHARDSON Bible; eb 1845; em 1869; res Snow Hill, MD;
     pub MDG 23-3:86.
B024 Ephraim BALDWIN Bible; eb 1717; em 1803; on SAGE, SHEPHEARD, ELDER, PEAK,
     WITBECK, JAMISON, CROXALL, GITTINGS; dep MHS/FCA.
B025 Silas BALDWIN Bible; pd 1791; eb 1747; res Harf. Co., MD;
     pub NGSQ 57-1:45; pub MDG 8-1:16.
B026 BALDWIN Bible; eb 1799; em 1828; on CHAPEL, SHELDON; res CT; OH;
     dep MHS/FCA.
B027 BALDWIN Bible; eb 1826; em 1853; on McVEIGH; dep MHS/FCA.
B028 BALL Bible; eb 1762; em 1789; on ADAMS, RICHARDSON, BRAWNER, BARNES,
     RAMES, MORRIS, MILLER, GILCHRIST; pub MBR 1:7 (in BCGS).

BIBLES

B029 BALL-POWELL Bible; pd 1846; eb 1810; em 1840; on RIGGIN; res Pocomoke
City, MD; dep MHS/FCA.
B030 BALLARD Bible; eb 1804; em 1857; on WOODWARD, LYMAN, HARRY , MITCHELL,
GRIFFIN, TURPIN, GASKINS, MARTIN, SHAWN; res Eastern Shore, MD;
Wash., DC; dep AAGS.
B031 BALLARD Bible; eb 1827; em 1926; on WATERS, LOOKERMAN, CRAIG, ROBERTSON;
res Soms. Co., MD; dep MHS/FCA.
B032 BALLARD Bible; eb 1838; em 1826; on ROBERTSON, CURTIS, LOOKLERMAN; res
Soms. Co., MD; dep MHS/FCA.
B033 BALLARD-SMITH Bible; eb 1811; em 1832; on SMITH, SNYDER, HOPKINS, DORMAN,
ADREAN, OGIER; res Soms. Co., MD; dep MHS/FCA.
B034 BALLIN Bible; rs 1800-1968; on BELL, CLEMENTS, DARDEN, EDGER, ELDRIDGE,
HALL, HICKS, HOPKINS, KNIGHTON; res Rockville, MD; Wash. DC; VA;
dep VSL (acc. #30433).
B035 BALTZELL Bible; eb 1752; em 1773; on HOUCK, GIBBS, RIDGELY, FORD, PARKER,
BUCHANAN, PARTRIDGE, WELCH, KENNEDY, MACKENHEIMER, RINGGOLD,
THOMAS, GILL; res Fred. Co. & Balto. Co., MD; VA; Germany;
dep MHS/FCA.
B036 BANDEL Bible; pd 1839; eb 1786; em 1805; on BAXTER, CLARKE, JOHNSON,
KERNER, McJILTON, SAGASER, THOMAS; pub BMGS 24-3:247; dep CCGS;
dep NGS Bible Records Collection.
B037 BANDY Bible; eb 1813; em 1841; on HUTCHISON, WARNER, LUSTER, PASCO,
McGUFFIN; pub MBR 1:39 (in BCGS).
B038 John BANKSON Bible; eb 1788; em 1787; on MICKLE; res MD; PA; pub LU 2:60.
B039 BARAKMAN Bible; pd 1843; eb 1846; em 1845; on BLAKE, GOODYEAR; res CA;
IL; pub BMGS 10-2:51.
B040 BARBER Bible; pd 1808; eb 1777; em 1803; on BRISCOE, HANSON, PLUMMER,
YATES; res St.M & PG Cos., MD; pub NGSQ 22-4:89.
B041 BARCLAY Bible; rb 1748; KEEN, MILLER, FORWOOD, FISHER, TALBOTT, WILLIS,
JACKSON, GEORGE; res Harf. Co., MD; dep HCGS.
B042 BARCLAY Bible; pd 1789; eb 1778; em 1801; on STOKES, FORWOOD, HALL,
SCARBOROUGH, JOHNS, ALBERT, ROBINSON, FISHER; res Harf. Co., MD;
dep MHS/FCA.
B043 BARCLAY-STOKES Bible; rb 1745; on STOKES, FORWOOD, SCARBOROUGH, HALL,
ROBINSON, CAVENDER, HARVEY, GILL, FISHER, ALBERT, JOHNS, LEWIN,
HEAPS, JOHNSON; res Harf. Co., MD; dep HCGS.
B044 BARICKMAN Bible; pd 1828; eb 1790; em 1816; pub BMGS 10-2:51.
B045 BARKER Bible; eb 1768; on METCALF; dep MHS/FCA.
B046 BARKLEY-STOKES Bible; pd 1789; eb 1778; em 1800; res prob. Harf. Co., MD;
dep BCHS.
B047 Henry F. BARNES Bible; eb 1755; em 1804; on WINDSOR, KING, HANDY, POLK,
BROUGHTON, STEWART; dep MHS/FCA.
B048 BARNES Bible; eb 1767; em 1782; on GILBERT, BAYLESS, BAYLEY, OSBORN; res
Harf. Co., MD; dep MHS (in HBFR, 56).
B049 Benjamin BARNES Bible; pd 1834; eb 1810; em 1833; on HENRY, BRENNISEN;
res How. Co., MD; dep MHS/FCA.
B050 Walter A. BARNES Bible; eb 1838; em 1865; on HARTSOOK, LINDSAY, FILLER,
ENSOR, DEVILBISS; dep BCGS.
B051 BARNES Bible; eb 1843; em 1873; on HUGHES, MITCHELL; res Harf. Co., MD;
dep MHS (in HBFR, 51).
B052 Michael D. BARNES Bible; ins 1880; eb 1873; em 1866; on DIXON, FISHER,
SWAM, TALBOT, NELSON, RIGNEY, GARDNER, ALBAN; dep MHS/FCA.
B053 William BARNES Bible; eb 1886; em 1866; pub O'Brien, 284.
B054 BARNETT Bible; pd 1898; res Balto. Co., MD; pub BMGS 15-1:26.
B055 BARNETT Bible; eb 1899; em 1898; res Dor. Co., MD; pub DOBR,10.

INVENTORY OF MARYLAND BIBLE RECORDS

B056 Jacob BARNITZ Bible; pd 1791; eb 1785; em 1784; on McCLEAN, BACON, TRUMP;
     res York Co., PA; pub MGB 10:4.
B057 BARNITZ Bible; eb 1807; em 1850; on SEIP, VANDERSTILL, TAYLOR, CLAGETT,
     RICHARDS; res Balto. Co., MD; pub DAR (in MdGRC 13:186).
B058 BARNS Bible; eb 1803; em 1827; on BARKER, PARKER, ROHNER, COGSWELL; res
     CT; OH; MA; pub BMGS 20-3:241; dep MHS/FCA.
B059 BARNWELL Bible; eb 1757; em 1783; on WILLIAMS, WIGG; res SC;
     pub MBR 1:19 (in BCGS).
B060 BARR Bible; eb 1740; em 1799; on KILLPATRICK, COWEN, HODGE, JONES;
     pub MBR 1:24 (in BCGS).
B061 BARR Bible; eb 1847; em 1911; on REED, ROBINSON, DIXON, SHARROCK, LONTOR,
     MILLER, POYSER; dep MHS/FCA.
B062 BARRETT Bible; eb 1716; em 1751; on LEWIS, LEE, WINSTON; res poss. ARK;
     pub MBR 1:29 (in BCGS).
B063 BARRICKMAN Bible; pd 1861; eb 1824; em 1857; on PITCHENGER, BROCK,
     TENECH; res CT; pub BMGS 10-2:52.
B064 BARRICKMAN Bible; pd 1881; eb 1890; em 1889; on REEVE, LEMANS, LAURENCE,
     GATES, HOCH, WERNER, CHRISISENSEN; pub BMGS 10-2:53.
B065 BARRIERE Bible; pd 1813; eb 1811; em 1810; on MAHON, FENLY, DALEY;
     dep MHS/FCA.
B066 BARROLL Bible; pd 1759; eb 1786; em 1785; on CROCKETT, DONELLAN; res
     Balto., MD; dep MHS/FCA.
B067 BARTLETT-ELLIS Bible; eb 1763; res Fred. Co., MD; ME; OH; dep MHS/FCA.
B068 BARTLETT-OREM Bible; eb 1713; re 1943; on OREM, JARDIN; pub MDG 15-3:68;
     dep MSA (G-289).
B069 BARTOL-CHARBONNIER Bible; eb 1813; em 1841; on CHARBONNIER; res Havre de
     Grace, MD; LA; dep MHS/FCA.
B070 BASHORE Bible; rs 1812-1898; pd 1880; res Miami Co., OH; dep HOGS.
B071 BASHORE-EARHART-WOOD Bible; pd 1893; rs 1873-1951; on EARHART, WOOD; res
     Miami Co., OH; ARK; Bexar Co., TX; pub HCMR 5:86, dep HOGS.
B072 BATTIS Bible; eb 1874; em 1869; on TARBUTTON, RICHARDSON, FOREST; res QA
     Co., MD; pub DAR (in MdGRC 13:145).
B073 John BAUM Bible; eb 1782; em 1830; on FORSHEY; res MD; Cambria CO., PA;
     pub LU 2:111.
B074 BAXTER Bible; eb 1758; em 1785; on ELSON, BROWN, McGRAW, HENDRICKS,
     BRADY, FARMER, CAIRNES, PERMAR, CUNNINGHAM, VEASEY;
     pub MBR 1:34 (in BCGS).
B075 BAXTER Bible; pd 1809; eb 1764; em 1805; on GAYER, BONNER, CHENOWETH,
     McGEE, BUTLER, BUCKINGHAM, THORLEY, ANDERSON, HANEY; pub MGB 12:37.
B076 Thomas C. BAYARD Bible; eb 1819; em 1860; on HOWLETT, DAVIS; dep BCGS.
B077 Sylvia BAYLEY Bible; pub HCMR 5:72 (See also A055 ANES Bible).
B078 BAYLY Bible; eb 1792; em 1791; on GERMAN; dep MHS/FCA.
B079 Thomas C. BAYLY Bible; pd 1825; eb 1773; em 1820; on JORDAN, COX, EVANS,
     DASHIELL; res Soms. Co.(now Wico. Co.), MD; dep WCFL.
B080 BEAL Bible; eb 1779; on EVERETT; dep MHS/FCA (in Hancock).
B081 BEAL Bible; eb 1807; em 1831; dep BCGS.
B082 Samuel BEALL Bible; eb 1749; em 1822; pub NGSQ 18-1:20.
B083 Elijah BEALL Bible; eb 1791; pub NGSQ 24-3:87.
B084 BEALL Bibles; pd 1852; eb 1796; res Fred. Co., MD; pub NGSQ 59-1:32.
B085 BEALL Bible; rs 1807-1902; res PG Co., MD; dep MSA (G-560:90).
B086 BEALL Bible; eb 1816; em 1839; on RINE, RYAN, SPURRIER; res Mont. Co., MD;
     pub BMGS 23-3:259.
B087 William R. BEALL Bible; eb 1817; em 1858; on STILLWELL; res Hancock, MD;
     pub DAR Mag, Aug-Sept 1980, p.927.
B088 Ninian BEALL Bible; eb 1846; em 1844; on BECKETT, WOOD; pub DAR Mag.,
     Aug-Sept 1980, p.927.

6

B089 BEALL Bible; eb 1879; em 1902; on TUCKER, BECK, McDONOUGH, KOENIG, WOSTER,
      LINGERFELT, SILVAS, GREGG, BETTES; dep MHS/FCA.
B090 BEAN Bible; rs 1848-1886; dep MSA (G-476).
B091 BEARD Bible; on JOHNS, MAGRUDER, GASSAWAY; res PG Co., MD; DC;
      dep MHS/FCA.
B092 BEARD Bible; pd 1878; eb 1828; em 1852; on CAYLOR, SMITH, YINGLING, ENGLE;
      res Carr. Co., MD; dep BCGS.
B093 BEARD Bible; rs 1847-1933; dep MSA (G-705 with G-824).
B094 BEASMAN Bible; eb 1775; res Carr. Co., MD; pub MGB 1:17.
B095 BEASMAN Bible; pd 1852; eb 1850; em 1849; pub MGB 1:17.
B096 BEAUCHAMP Bible; eb 1843; em 1842; on MARINER, TEW, TAPP, LONG, THOMAS,
      QUINTON, DENNIS, HARLOW, BROUGHTON; res Pocomoke & Soms. Co., MD;
      dep MHS/FCA.
B097 BEAVEN Bible; pd 1857; eb 1819; em 1852; on STERRETT, McNULTY, STEBBING;
      dep MHS/FCA.
B098 BEAVEN Bible; rs 1821-1942; res Cecil Co., MD; dep MSA (G-214).
B099 BECK Bible; eb 1785; em 1784; on MILLER; res Kent Co., MD; Ohio Co.,WVA;
      pub LU 3:14.
B100 BECK Bible; eb 1793; em 1793; on CASH; res Kent Co., MD; pub LU 3:15.
B100 BECK Bible; eb 1774; em 1773; on ERNST; res Balto., MD; PA; pub MGB 19:58.
B101 BECKLEY-HAGMEIR-STONEBRAKER Bible; pd 1824; eb 1820; em 1819; on HAGMEIR,
      STONEBRAKER; res Wash. Co., MD; pub MDG 10-1:21.
B102 BECKLEY Bible; pd 1835; eb 1825; em 1853; on WATKINS, KERSHNER; res Wash.
      Co., MD; pub WMG 1-4:169.
B103 Thomas BEDDOW Bible; eb 1779; em 1777; res PG Co., MD; OH; pub LU 3:19.
B104 BEDFORD Bible; eb 1752; dep MHS/FCA.
B105 BEDFORD Bible; eb 1769; em 1790; on CLAY, DAWSON, KENNEDY, ROLLINS, KING,
      LEWIS, HOREN, GARRARD, de GRAFFENRIED, EMMON, HORTON, COLEMAN;
      pub MBR 1:26 (in BCGS).
B106 BEEDLE Bible; eb 1752; em 1752; on THOMAS, RASIN, CLAYTON, PERKINS;
      dep MHS/FCA.
B107 BEESON Bible; eb 1741; em 1764; on HEDGES, TUMLESTON, CLARK, VALE, MILLER,
      BARRACKMAN, FULTON, SKILES, RIDGERS; pub MBR 1:30 (in BCGS).
B108 BEESON Bible; eb 1743; em 1765; on MARTIN, CAMPBELL, WHITE, MORRIS,
      OLIPHANT, SKILES; res Martinsburg, VA; OH; pub MBR 1:31 (in BCGS).
B109 John BELL Record Bible; eb 1774; em 1773; res Balto. Co., MD;
      pub LU 3:31.
B110 BELL Bible; pd 1817; eb 1719; em 1797; dep MSA (D-531); dep BCGS.
B111 BELL Bible; eb 1719; em 1797; on MARSHALL, BOSTON; res Worc. Co., MD;
      dep MHS/FCA.
B112 BELL Bible; rs 1763-1878; dep MSA (G-503:4).
B113 BELL Bible; pd 1893; eb 1880; em 1879; res Jasper Co., TX;
      dep MdSAR (#2524).
B114 BELT-WATERS Bible; pd 1812; eb 1786; em 1785; on SMITH, WATERS, SHAW,
      McELFRESH, LINTHICUM, MONROE, KEPHART, STOVER, PIERCE;
      pub DAR (in MdGRC 33:68).
B115 BELT Bible; pd 1839; eb 1824; em 1849; on BOONE, TYLER, HELMUTH; res
      Fred. Co., MD; Richmond, VA; dep FCHS.
B116 BENER-BAINNER Bible; eb 1767; em 1796; on BAINNER, SEBACK, OBERKANDER,
      GUEERIA, GILLION; dep FCHS (some entries in German).
B117 BENNER-COBB Bible; rs 1869-1964; on COBB, BIRT, BRISCOE, CARLSON, CRAIG,
      DROGESON, FRY, GOODIN, MENDENHALL, PILCHER; res MD; MD; PA; and
      others; pub VSL (acc. #30435).
B118 BENNETT Bible; eb 1779; em 1845; on TRADER, BRITTINGHAM, GIRDLETRE;
      dep MHS/FCA.

B119 BENNETT Bible; pd 1770; eb 1766; em 1857; on SPEDDIN, PHILLIPS, COLE,
     THILLIPS; dep MHS/FCA.
B120 BENNETT Bible; pd 1859; eb 1812; em 1836; on KOLLER, PRUGH, BEASMAN,
     HARDEN, CONAWAY, RANDALL, DeVRIES; pub BMGS 18-1:38.
B121 BENNINGTON Bible; rb 1763; on ROGAN, GUYTON, STUBBINS, MYRES, AUBLE,
     NAYLOR; dep HCGS.
B122 BENNINGTON Bible; pd 1771; eb 1784; em 1783; on ROGAN; dep BCGS.
B123 BENSON Bible; eb 1793; em 1816; on DAKES, LOND, ADAMS; res Westover, MD;
     dep MHS/FCA.
B124 BENSON Bible; pd 1843; eb 1803; em 1846; on ROBINSON, THOMPSON; res Soms.
     Co., MD; DE; pub DBR 12:30 (in DSA).
B125 BENSON Bible; eb 1806; em 1830; on LONG; res Soms. Co., MD; dep MHS/FCA.
B126 BENTON Bible; rb 1834; on HEIDLER; res Harf. Co., MD; dep HCGS.
B127 BENTON Bible; eb 1834; em 1853; on KNIGHT, HEIDLER, BARNES; res Harf. Co.,
     MD; dep MHS/FCA.
B128 BEAKELEY Bible; eb 1803; em 1833; on BUTLER, BROOKE, DOWELL; dep MHS/FCA.
B129 BERRY Bible; eb 1752; em 1775; on ANTHONY, ARNOLD, HALBERT, GRACE, GAINES,
     HIATT, WILLIAMS, KELLY, SULLIVAN; pub MBR 1:13 (in BCGS).
B130 BERRY Bible; eb 1784; pub MGB 13:31.
B131 BERRY Bible; eb 1788; em 1787; on DORSEY; dep MHS/FCA.
B132 BERRY Bible; rs 1820; on ELLERBE, HASELDEN, FORE, MACE, ALFORD, WATSON;
     dep MHS/FCA.
B133 BEVANS Bible; eb 1781; em 1808; on CLARK, HIGGINS, SNIDER, CROSS,
     RIDGELY; res Clear Spring, MD; dep MHS/FCA.
B134 BIB Bible; ins 1813; eb 1703; em 1736; on BIGGER, BOOKER, SCOTT, SLAUGHTER,
     LEWIS, ROBERTS, JACKSON, BACON, HOPKINS, BURGESS, KING, HORSLEY;
     pub MBR 1:15 (in BCGS).
B135 BIBB Bible; eb 1814; em 1851; on SNEED, THOMPSON; res TX; KY;
     pub MBR 1:17 (in BCGS).
B136 Levi BIGELOW Bible; eb 1785; em 1814; res VT; PA; NY;
     pub DAR (in MdGRC 33:32).
B137 BIGELOW Bible; pd 1853; eb 1845; em 1844; on DUFF, NICHOLAS, SHORT,
     WEBSTER; res Buckingham & Franklin Cos., VA; pub BMGS 24-4:362.
B138 BIGGS Bible; eb 1758; em 1782; pub NGSQ 10-3:110.
B139 BIGHAM-BINGHAM Bible; eb 1822; em 1849; pub MGB 12:55.
B140 BILLINGSLEY Bible; pd 1870; eb 1913; em 1911; on MOORE, SHERTSER,
     UPPERCO; res Balto. Co., MD; pub BMGS 23-2:170.
B141 BILLINGSLEY Bible; pd 1876; em 1867; on BRISCOE, ABELL; dep MHS/FCA.
B142 BILLIPS Bible; eb 1815; em 1843; on NORMAN, HIGGINS, BRADLIE, WILLIAMSON;
     res Dor. Co., MD; pub DCGM 2-4:3.
B143 Samuel BINGHAM Bible; pd 1849; eb 1772; em 1921; on LINDSAY, DORSEY,
     PRUGH, FIELD, CRAWFORD, FAY; res Sykesville & Ellicott City, MD;
     NY; pub BMGS 19-3:179.
B144 BINGHAM Bible; pd 1740; eb 1779; res Balto., MD; County Mayo, Ireland;
     pub MGB 12:53.
B145 BINKLEY Bible; pd 1849; eb 1820; em 1845; on SNIVELY, LESHER, KERSHNER;
     pub DAR (in MdGRC 33:92).
B146 BINNANZER Bible; pd 1832; eb 1828; on BENNANZER; dep MHS/FCA (in German).
B147 BIRD Bible; eb 1798; em 1817; on HILL, WILLIAMS, MARTIN, CLARK, SKINNER,
     POLLARD, BOLES, LOYD, KNOW, McLANE, WARD, HARDING;
     dep MBR 1:10 (in BCGS).
B148 BIRD Bible; eb 1823; em 1825; on BLOXOM, MASON, BYRD; dep MHS/FCA.
B149 BISHOP Bible; em 1854; dep MHS/FCA (no births or deaths).
B150 BISSELL Bible; pd 1833; eb 1811; em 1834; on WEBSTER, RICHARDSON, HOLLAND,
     WILSON, BALDWIN, HENSHAW, WILKENSON; res Harf. Co., MD;
     dep MHS (in HBFR, 22); dep BCGS.

B151 BISSELL Bible; eb 1852; em 1834; on WEBSTER, HENSHAW, PASSANO, SHAW, LITTIG, REICHE, KERN; res Harf. Co., MD; dep MHS (in HBFR, 19); dep BCGS.

B152 BIXLER Bible; pd 1878; eb 1848; em 1871; on MYERS, GRAYBILL, ENGLER, EARLY; res Carr. Co., MD; dep BCGS (in Yingling).

B153 BLACK Bible; eb 1740; em 1762; on ADAMS, LAYCROFT, BOWMAN, BLYTHWOOD, SALTREEE, BAYNARD, REID, DUPONT, GRAYSON; res poss. GA; pub MBR 1:24 (in BCGS).

B154 BLACK Bible; pd 1843; eb 1786; em 1838; dep BCHS.

B155 Noah BLACK Bible; pd 1828; eb 1791; em 1837; on ROE, JUMP, EMERSON; res Caro. Co., MD; pub MDG 20-2:57; dep MGS/FCA (typed).

B156 BLACK Bible; eb 1833; em 1855; on WELLSLAGER; res Balto. MD; dep MHS/FCA.

B157 David BLACKWELL Family Record; eb 1777; em 1776; on LEWIS; res Fauquier Co., VA; MD; pub LU 3:98.

B158 Philemon BLACKWELL Bible; eb 1754; em 1818; on WOOLSEY, MARTINDELL, ARMSTRONG, THOMPSON, THOMAS, JOHNSON; res Cowenton, MD; Hopewell, NJ; pub OBR p.16 (at MSA).

B159 BLAINE Bible; eb 1786; on HARRIS; dep MHS/FCA (no Blaine dates).

B160 BLAIR Bible; pd 1704; eb 1706; em 1817; on RAY, TAGGART, KNOX, CAMPBELL, MACKEY, SMALL, CHAMBERS, ORR, ROSS; res Lancaster Co., PA; Ireland; dep MHS (in HBFR, 33).

B161 Walter D. BLAIR Bible; rb 1785; res MD; VA; KY; dep VSL (#250, acc. #29785).

B162 BLAISDELL Bible; rb 1826; on CARLTON, PIPER, GIFFORD, TUTTLE, BRADSTREET, on LITTLEFORD; res York, ME; dep BCGS.

B163 BLAND Bible; eb 1800; em 1826; dep BCHS (original pages).

B164 BLAND Bible; eb 1827; res Balto., MD; VA; dep BCHS (original pages).

B165 BLANEY Bible; pd 1881; eb 1842; em 1870; on NAGLE; res Harf. Co., MD; dep BCGS.

B166 BLEAKLEY Bible; pd 1832; eb 1835; em 1834; on SHIPLEY, SHIRK, SOMMERVILLE, PARK, DUVALL; dep MHS/FCA.

B167 BLESSING Bible; pd 1855; eb 1792; em 1821; on PETERS; dep CCGS #24.

B168 BLIZZARD Bible; eb 1816; em 1835; on GIBSON; res Fred. & Wash. Cos., MD; dep MHS/FCA.

B169 BLOCK Bible; pd 1868; eb 1863; em 1894; on KNOLL, FOWLER, SCHIPPER; res Balto., MD; dep MHS/FCA.

B170 BLOODSWORTH Bible; eb 1824; em 1847; on MURRELL; pub MDG 1-4:89.

B171 BLOUNT Bible; eb 1838; em 1866; on BOOKHART, WEEKLY, LEGGETT; dep MHS/FCA.

B172 BLUEFORD Bible; eb 1781; em 1780; on GARDNER, ZIMMERMAN; res MD; VA; pub LU 4:11.

B173 BOCKMILLER Bible; pd 1808; eb 1828; em 1777; on BOLGIANO, HARRISON; res Balto., MD; pub BMGS 22-1:317; dep BCGS.

B174 BODDER-GRIER Bible; eb 1832; em 1866; on GRIER, MICHAEL; res Harf. Co., MD; dep BCGS.

B175 BOLLINGER Bible; pd 1867; eb 1797; em 1818; on OVERHOLTZER, SHINGLEDECKER; dep CCGS.

B176 BOLLINGER Bible; pd 1868; eb 1808; em 184(?); on OBERHOLZER, HOOVER, BOYD, BAKER, SHRINER, SHINGLEDECKER; dep BCGS.

B177 James BOND Bible; eb 1731; em 1730; pub GPF/PGM 3:581.

B178 BOND Bible; pd 1733; eb 1735; em 1762; on WILMER, HATTON, BLACKISTONE, OWINGS, WORTHINGTON; dep MHS/FCA.

B179 BOND Bible; eb 1870; em 1853; on WELLS, ELLENDER; res Balto. Co., MD; dep MHS/FCA.

B180 BOND Bible; rb 1858; on ELLENDER; res Balto. & Harf. Cos., MD; dep HCGS.

INVENTORY OF MARYLAND BIBLE RECORDS

B181 Stephen BOONE Bible; eb 1813; em 1774; on BUCKMASTER, CRAIG, WALTON,
     BLADES, STEPHENS, HUDSON, RUSSELL, JESTER, JARRELL; res Kent Co.,
     MD; pub DBR 12:141 (in DSA).
B182 William BOOTH Bible; rb 1798; res Balto., MD; Richmond, VA;
     dep VSL (#295, acc. #29648).
B183 BORING Bible; eb 1749; em 1772; pub DAR (in MdGRC 16:3).
B184 BOSE Bible; pd 1770; eb 1760; em 1802; on DOBBIN, BULL; res Balto., MD;
     dep MHS/FCA.
B185 BOSLEY Bible; eb 1797; em 1796; on LITTIG, JESSOP, SCOTT, HARRISON,
     SLAGLE; dep MHS/FCA.
B186 BOSSERMAN Bible; eb 1781; em 1808; on COLLINSON, LEE, WHITTINGHTON, BEARD,
     STEPHENS; dep MHS/FCA.
B187 BOSTON Bible; pd 1815; eb 1759; em 1817; on MARSHALL, TAYLOR; res Worc.
     Co., MD; dep MHS/FCA.
B188 BOTELER Bible; rs 1766-1860; dep MSA (G-415).
B189 Isaac H. BOTTS Bible; pd 1866; eb 1839; em 1837; on SHERIDAN, GARRETTSON;
     dep BCGS.
B190 Thomas BOTTS Bible; pd 1895; eb 1858; em 1886; on McNUTT, JONES, KILGORE;
     res Street, MD; dep BCGS.
B191 BOULDEN Bible; eb 1774; em 1800; on GRIFFITH; res Pencader Hundred, DE;
     pub MDG 2-2:42.
B192 BOVEY Bible; eb 1819; em 1842; on MARTIN; res Concord, NH; dep BCGS #520.
B193 BOVEY Bible; pd 1874; eb 1850; on FUNK; pub DAR (in MdGRC 33:108).
B194 BOWDLE Family Record; rs 1792-1869; dep MSA (G-925:1)(kept in flyleaves
     of Armenian Mag. vol.1).
B195 BOWDLE-JONES Bible; pd 1817; eb 1832; em 1858; on DAIL, JONES, PATTISON,
     ROBINSON, CARROLL, BROHAWN; res Dor. Co., MD; pub DOBR,10.
B196 Benjamin I. BOWEN Bible; eb 1828; em 1853; res CV, MD; pub O'Brien,297.
B197 Briscoe Brurdell BOWEN Bible; eb 1939; em 1936; pub O'Brien p.285.
B198 Daniel Frazier BOWEN Bible; eb 1803; em 1827; pub O'Brien p.285.
B199 Daniel Wilson BOWEN Bible; eb 1879; em 1902; pub O'Brien p.287.
B200 Hezekiah BOWEN Bible; eb 1901; em 1877; pub O'Brien p.288.
B201 Hilery E. BOWEN Bible; eb 1880; em 1897; pub O'Brien p.228.
B202 Holdsworth BOWEN Bible; eb 1838; em 1837; pub O'Brien p.289.
B203 James Franklin BOWEN Bible; eb 1876; em 1875; pub O'Brien p.291.
B204 Jesse BOWEN Bible; eb 1791; em 1810; pub O'Brien p.296.
B205 Joseph BOWEN Bible; pd 1809; eb 1747; em 1798; res NJ; IN; pub MGB 5:17.
B206 Somerset BOWEN Bible; eb 1863; em 1890; pub O'Brien p.292.
B207 William Henry BOWEN Bible; eb 1843; em 1864; pub O'Brien p.293.
B208 BOWEN Bible; rs 1818-1861; dep MSA (G-550:1).
B209 BOWEN Bible; eb 1847; em 1845; on HAYWARD, SPENCE, CURTIS, PURNELL,
     GREGOR, RUSSELL; dep MHS/FCA.
B210 BOWER Family Record; eb 1754; on ROHRER; res Wash. Co., MD; Lancaster Co.,
     PA; OH; pub LU 4:46.
B211 BOWERS Bible; pd 1895; eb 1748; em 1866; on WHEELER, CHAPMAN, WORTHINGTON,
     BROWN, GRAY, HIPP, GLENN, SUMMERS; res Newberry, SC; dep AACG;
     dep MHS/FCA.
B212 BOWERS Bible; eb 1760; em 1785; on NAVE; res MD; TN; pub LU 4:42.
B213 BOWERS Bible; pd 1907; eb 1790; em 1922; on HIPP, SUMMER, COUNTS,
     HOLLOWAY, RAMAGE, FOLK; res Newberry, SC; dep AAGS.
B214 BOWERSOX Bible; eb 1823; on HELTIBRIDLE; res Carr. Co., MD; dep CCGS.
B215 BOWIE Bible; pd 1816; eb 1832; em 1776; on BURGESS, HALL, MAGRUDER,
     HILLEARY, COOMBS, SUTER, SMITH, McCENEY; pub MGB 11:40.
B216 BOWIE Bible; rs 1854-1942; res Hagerstown, MD;
     dep NGS Bible Records Collection.

10

B217 BOWLAND Bible; eb 1815; em 1847; on HAYMAN, COOPER, BENSON, DAVIS,
     LANDING, WHITTINGTON, POLLITT, MORRIS, GRIFFIN, ADAMS, HOLLAWAY,
     HUFFINGTON, REVELL, MONROE, MOORE, SMITH, LONG, STAGG; res Kingston,
     MD; dep MHS/FCA (Hayman, Daughtery, Turner Genealogical Collection).
B218 BOWLER Bible; eb 1766; res Wash. Co., MD; pub DAR Mag. 70:1021.
B219 BOWMAN Bible; rb 1817; on DILL, BECHTOLD, BONNETT, SCHAADT, BAUER, SMITH,
     SPRY, McCANN, MITCHELL, COALE, CARICO;
     res Balto. City & Harf. Co., MD; Germany; dep HOGS.
B220 BOYCE Bible; eb 1798; em 1825; on LEE; res Havre de Grace, MD; Phila., PA;
     dep MHS/FCA.
B221 BOYCE Bible; eb 1898; em 1921; dep BCGS (photocopy).
B222 BOYCE Bible; eb 1877; em 1880; res Balto., MD; dep BCGS (photocopy).
B223 James Caleb BOYD Bible; eb 1882; em 1880; pub O'Brien p.294.
B224 BOYD Bible; eb 1749; em 1783; on McKAY, MICHEL; dep MHS/FCA.
B225 BOYD-CHENEY-ADAMS Bible; pd 1808; eb 1777; em 1814; on CHENEY, ADAMS;
     pub NGSQ 66-2:126.
B226 BOYD Bible; pd 1793; eb 1798; on GREEN, McGINNES, STINCHCOM;
     pub BMGS 11:139.
B227 BOYER Bible; eb 1762; em 1786; on ZEALER, LOCOM, McCOY; res MD; KY;
     pub LU 4:58.
B228 BOYER Bible; pd 1859; eb 1850; em 1849; on BREWER, NEILSON; dep MHS/FCA.
B229 BOYLEN Bible; rb 1763; on ARGY, MEGEE; res Chester Co., PA; dep HOGS.
B230 BRADFIELD Bible; eb 1807; on FORD, RICKETTS, SHAY;
     dep MHS (in HBFR, 15).
B231 BRADLEY Bible; eb 1830; em 1959; on PHILLIPS, LOWE, SEABREASE, MAJORS,
     INSLEY, COBB, REDDISH; dep MHS/FCA.
B232 BRADLEY Bible; eb 1851; em 1969; res DE; dep MdSAR #2653.
B233 BRADLEY-JONES Bible; eb 1856; em 1880; on COOK, JONES; res Caro. Co., MD;
     dep BCGS (from DAR).
B234 Francis BRADY Bible; rb 1777; res Quantico, MD;
     dep VSL (#331, acc. #29099).
B235 BRADY Bible; eb 1849; em 1869; on MERSON, STOCKETT, WEDMORE, TAYLOR,
     NICHOLS; res Balto., MD; pub DAR (in MdGRC 35:19).
B236 BRALY Bible; pd 1876; eb 1791; em 1818; on HERBERT, DOYLE, LEA, BILLUPS,
     NORRIS, CAVANAUGH, COST, CROMWELL, SWARTZ, MYERS, WILLIS; res
     Hagerstown, MD; dep AAGS.
B237 BRAMBLE Bible; eb 1836; em 1863; on NEWTON, CHAVER, MORRIS, DILLEHUNT,
     CLEAVER; dep MHS/FCA.
B238 BRAMBLE Bible; pd 1847; on CLARK; dep BCGS.
B239 BRAMBLE Bible; ins 1901; eb 1872; em 1899; on MURPHY; res Dor. Co., MD;
     pub DCGM 3-6:18.
B240 BRANDAN Bible; eb 1892; em 1891; on EGERTON, POHL, STEEN, WHETTLE,
     GILBERT; res Balto., MD; dep MHS/FCA.
B241 BRASSEUR Bible; eb 1731; em 1800; on BRASHEARS, HORTON;
     pub DAR Mag. 80:153.
B242 Nacy BRASHEARS Bible; eb 1734; on EDMONSTON, BERRY, ORME; res PG Co., MD;
     KY; pub Lester,34.
B243 BRASWELL Bible; eb 1755; em 1780; on BLOW; pub MBR 1:33.
B244 BRATTEN Bible; eb 1781; em 1780; on POLK, PORTER, MISTER, TAYLOR,
     WHITTINGTON; dep MHS/FCA.
B245 BRATTEN Bible; pd 1792; eb 1744; em 1766; on CORD, ATKINSON, MORRIS,
     HOPKINS, SPENCE, SPENCER; dep MHS/FCA.
B246 BRECHBIRL Bible; eb 1788; em 1784; res Wash. Co., MD; TN; PA; pub LU 4:81.
B247 BREMERMAN Bible; eb 1814; em 1834; on BANGS, PECK, REAVER, DARBY,
     HACKNEY, RHINEHART; dep MHS/FCA.

B248 BRENT Bible; pd 1736; eb 1739; on SLAUGHTER, THOMAS, WALLIS, WILLIAMS; dep MHS/FCA.
B249 BRENT Bible; eb 1784; on FENWICK; pub MGB 21:52.
B250 BRENT Bible; eb 1784; em 1809; on WATKINS, SIMPSON, FENWICK; dep MHS.
B251 BRESSLER Bible; pd 1830; eb 1765; em 1802 ; on KOLLER; res vicinity of Sykesville, MD; dep CCGS.
B252 BREVITT Bible; pd 1769; eb 1717; on SKATT, BORASTON, POWERS, WILKES, WOODLAND, COALE; res Balto., MD; Staffordshire, England; dep MHS/FCA.
B253 BREWER Bible; rs 1738-1876; res PG Co., MD; dep MSA (G-560:92 with D-150).
B254 BREWER Record; eb 1780; em 1783; on LAMPLEY; res AA Co., MD; pub LU 4:85.
B255 BRIDGEMAN Bible; pd 1869; eb 1805; em 1833; on NOYES, BROOKS, FLETCHER; res MA; OH; pub BMGS 8-1:4.
B256 BRIGGS Bible; pd 1855; eb 1763; em 1794; on BROOKE; dep MHS/FCA.
B257 BRIGGS Bible; eb 1862; em 1861; on BROOKS, SIDAWAY, JOY, BUCKNER, CLARK, SHERMAN; pub BMGS 19-2:130; dep MHS/FCA.
B257A BRIGGS Bible; pd 1864; eb 1876; em 1874; on EARP, RAY; res Burtonsville, MD; dep MHS/FCA.
B257B BRIGGS Bible; pd 1881; eb 1886; em 1861; on BECKWITH, PETLETTE, MUSGROVE, BAGLEY, GLOVER, EARP; res Mont. Co., MD; dep MHS/FCA.
B258 BRIGGS Bible; pd 1882; eb 1863; em 1861; on BECKWITH, PETLETT, MUSGRAVE, BAGLEY, GLOVER, EARP; res Burtonsville, Mont. Co.,MD; dep MHS/FCA.
B259 BRIGHT Bible; on HENDERSON, RIGGS, SMEDBURG; dep MHS/FCA (contains deaths only).
B260 BRINSON Bible; eb 1763; em 1787; on WRIGHT, PARKE, PURVES, TURNER, FREEMAN, YOUNG, TARVER, JORDON, SHIN; pub MBR 1:20.
B261 Benjamin BRISCOE Record; pd 1774; eb 1767; pub DAR (MdGRC 7:53).
B262 Hezekiah BRISCOE Bible; pd 1762; eb 1693; em 1776; res P.G. Co., MD; VA; pub MG 1:87.
B263 BRISCOE Bible; eb 1743; em 1743; on MILLS, COMPTON, HESLETINE, SMITH; pub DAR Mag. 73:89 (May 1939).
B264 BRISCOE Bible; eb 1752; em 1784; on MAGRUDER, LACY; res Fred. Co., MD; dep MHS/FCA.
B265 BRISCOE Bible; pd 1806; eb 1782; em 1809; on BRINKLEY, BOGGS, FOWLER; res Balto., MD; Wash., D.C.; dep MHS/FCA.
B266 BRISCOE Bible; pd 1815; eb 1796; em 1817; on THOMPSON; res Leonardtown, MD; dep MHS/FCA.
B267 BRITTINGHAM Bible; eb 1765; em 1806; on BROWN; res MD; Fairfield Co., OH; pub LU 4:106.
B268 BROHAWN Bible; eb 1864; on CREIGHTON, JOHNSON; res Dor. Co., MD; pub DCGM 1-1:2.
B269 BROOKE Bible; pd 1819; eb 1800; em 1827; on HUNTER, BALDWIN, CATESBY, RILEY, TROWBRIDGE, GREGORY; dep MHS/FCA.
B270 Martha Hawkins BROOKS Bible; eb 1733; on CROWDER, DICK, WALLER, WEBLEY, GREEN; res Balto. Co., MD; VA; NC; pub Austin,287.
B271 BROOKS Bible; on STRODE, DUNCAN, LAFFERTY, BRECKENRIDGE, SCOTT, KERR, HOPKINS, ACTON, YOUNG; pub MBR 1:12.
B272 BROOME Bible; eb 1851; em 1879; on HENSCHEL, MAYHEW, DUKEHART, BLOOM; res Balto., MD; dep MHS/FCA; dep BCHS.
B273 BROWDRESS Bible; eb 1888; on ADAMS; res Dor. Co., MD; pub DOBR,11.
B274 BROWN Bible; eb 1745; em 1773; on RIGGS, DORSEY; dep MHS/FCA.
B275 Samuel BROWN Bible; ins 1817; eb 1745;em 1773; pub BMOS 3:34.
B276 BROWN Bible: in 1804; on DAWSON, HOWARD, PRITCHARD, SHANKS, LEACH, LEWIS, LINTHICUM; res Georgetwon, DC; pub DAR (in MdGRC 1:6).
B277 BROWN Bible; rs 1779-1899; res Cecil Co., MD; dep MSA (G-863:2).

B278 BROWN Bible; eb 1781; em 1810; on HUGHES, PHILLIPS, RANSON, CASE, WOOD;
dep MHS/FCA.
B279 BROWN Bible; eb 1799; on LAWS, QUINTON; res Dor. Co., MD; pub DCGM 2-2:11.
B279A BROWN Bible; rb 1798; on REYNOLDS; res Lancaster Co., PA; dep HOGS.
B280 BROWN Bible; pd 1848; eb 1812; on BOUNDS; res Wico. Co., MD;
pub DAR (in MdGRC 11:137).
B281 Edmund BROWN, Sr. Bible; pd 1846; eb 1814; em 1812; on HAINES; res Elkton,
MD; pub BRP 1:109.
B282 BROWN Bible; rb 1820; on LIPPOLD, SANDERS; res Cumberland, MD; dep HOGS.
B283 BROWN Bible; eb 1821; on NELSON, SLINKMAN; dep MHS/FCA.
B284 BROWN Bible; pd 1852; eb 1823; em 1853; on MALONE, TOADVINE, McGRATH;
res Wico. Co., MD; pub DAR (in MdGRC 11:137).
B285 BROWN Bible; ins 1888; eb 1831; em 1849; on WOLF, BUHRMAN; res Mt. Zion,
Foxville, MD; dep MHS/FCA.
B286 James BROWN Bible; ins 1888; eb 1831; em 1849; on BUHRMAN; res Foxville,
MD; dep MHS (in MdSAR #2719).
B287 BROWN Bible; eb 1837; em 1822; on TYSON, FREDERICK, MUMMAUGH; res Carr.
Co., MD; dep CCGS.
B288 BROWN Bible; eb 1837; em 1863; on BIDDISON, CLARK, LOGSDON, KAUFFMANN,
ERK; res Balto., MD; dep MHS/FCA.
B289 Thomas W. BROWN Bible; eb 1837; em 1864; res Balto., MD; VA; dep BCHS.
B290 BROWN Bible; pd 1873; eb 1855; em 1854; on FREDRICH, PRICE, COANE; res
Carr. Co., MD; dep CCGS.
B291 BROWN Bible; rb 1877; res York Co., PA; dep HOGS.
B292 BROWNYARD Bible; pd 1850; eb 1822; em 1847; res Silver Spring, MD;
pub DAR Mag. Feb. 1977 p.131.
B293 BRUFF Bible; pd 1801; eb 1799; dep MHS/FCA.
B294 BRUFF-MANSFIELD Bible; on MANSFIELD; pub CC 10-1:6.
B295 BRUFFEY Bible; eb 1811; em 1842; res IL; TX; dep MHS/FCA.
B296 BRUGH Bible; ins 1891; eb 1815; em 1855; on GESH, WEBB, GRAYBILL, JEWELL;
res Botetourt Co., VA; pub BCGS (in Yingling).
B297 BRUNER Bible; eb 1766; on STOOKY, DUNICAL, WRIGHT, BLACKMAN, DOFGE,
CLUTTER, COCKRUM, SPARKS, KEY, COTTER, BALDWIN; res MD; KY; IN; MI;
pub DAR Mag 79:187.
B298 BRUNER Bible; pd 1788; eb 1785; em 1783; on CLINE, MERCER, STARNS,
BAYLIE; res Fred. Co., MD; TN; pub LU 5:53.
B299 John BRYAN, Sr. Bible; eb 1763; on OFFUTT; pub MGB 9:26.
B300 Samuel BRYAN, Sr. Bible; em 1824; on RUDDELL, DOWLEY, McDOW, ROSS,
OFFUTT, OWEN; res Monroe Co., MO; pub MGB 9:27.
B301 BRYAN Bible; eb 1753; em 1783; on STONE; pub LU 5:55.
B302 BRYAN Bible; eb 1799; em 1825; on HARRIS, COOK, BUTLER, MACKUBIN, MURPHY,
TELSON; dep MHS/FCA.
B303 BRYAN Bible; rs 1799-1852; res QA Co., MD; dep MSA (G-560:73 with D-150).
B304 BRYAN-MOFFETT Bible; pd 1769; eb 1771; on SMITH, HAYES; res Kent Co., MD;
pub DAR (in MdGRC 7:323).
B305 BUCHANAN Bible; eb 1763; on GILLINGS, BROWN, PERINE, FEYE, COCKEY; res
Balto. Co., MD; dep MHS/FCA.
B306 BUCHANAN-WINDER Bible; pd 1846; eb 1811; em 1850; pub BMGS 23-1:91.
B307 BUCK Bible; rs 1778-1891; eb 1756; em 1778; on CROOK, COLLINS, STANSBURY,
GORSUCH, ROGERS, BARTLETT; pub DAR (in MdGRC 1:11).
B308 BUCK Bible; eb 1767; em 1827; on SHANNON, ROGERS, BROWN, JACOBS;
dep MHS/FCA.
B309 BUCK Bible; eb 1767; em 1790; dep BCHS (typed manuscript).
B310 BUCK Bible; pd 1768; eb 1756; on STANSBURY, BEARY; res Eastern Shore;
dep MHS/FCA.

13

B312 Benjamin Alpheus BUCK Bible; eb 1716; em 1793; res Balto. Co., MD; IL;
     dep BCHS (typed manuscript).
B313 BUCKINGHAM Bible; pd 1830; dep MHS/FCA.
B314 BUCKINGHAM Bible; eb 1798; em 1821; res Balto. Co., MD; pub NGSQ 22:45.
B315 BUCKINGHAM-CONAWAY Bible; pd 1872; eb 1827; em 1849; on SKIDMORE,
     CONAWAY; dep MHS/FCA (31).
B316 Joseph F. BUCKLER Bible; eb 1866; em 1914; pub O'Brien p.295.
B317 Joseph William BUCKLER Bible; eb 1840; em 1865; pub O'Brien p.295.
B318 Robert BUCKLER Bible; eb 1832; em 1831; pub O'Brien p.296.
B319 BUCKLER Bible; rs 1831-1878; dep MSA (G-550:2).
B320 BUDD Bible; eb 1740; em 1779; on MORROW, DOBBINS, MURIELL, BURR, BEATTY,
     BISPHAM, CAMBLESS; dep MHS/FCA (Dobbins-Budd).
B321 BUFFINGTON Bible; eb 1904; em 1899; on LIPPY, HAINES, CRABBS, TRIMMER,
     THOMAS, YINGLING, HALL, MYERS; pub BCGS (in Yingling).
B322 John BUHALO Bible; eb 1842; dep MGS (typed copy).
B323 BULLARD Bible; eb 1875; em 1873; on HEATON, WHEATON, BAILEY, ALMY, YATES;
     res Balto., MD; CT; MA; dep MHS/FCA.
B324 BULLITT Bible; rs 1733-1951; dep MSA (G-464).
B325 BULLITT Bible; eb 1754; em 1733; on HARRISON, HAYWARD, CHAMBERLAIN; res
     Dor. Co., MD; dep MSA (G-464).
B326 BULLOCK Bible; eb 1791; em 1817; on MORTON, CLAYTON, VENABLE; res KY;
     dep BCGS (Miller Collection).
B327 BURCH Bible; eb 1768; em 1821; pub Audery 2:193.
B328 BURCH Bible; eb 1781; em 1805; res Chas. Co., MD; dep MHS/FCA.
B329 BURCH Bible; eb 1807; em 1834; on MORRISON; res Worc. Co., MD; IN;
     dep MHS/FCA.
B330 BURCH Family Record; em 1834; on MORRISON; res Worc. Co., MD; dep MHS/FCA.
B331 BURGESS Bible; eb 1784; em 1783; on WARFIELD; res Balto., MD; dep MHS/FCA.
B332 BURGESS Bible; rs 1790-1804; dep MSA (G-159).
B333 BURGESS Bible; pd 1872; eb 1817; em 1840; on MILLER, BENNETT, GIBBONS,
     LEACH, HERR, CROMWELL, MATHIESON, TRACY, LUCY, FIZZEL, LIVESAY; res
     Balto., MD; dep AAGS.
B334 BURGESS Bible; pd 1881; eb 1834; em 1882; on JONES, HAMILTON; res Balto.,
     MD; dep BCGS (from DAR).
B335 BURGESS Bible; pd 1829; eb 1841; on O'LAUGHLIN, KERR; pub BMGS 17-1:18.
B336 BURK Bible; eb 1877; em 1905; on ALLEN; res Baldwin & Glen Arm, MD;
     dep MHS/FCA.
B337 BURNHAM Bible; pd 1751; eb 1748; em 1784; on TAYLOR, HART, NOVINGTON;
     dep MHS/FCA.
B338 BURNHAM Bible; pd 1824; eb 1789; em 1817; on BURGESS, HARPER,
     VAN LOUVENEIGH, BIRD, HAMILTON; pub MDG 3-3:65.
B339 BURR Bible; pd 1872; eb 1817; em 149S; on QUIRE, KIER, BAKER, BORMAN,
     CROFT; res Columbia, OH; dep AAGS.
B340 BURR Bible; eb 1798; em 1833; on NEWBOLD, GETTY, ARMSTRONG, FINCHAM,
     MARBURY; res Olney, MD; dep MHS/FCA.
B341 BURR Bible; eb 1849; em 1848; on NEWBOLD, GETTY, ARMSTRONG, FINCHAM; res
     NJ; pub DAR (in McGRC 25:18).
B342 BURROUGHS Bible; rs 1786-1844; res Harf. & Cecil Cos., MD;
     dep MSA (G-236:56 with D-150).
B343 BURROUGHS Bible; pd 1904; eb 1786; em 1823; on ARMSTRONG, HAYES, MAHAN,
     BERRY; res Harf. Co., MD; dep MHS/FCA.
B344 BURTON Bible; eb 1788; em 1846; on MORGAN, MITCHELL, MURPHY, BOWDIN; res
     Burtonsville, MD; dep MHS/FCA.
B345 BURTON Bible; rs 1813-1971; on OWENS, TRUITT; dep MSA (G-853).
B346 BURK Bible; eb 1877; em 1905; res Balto. Co., MD; dep DAR (MdSAR).

BIBLES

B347 Ulick BURK Bible; eb 1766; em 1806; res Balto. Co., MD; IL; dep BCHS.
B348 Joseph BURNESTON Bible; eb 1746; on BARTON, MEYERS, EICHELBERGER,
     HAGERTY; dep MHS/FCA (6).
B349 BURWELL Bible; eb 1810; em 1809; on DIGGES, CARTER, JOHNSTON, PENDLETON,
     LOGAN; res VA; dep MHS/FCA (Harvey Family Bible Records).
B350 BURWELL Bible; eb 1750; em 1772; on GRYMES, BAYLOR, RANDOLPH, PAGE; res
     VA; pub MBR 1:36.
B351 BUTLER Bible; eb 1748; em 1770; on WINGFIELD, TERRELL, SHACKLEFORD,
     MERRIWETHER, STONE; pub MBR 1:22.
B352 BUTLER Bible; eb 1759; em 1758; on MOORE; res Loudoun Co., VA;
     pub MBR 1:9.
B353 BUTLER Bible; pd 1867; eb 1781; em 1807; on BAXTER, McGEE, WORRELL,
     PALMER, YOUNGER, CLAYTON, on WELLS; pub MGB 15:22.
B354 BUTLER-ROBERTS Bible; pd 1853; eb 1793; em 1821; res Harf. Co., MD; PA;
     dep BCHS (typed manuscript).
B355 BUTLER-ROBERTS Bible; rb 1807; on STREETT, DAVIS, MITCHELL, FENDALL,
     WHITEFORD, MORGAN, DALLAM, HUSTON, JONES, JULIANO, McCABE, WYATT,
     CUTSAIL, WOLFE, WILSON, CROPPER, ROUZER. BROWN, HURLOCK, GRISE,
     USILTON, CHESTER, HOWARD, ROBERTS; res Harf. Co., MD; dep HCGS.
B356 Joseph Butler Bible; pd 1854; eb 1816; on GRAY, WILBER; res MD;
     pub MGB 17:65.
B357 Mathew BUTLER Bible; rs 1816-1950; pd 1892; on DAMERON, DEVERS, FINKS,
     HUGHES, JONES, KNOWLES, KRISE; res Balto. & Rockville, MD; Wash.,
     DC; VA; dep VSL (#463).
B358 BUTLER Bible; rs 1824-1953; res QA Co., MD; dep MSA (G-560:74 with D-150).
B359 Norman G. BUTLER Bible; pd 1849; eb 1830; on BROWN, THRAP, VAN CAMP,
     SUMMERS, KELLY, GORSUCH; pub MGB 17:39.
B360 BUTLER Bible; eb 1848; em 1847; on WALTERS, PRICE, REEVES; res QA Co., MD;
     dep MHS/FCA.
B361 BUTLER Bible; eb 1878; em 1876; on BRYAN; dep MHS/FCA.
B362 BYRD-TAYLOR Bible; eb 1908; em 1848; on KEEN, MARTEN, TAYLOR;
     dep CCGS (#22).
B363 James A. BYUS Bible; pd 1844; eb 1845; em 1844; on ECCLESTON, TRAVERSE,
     HARRISON, JOHNSTON; res Dor. Co., MD; pub DOBR,11.
B364 William BYUS Bible; eb 1729; em 1727; on HICKS, ENNELS; pub DOBR,12.
B365 BYUS Bible; pd 1762; eb 1729; em 1727; on HICKS, ENNALLS; pub DOBR,12.

C001 CABLE Bible; pd 1811; eb 1771; on GUYER, ALEXANDER, McVEY;
     dep MHS (HBFR,36).
C002 CADLE Bible; eb 1877; em 1877; on PILES, McNEY, HAMILTON, PUMPHREY; res
     Broad Creek, PG Co., MD; pub PGCGS Bulletin, Jan. 1987, 18-5:82.
C003 CALHOUN Bible; pd 1723; eb 1774; em 1792; on CATTELL, HALL; dep MHS/FCA.
C004 CALLAHAN Bible; eb 1840; em 1839; on LEDNUM, FREY, WILSON, COOPER, WRIGHT;
     res Dor. Co., MD; pub DCGM 3-1:9.
C005 CALLAWAY Bible; eb 1754; em 1777; on MORGAN; pub MBR 1:73.
C006 Peter CALLAWAY Bible; eb 1792; em 1839; on HARRINGTON, VERGEN, WILLIAMS;
     res Kent Co., Del.; pub Callaway Journal, 1976, 1:54.
C007 CALLIS Bible; pd 1826; eb 1818; em 1820; on SUNDERLAND, FOSTER, BARTLETT,
     TILDON, LARRABEE; dep MHS/FCA.
C008 CALVERT Bible; eb 1720; em 1719; on SAUNDERS; dep MHS/FCA.
C009 CALWELL Bible; ins 1793 Bible; eb 1794; em 1793; on GALLION, JOHNSON;
     res Balto., MD; dep MHS/FCA (21).
C010 CAMPBELL Bible; rs 1751-1840; dep MSA (G-560:75).
C011 CAMPBELL-FOWLER Bible; pd 1712; eb 1752; em 1751; on FOWLER, HAMMOND,
     DUFF; dep MHS/FCA (21).
C012 CAMPBELL Bible; eb 1742; em 1768; on CLARK; pub MBR 1:58.

15

INVENTORY OF MARYLAND BIBLE RECORDS

C013 CANBY Bible; eb 1824; res Balto. MD; dep HCGS.
C014 CANNON-KENNARD Bible; pd 1761; eb 1732; em 1793; on KENNARD, DREW,
     MITCHELL, McCONNIER, OGLIVIE, HOUSTON, McEWEN, FLEMING, CRUMP,
     STEVENS; res MD, NC, TN; dep MHS/FCA (21).
C015 CANNON Bible; eb 1749; em 1832; on BUSH, McGUIRE, DAVIS; res Dor. Co.,
     MD.; pub DCGM 3-5:19.
C016 CANNON Family Records; pd 1686; eb 1749; em 1792; on DAVIS, BUSH,
     SATTERFIELD, CALDER, JOINER, MEEKS; res Kent and QA Cos., MD;
     pub KBR p.24 (typescript in MHS)
C017 CANNON Bible; eb 1864; em 1893; on WILLEY, MORRIS, HALES, TAYLOR; res
     Dor. Co., MD; pub DCGM 3-2:16.
C018 CARBACH Bible; rs 1763-1874; eb 1763; em 1783; on HUGHES, BEVAN, GAWTHROP,
     JONES, FISHER; pub DAR (in MdGRC 1:16), dep MHS/FCA,
     pub CMF (copy in BCGS).
C019 CARCAUD Bible; ins 1863; eb 1827; em 1859; res Balto., MD. and LA;
     dep BCGS (photocopy).
C020 CARDEAU Bible; pd 1865; eb 1894; em 1893; on LOWRY, CONNALLY, NEILL,
     TARLTON, GIBSON, CORSON; dep MHS/FCA (21).
C021 CAREY Birth Record; pd 1804; eb 1751; res Balto., MD; dep MHS/FCA (21).
C022 CAREINS Bible; pd 1834; eb 1812; em 1836; on BAY, JOHNSON, PATTERSON,
     NELSON, CAIRNES, BURTON;; dep MHS (HBFR,43)
C023 CAREONS Bible; eb 1768; em 1803; dep BCGS.
C024 CARLISLE Bible; eb 1882; em 1880; on MOORE; res Marydel, MD; dep MGS
     Library (typed copy).
C025 CARMACK Bible; eb 1759; res Fred. Co., MD; dep MHS/FCA (21).
C026 CARMACK Bible; dep MHS/FCA (21).
C027 CARNAN Bible; pd 1866; eb 1831; dep DAR (MdSAR #2614).
C028 CARNAN-VALIENT Bible; eb 1905; em 1904; on BROWN, WINN, VALIENT; res
     Balto., MD; VA; dep MHS/FCA.
C029 CARR Bible; eb 1812; em 1809; on CLAYTON, HARRISON, WELLS, PORTER;
     res AA Co., MD; dep MHS/FCA (21).
C030 CARR Bible; eb 1796; em 1855; on OWENS, PORTER, HARDESTY, HARVEY, ABBEY;
     dep MHS/FCA (21).
C031 CARRICK Bible; pd 1819; on MILLER; dep MHS/FCA.
C032 CARRICK Bible; eb 1841; res Balto. Co., MD; dep HCGS.
C034 CARRICK Record; eb 1841; pub BMGS 23-2:154; dep MHS/FCA.
C034 CARRICK Bible; eb 1854; dep DAR (in MdSAR #2627).
C035 Thomas CARRINGTON Bible; eb 1782; em 1804; on CAYWOOD, WILSOMON; res MD;
     KY; IN; pub MGB 18:69.
C036 CARROLL Bible; eb 1690; em 1689; on UNDERWOOD, DARNALL; res AA Co., MD;
     dep MHS/FCA (22).
C037 CARROLL Bible; eb 1751; on CORKRILL; res York, PA; Balto., MD.;
     dep MHS/FCA.
C038 Patrick CARROLL Prayer Book; pd 1793; eb 1796; res Bladensburg, MD;
     pub MGB 2:6.
C039 Henry H. CARROLL Bible; pd 1831; eb 1822; em 1821; dep BCHS (typed copy).
C040 Thomas King CARROLL Bible; eb 1829; em 1814; on STEVENSON, BOWDLE,
     ROBINSON; pub DOBR,13.
C041 CARROLL Bible; pd 1860; eb 1862; em 1861; res Dor. Co., MD; DE;
     dep BCGS.
C042 CARROTHERS Bible; eb 1807; em 1827; on GAITHER, HARPER, TUCKER, HILL,
     FOWLER, MORRIS, HARRIS, LAVELL, LEIPER, JOHNSON; res TN; AR; MI;
     dep MHS/FCA, dep BCGS.
C043 Sadie CASEY Bible; eb 1857; on FRENCH, PIQUETT, BROWN; res Mont. and How.
     Cos., MD; Lincolnshire, England; dep AAGS.

16

C044 Jacob CASHO Bible; pd 1790; eb 1800; em 1827; res Cecil Co., MD;
    pub NGSQ 44:77.
C045 CASPARI Bible; eb 1850; em 1874; on HEINICKEN, WIGET, BARRON, McLELLEN,
    KIRKMAN, ABEL; WYMAN; dep BOGS.
C046 CASTLE Bible; pd 1765; eb 1783; em 1808; on LONG, SHANABARGER, ROUTZAHN,
    MILLER, ALBOUGH; res Fred. and Wash. Cos., MD; IN; pub BMGS 14:28.
C047 CASWELL Bible; pd 1797; eb 1710; em 1732; on AVERILL, BROWN; res CT; MA;
    dep MHS/FCA.
C048 CASWELL Bible; pd 1789; eb 1799; em 1830; on THOMPSON, ANGELL, BALDWIN,
    FORD, EDMANDS; dep BOGS (from DAR).
C049 CATELL Bible; pd 1723; eb 1774; em 1792; on CALHOUN, HALL;
    dep MHS/FCA (23).
C050 CAUSEY Bible; rs 1778-1921; dep MSA (in G-305:1).
C051 CAUSEY Bible; rs 1804-1927; dep MSA (in G-308).
C052 Thedosha CAUSEY Bible; eb 1808; em 1862; on LOKEY, PARSONS, LEONARD,
    GORDY, WALLER, FOOKES; dep WCFL.
C053 CAUSEY Bible; rs 1811-1847; dep MSA (in G-305:2).
C054 CAZIER Bible; eb 1770; em 1793; on FOSTER, FORD, ALDRIDGE; pub DAR
    (in MdGRC 7:321),(photocopy).
C055 CHAFEE Bible; eb 1802; em 1801; on UNDERWOOD, CLARK, HOFFMAN; res Balto.,
    MD; dep MHS/FCA (27).
C056 CHAIRES Bible; pd 1815; eb 1780; em 1797; on START, DODD, GRAY;
    res QA Co., MD; pub DAR (in MdGRC 11:70); dep MHS/FCA (27).
C057 CHAMBERLAINE Bible; rs 1733-1951; dep MSA (in G-464).
C058 CHAMBERS Bible; pd 1854; eb 1796; em 1854; on WARD, AUSTIN; res AA Co.,
    MD; pub DAR (in MdGRC 35:1).
C059 CHAMBERS Bible; eb 1747; em 1782; on FORMAN, HEMSLEY, VAN BIBBER, HOUSTON,
    PORTER, BOWERS, MARSH, SPEAR; res Kent and QA Cos, MD; pub KTR;
    pub DAR (in MdGRC 12:94).
C060 CHAMBERS Bible; eb 1827; on CHILDRESS, TEEL; res Roanoke, VA; dep HOGS.
C061 CHANCE Bible; eb 1758; em 1777; on TAYLOR, DOUGHTY, HAVELL; res MD; LA;
    SC; pub MGB 8:27.
C062 CHAPMAN Bible; ins 1867; pd 1842; on TYDINGS; res Balto. Co., MD;
    dep MHS/FCA (27)(deaths only).
C063 CHAPMAN Bible; rs 1764-1881; pd 1851; eb 1764; em 1789; on HANSON,
    DAVIDSON, GATES, DODGE, WHEELOCK, MAGRUDER, FORREST; res PG Co., MD;
    dep MSA (G-560:76); dep MHS/FCA (27).
C064 CHAPMAN Bible; pd 1840; eb 1834; em 1831; on COOPER, OURSLER; res Balto.
    Co., MD; dep MHS/FCA (27).
C065 CHAPMAN Bible; ins 1879; eb 1847; em 1879; on HAYES, STUART, WEBB, McCORD;
    res Balto. Co., MD; dep MHS/FCA (27).
C066 CHAPMAN Bible; pd 1837; eb 1847; on OURSLER; dep MHS/FCA (27);
    dep BCHS (transcript).
C067 CHAPMAN Bible; eb 1880; dep MHS (original); dep BCHS (photocopy).
C068 CHAPPELEAR Bible; pd 1751; eb 1766; em 1796; dep MHS/FCA (27).
C069 CHASE Bible; pd 1770; eb 1736; em 1758; on MARTIN; res New Bedford, MA;
    dep AAGS; dep MHS/FCA.
C070 CHASE Bible; pd 1770; eb 1741; on WALKER, COLE, JACKSON, BARNEY; res Som.
    Co. and Balto., MD; dep MHS/FCA (27); dep BOGS.
C071 Samuel CHASE Bible; rs 1762-1905; dep MSA (in D-603:3).
C072 Nathaniel CHEAIRS Bible; rb 1764; pd 1820; on RUSH; res QA Co.,MD; NC;
    TN; dep VSL (#564, acc. #22435).
C073 CHELTON Bible; eb 1812; em 1809; on CHROSWELL, TOWNSEND, CLARVOE, NEVIT,
    ADAMS, HOLLAND; dep MHS/FCA (27).
C074 CHESHIRE Bible; eb 1791; em 1818; on CAIN, GOWAN, MOCK, BLACKWELL, WILSON,
    NEELY; pub MBR 1:51.

C075 CHESNEY Bible; eb 1784; dep MHS (HBFR,62); pub BCGS.
C076 CHESNEY Bible; pd 1845; eb 1785; em 1812; on McCAULEY, FLETCHER, FOSTER,
     OSBORN, HAWKINS, GORRELL, THOMPSON, BARNES; dep MHS (HBFR,62);
     pub BCGS.
C077 CHESTER Bible; pd 1875; eb 1862; on FURTZ; dep BCGS.
C078 CHEW Bible; pd 1716; eb 1728; em 1727; on LLOYD, DULANY, BORDLEY;
     dep MHS/FCA (28).
C079 CHEW Bible; pd 1752; eb 1755; em 1749; on LENGAN; dep MHS/FCA (27).
C080 CHEW; Bible; rs 1749-1775; dep MSA (in G-541)..
C081 CHILCOTE Bible; eb 1834; em 1858; res Frederick. MD; TN;
     dep BCHS (photocopy of original pages).
C082 Charles CHILTON Bible; eb 1741; em 1760; on BLACKWELL, TURNER, CORBIN,
     GILSON; res VA; pub MBR 1:69.
C083 John CHILTON Bible; eb 1739; em 1765; on BLACKWELL, BALL, RANSDELL,
     CORBIN, SMITH; pub MBR 1:71.
C084 Orrick CHILTON Bible; eb 1769; em 1791; on CORBIN, PICKETT, MARSHALL;
     pub MBR 1:72.
C085 CHISWELL Bible; pd 1816; eb 1747; em 1809; on FLETCHALL, WHITE, GRIFFITH;
     res Mont. Co., MD; dep MCHS.
C086 CHISWELL Bible; eb 1783; em 1809; on FLETCHALL, WHITE, GRIFFITH, JONES,
     GOTT; dep MHS/FCA (27).
C087 CHISWELL Bible; pd 1816; eb 1810; em 1807; on FLETCHALL, WHITE, GRIFFITH,
     JONES, GOTT, LYONS; res Mont. Co., MD; pub DAR (in MdGRC 7:220).
C088 CHRISSINGER Bible; eb 1813; em 1860; on CLEVIDENCE, CLAWSON, MUMMA, PIKE,
     HOFFMAN; pub BMGS 14:9.
C089 CHRISTIAN Bible; eb 1774; em 1811; on BATES, TURNER, LAWRENCE, BOWE,
     CLARKE, ESTILLE, SHEILD, CARVER; pub BMGS 20-4:335; dep MHS/FCA.
C090 CINNAMOND Bible; eb 1814; em 1840; on BURDICK, HOWARD, ROSEBERRY;
     dep MHS/FCA (27).
C091 CLABAUGH Bible; eb 1781; em 1805; on HARRIS; dep MHS/FCA (27).
C092 CLAGETT-SUMMERS Bible; eb 1729; em 1774; on SUMMERS; pub NGSQ 32-1:43.
C093 CLAPHAM Bible; pd 1801; eb 1765; em 1791; on PAULING, PRICE, GRIFFITH,
     THOMSON, MASON; res VA; TX; dep MHS/FCA (29).
C094 CLARKE Bible: rs 1743-1891; dep MSA (in G-598).
C095 CLARK Bible; pd 1752; eb 1750; res Balto., and Harf. Co., MD;
     pub DAR (in MdGRC 25:3); dep MHS/FCA (29.
C096 CLARK Bible; eb 1778; em 1811; on BURRESS, MERRITT, NEWMAN, WILKINSON,
     GLASCOW; res Kent Co., MD; dep MHS/FCA (29).
C097 James CLARK Bible; pd 1853; eb 1800; em 1823; on FEINOUR, JAMESON, BURTON;
     res How. Co., MD; LA; AL; pub DAR (in MdGRC 35:76).
C098 James T. CLARK Bible; pd 1881; eb 1815; em 1836; on CRAWFORD, DORSEY,
     BRANCH, GARRISON, HAMMOND, HOWARD; res How. Co., MD;
     pub DAR (in MdGRC 35:80).
C099 CLARK Bible; pd 1852; eb 1837; on WITTS, BLACK, WILSON, POOLE; res Harf.
     Co., MD; pub BMGS 17-1:19.
C100 CLAWSON Bible; eb 1798; em 1824; res CA, Cecil, and QA Cos., MD;
     pub GPF/PMG 3:782.
C101 John W. CLAY Bible; rs 1824-1933; res MD; DC; dep VSL (#616, acc. #21403,
     also refers to #2413).
C102 CLAYPOOLE Bible; pd 1772; eb 1770; em 1793; on ANDERSON, YEWELL, BROWNE,
     RAISIN, HARRISON, COLLINS; res Chestertown, Balto., MD; NY;
     dep MHS/FCA; dep BCHS.
C103 CLAYPOOLE Bible; pd 1873; eb 1848; em 1812; on LLOYD, CLARKE, ORR,
     CLEMENTS, VOIGHT, BRASHER, NOTTINGHAM, ANGIER; res Balto. MD;
     Phila. PA; MO; dep MHS/FCA; dep BCHS.

C104 CLAYTON Bible; pd 1844; eb 1778; em 1796; on LUKENS, WELLS,
      ARCHER; res Balto. and Harf. Cos. MD; dep BGS Harf. Co.
C105 CLAYTON Bible; pd 1844; eb 1823; em 1796; on ARCHER, GRIER, LUKENS, WELLS;
      dep MHS (HBFR,30).
C106 CLAYTON Bible; eb 1814; res QA Co., MD; dep MHS/FCA (29).
C107 CLEAVER Record; pd 1828; eb 1774; dep BGS (from DAR).
C108 CLEMENTS Bible; eb 1781; em 1778; res CA and Kent Cos., MD; pub MG 2:40;
      dep MHS/FCA (29).
C109 CLEMENTS Bible; pd 1834; eb 1783; em 1803; on BAGGS, MORRIS; res Caro.
      Co., MD; dep MHS/FCA (29).
C110 CLEMENTS Bible; eb 1788; dep MdSAR #2354.
C111 CLEMENTS Bible; pd 1846; eb 1821; dep MdSAR 2354 (partial photocopy).
C112 CLEMENTS Bible; eb 1888; em 1906; dep MdSAR 2354.
C113 CLEMSON Bible; eb 1757; on HAINES, HOWARD, SIMPSON, CRUMSON, VARDEN,
      BROWER, BENNETT; pub DAR (in MdGRC 8:146).
C114 CLEMSON Bible; eb 1780; on HAINES, WHITEHALL, JAMES; res MD; Lancaster
      Co., PA; dep MHS/FCA (29).
C115 George W. CLOMAN Bible; eb 1819; em 1843; on NAGLE; res Harf. Co. MD;
      York Co. PA; dep BGS.
C116 George W. CLOMAN Bible; eb 1819; em 1843; on NOGGLE; dep BGS.
C117 Samuel Stringer COALE Bible; eb 1754; em 1775; on HOPKINSON, BUCHANAN,
      BRUNE, OLIVER, DONALDOSN, ATKINSON, BROWN; res MD; MA; England;
      dep MHS/FCA (29).
C118 COALE Bible; rs 1823-1934; res Harf. Co. MD; dep MSA (in G-560:77).
C119 Jesse COBB Bible; eb 1772; em 1771; on HERITAGE, JONES, ISLER, KILPATRICK,
      WHITFIELD, BRYAN, WASHINGTON, GIST; res NC; pub MBR 1:59.
C120 COCKEY Bible; pd 1819; eb 1787; em 1816; on WORTHINGTON, OWINGS, HILL,
      BROWNE, CARLISLE; res Balto. Co. MD; pub BMGS 26-2:186.
C121 COCKEY Bible; rs 1796-1855; res Balto. Co. MD; dep MSA (in G-236:57).
C122 COCKEY Bible; eb 1851; em 1850; dep BGS (photocopy).
C123 COCKEY-WARFIELD Bible; pd 1884; eb 1855; em 1885; on WARFIELD, REGESTER,
      WERTH, HELFRECH, BRADLEY, HALLING; res Balto. and How. Co., MD;
      pub BMGS 26-2:188.
C124 COCKEY Bible; eb 1856; em 1885; on WARFIELD, REGESTER, WERTH, HELFRECH,
      BRADLEY; res Balto. MD; dep MHS/FCA (30).
C125 William COFFIN Bible; eb 1720; em 1740; on PADDOCK, TURRELL, BERNARD,
      SLARLUCK, COLEMAN, MARSHALL, MENDENHALL, DIGGS; pub MBR 1:67.
C126 COGSWELL Bible; pd 1797; eb 1710; em 1732; on BROWNE,
      CASWELL, KINNEY; dep MHS/FCA.
C127 COHEN Bible; eb 1797; em 1819; on ETTING; dep MHS/FCA (30).
C128 COLE Bible; pd 1859; eb 1806; em 1829; on SCOTT, MYERS, BANKERT, ZEPP,
      GRISCOM; res Carr. Co., MD; DC; NC; dep COGS.
C129 COLE Bible; rs 1910-1959; res Harf.Co. MD; dep MSA (in G-560:78).
C130 Thomas COLEMAN Bible; eb 1688; em 1713; on ROBINS, THOMPSON; pub MBR 1:66.
C131 COLES Bible; eb 1745; em 1769; on TUCKER; pub MBR 1:60.
C132 Isaac COLES Bible; eb 1747; em 1771; on LIGHTFOOT, THOMPSON, CARRINGTON,
      PAYNE, PATTON, WHITTLE, WINSTON, HOWELL; res Richmond, VA;
      pub MBR 1:61.
C133 COLLIER Bible; eb 1660; em 1704; on EYERS, GRANER, BALLARD, IRONMENGER,
      EPPES, TUNSTALL; pub MBR 1:40.
C134 COLLIER Bible; eb 1720; em 1763; on WYATT; pub MBR 1:43.
C135 COLLIER Bible; eb 1747; on BROWN, WALTERS, EVERETT, COUNTISS;
      dep MHS/FCA ("Hancock").
C136 COLLIER Bible; eb 1757; em 1788; on BOULDIN, SLAUGHTER, BLACKWELL;
      res probably in AL; pub MBR 1:45.

INVENTORY OF MARYLAND BIBLE RECORDS

C137 COLLIER Bible; eb 1805; em 1828; on STEWART, PICKETT, WILKINS, JONES, WHITE, ELLIOTT; res probably in AL: pub MBR 1:48.
C138 COLLIER Bible; eb 1791; em 1828; on WALKER, MAGUIRE, SIMPSON; res TN; pub MBR 1:50.
C139 COLLINS-LAW-POLK Bible; eb 1738; em 1797; on LAW, POLK; res MD; DE; pub MGB 6:13,25.
C140 COLLINS Bible; pd 1818; eb 1758; em 1813; on MACKEY, ROSSE, GUDLER, WEBSTER, MAGRUDER, DOWNE; res Dor. and QA Cos., MD; RI; dep MHS/FCA; dep MSA (in G-544:1).
C141 Charity COLLINS Bible; eb 1769; dep MHS/FCA (31).
C142 COLLINS Bible; eb 1848; em 1847; on GRIFFIN, PECK, MERRICK, MARTEN, McNAB, MURRAY, MENEFEE, HORATH, COMPTON; res Dor. Co. MD; pub DCGM 2-3:5.
C143 COLSON Bible; pd 1902; eb 1875; em 1904; on OWENS, WAGNER, VERMILLION, WOODS, COLSTON; res PG Co., MD; pub PGCGS Bulletin 18-9:150, May 1987.
C144 COLT Bible; eb 1862; em 1790; on BORROWS, HALLETT, BEEKMAN, NEILSON, CAMPBELL, BROWN, BARCLAY, BOUGHERT, JOHNSON; res NY; dep MHS/FCA.
C145 COLVIN Bible; eb 1778; res PA; OH; dep MHS/FCA (31).
C146 COMBS Bible; ins 1779; eb 1740; em 176(?); on WILLIAMS; res St.M. Co., MD; dep MHS/FCA (31).
C147 COMB Bible; eb 1789; dep FCHS (original in German).
C148 COMPTON Family Record; eb 1667; em 1717; on CLARK; dep MHS/FCA.
C149 COMPTON Bible; eb 1702; on HOWARD, BRISCOE; res St.M. & Chas. Cos., MD; dep MHS/FCA.
C150 COMPTON Bible; eb 1720; em 1719; CLARKE, WOOD; dep MHS/FCA (31).
       Note: Pages catalogued as one Bible may be from two separate Bibles.
C151 CONNELL Bible; pd 1857; eb 1820; em 1844; on HOBBS, THOMPSON, HOOD, HIGGINS, ATCHISON, SWAN, FARBER, COOK, PRICE, BARLOW; res How. Co., MD; pub BMGS 15-3:149.
C152 CONNELL Bible; eb 1829; em 1852; on HOBBS, THOMPSON, HIGGINS, ATCHISON, SWAN; res How. Co., MD; dep MHS/FCA (in Hobbs-Howard file).
C153 CONNIX Bible; eb 1820; em 1818; on COLEMAN, TALBOTT, TERRY, FAUTH, ROSS, POTTER, GALPIN; res Balto.MD; DC; CT; pub DAR (in MdGRC 13:8).
C154 CONNOLLY Bible; pd 1816; eb 1815; res MD; NJ; Ireland; pub NGSQ 56-1:46.
C155 CONRAD Bible; eb 1836; em 1835; on LEWIS, PENN, WORTHINGTON; res Balto. MD; dep MHS/FCA (31).
C156 CONTEE-DENT Bible; eb 1848; em 1874; on NAYLOR, TOWNSHEND, DENT; res MD; dep MHS/FCA (31).
C157 COOK Bible; eb 1752; em 1809; on LINSTED, FARMER, BLOWER, DUNBAR; res AA Co., MD; dep MHS/FCA (32).
C158 Robert COOK Bible; eb 1769; em 1801; on WILSON, DAVIS, MACARTNEY, PULLEN, BIBB, AROSEMENA; res Balto. MD; Phila. PA; dep MHS/FCA (32).
C159 COOK Bible; eb 1818; em 1865; on HAWYER, EDE; res Carr. Co. MD; Cornwall, England; dep MHS/FCA (32).
C160 COOK Bible; pd 1860; eb 1833; em 1857; on THOMAS, MOORE, MARSHALL, WINGATE, SPEDDEN; pub DOBR,13.
C161 COOKERLY Bible; pd 1828; eb 1809; on MYERS, HIGHBARGER; dep MHS/FCA.
C162 COOPER Bible; eb 1750; em 1780; on McCLURE; pub MBR 1:46.
C163 COOPER-JACKSON Bible; eb 1734; em 1795; on MOORE, JACKSON, BUCKLEY; res Cecil Co., MD; dep MHS/FCA.
C164 COOPER-AULD Bible; eb 1767; em 1788; on HARRISON, PORTER, FILLESON, FANNING, TILLOTSON, AULD; dep MHS/FCA (32).
C165 COOPER Bible; pd 1796; eb 1785; on LUKENS; res York Co., PA; dep MHS (HBFR,29).
C166 COOPER Bible; pd 1754; eb 1790; dep MHS/FCA (32).

C167 COOPER Bible; eb 1793; em 1818; on McDANIELS; pub MBR 1:47.
C168 COOPER Bible; pd 1797; on SIMON; res Balto. MD; Wales; dep MHS/FCA (32).
C169 COPE Bible; pd 1895; eb 1882; em 1905; on STTARNER; dep COGS (25).
C170 CORDELL Bible; ins 1832; eb 1847; on STULL; dep BCGS (521).
C171 CORKRAN Bible; pd 1863; eb 1812; em 1840; on CANNON, GAMBRILL, FAIRBANK;
     res Dor. Co., MD; dep COGS (36).
C172 CORNELL Bible; eb 1817; em 1838; on HANN; res Bedford Co., PA;
     dep MHS/FCA (32).
C173 CORNWELL Bible; pd 1824; eb 1819; on SHANBERGER, SMITHSON; res Harf. Co.,
     MD; dep MHS/FCA (32).
C174 Henry CORTELYON Bible; rs 1761-1879 on DeHART, DEMOTT, NEIRNS, VOORHIES;
     res MD; VSL (#697).
C176 COURSEY Bible; eb 1812; dep BCGS (transcript).
C177 COURTNEY Bible; res Harf. Co., MD; dep MSA (G-214, and G-560:32,84).
C178 COURTS Bible; eb 1785; pub MGB 20:8.
C179 COURTS-WILLIAMS Bible; eb 1776; em 1796; on WILLIAMS; res VA; NC; TN;
     pub BMGS 20-2:118.
C180 COVINGTON Bible; eb 1801; em 1826; on FRANKLIN, TOADVINE; dep MHS/FCA (33).
C181 John COWART Bible; eb 1756; em 1782; on WILLIAMS, PRICE, HORN, DRAKE,
     JACKSON, POWELL, TOMLINSON, HOLMES, CAUSEY, SPIVEY, BURNHAM; res GA;
     pub MBR 1:64.
C182 COWDEN-JAMESON Bible; eb 1725; em 1724; on JAMESON, RIDGELY, WALLICE,
     WILLIAMS; res PG Co., MD; pub DAR (in MdGRC 7:40).
C183 COYNER-KOINER Bible; eb 1789; em 1815; on KOINER, PATTERSON, FISHER,
     KYNER, HENKLE, YOUNT; res Augusta Co., VA; dep MHS/FCA (33).
C184 COX Bible; eb 1748; em 1775; on DECKER; pub MBR 1:52.
C185 James COX Bible; eb 1784; em 1813; on PRICE; res MD; DE; OH; IN;
     pub BMGS 22-1:88.
C186 Richard COX Bible; pd 1832; eb 1827; em 1851; on NEWELL, EMERSON,
     HARDEBECK, SLEETH; res OH; IN; pub BMGS 22-1:88.
C187 Walter COX Bible; eb 1821; em 1818; on BERRY, WALKER;
     pub DAR Magazine, Oct. 1980 p.1033.
C188 Walter W. COX Bible; pd 1848; eb 1810; em 1831; pub O'Brien p.298.
C189 COX-COHAGAN-NEIRTT Bible; pd 1808; eb 1774; em 1772; on COHAGAN, NEIRTT;
     pub NGSQ 52-1:37.
C190 CRABTREE Bible; pd 1879; eb 1879; res MD; VA; dep BCGS (502).
C191 CRAIG Bible; pd 1760; eb 1776; em 1837; on ENNALS, BOWIE, DENNIS,
     GOLDSBOROUGH; dep MHS/FCA (33).
C192 CRAIG Bible: rs 1816-1943; res Cecil Co., MD; dep MSA (G-205:16).
C193 CRAIG Bible; pd 1846; eb 1840; em 1861; on JACKSON, GILLISPIE, RUTTER;
     res Cecil Co., MD; dep MHS/FCA (6).
C194 CRAIG-KEENE Bible; eb 1869; em 1901; on RASIN, KEENE; res Balto. Co., MD;
     dep MHS/FCA (Keene).
C195 CRAMPHIN Bible; eb 1813; em 1831; on SMITH, BEAUMONT, JACKSON, JONES,
     MASON, MORSE, PALMER, BRILLINGHAM, GRISWALD, BARLOW; res DC; Phila.
     PA; NY; dep MHS/FCA (33).
C196 CRANDALL Bible: rs 1856-1953; res AA Co., MD; dep MSA (G-838:2).
C197 CRAWFORD Bible; pd 1854; eb 1819; em 1853; on BATES, WARFIELD;
     res Carr. Co., MD; dep COGS (2).
C198 CREAGH-WHITAKER Bible; eb 1773; em 1771; on WHITAKER; res Allegany and
     Harf. Cos., MD; dep BCGS (typed copy).
C199 CREIGHTON Bible; pd 1801; eb 1772; em 1801; on REA, MEEKENS, ENNALS,
     BIRDAEL; res Cambridge, MD; dep MHS/FCA (34).
C200 CREIGHTON Bible; eb 1857; em 1884; on FLOWERS, ADAMS; res Dor. Co., MD;
     pub DCGM 3-2:8.

C201 CRESWELL Bible; eb 1734; em 1807; on GATCHELL, POWLEY, SHIPPEY; res Cecil
Co., MD; dep MHS/FCA (33); dep MSA (in G-236:58).
C202 CREVENSTEN Bible; pd 1834; eb 1819; em 1818; on GREENFIELD;
dep MHS (HBFR,41).
C203 CRISFIELD Bible; eb 1805; on FINLEY, DENNIS; res Balto.,MD; Eastern Shore;
dep MHS/FCA (34).
C204 CROMWELL Bible; rs 1740-1957; res AA Co., MD; dep MSA (G-711).
C205 CROMWELL Bible; eb 1752; res Balto., MD; KY; McAdams p.251.
C206 CROMWELL Bible; eb 1770; res Cecil Co., MD; dep MHS/FCA (34).
C207 CROMWELL Prayer Book; dep BCGS (typed copy).
C208 CROMWELL Bible: rs 1814-1839; dep MSA (in G-823:1).
C209 CRONISE Bible; pd 1803; eb 1758; em 1781; on KNAUFF; dep MHS/FCA (34).
C210 CRONMILLER Bible; rs 1793-1954; on WELLING, CHAMPAYNE, GARDNER, HEATH,
BASTER, OBERWEISER, CONNER, PARSLOW, COALE, BANSEMER, SMITH,
HALVERSON, STEIGER, MARBURY, HUTTON, GRARATLE, OGLE; dep HOGS.
C211 CROOK Bible; eb 1859; em 1880; on HOPKINS, BRYAN, JOHNS; res Balto. and
PG Cos., MD; dep AAGS.
C212 CROOM Bible; eb 1761; em 1787; on RASBERRY; pub MBR 1:63.
C213 CROSBY Bible; pd 1712; eb 1690; em 1753; res How. Co., MD; dep MHS/FCA.
C214 CROSS Bible; pd 1802; eb 1897; dep MHS/FCA (34).
C215 CROTTY Bible; eb 1836; em 1861; on GILLETT, SCHOENLEBER, ARMSTRONG,
DAVENPORT, MOSHER; res Bladensburg, MD; KS; IL; dep MHS/FCA (34).
C216 CROW Bible; eb 1758; em 1793; res MD; KY; pub DAR Magazine, Feb.1972.
C217 Isaac H. CROWTHER Bible; eb 1858; em 1890; dep BCHS (photocopy of original)
C218 CRUIKSHANKS Bible; rs 1772-1853; res Cecil Co., MD; dep MSA (G-560:79).
C219 CRUMBACKER Bible; pd 1777; dep CCGS.
C220 CRUSE Family Record; em 1790; dep MHS/FCA (34).
C221 Sibert CRUTCHER Bible; eb 1772; em 1788; on GILBERT, VAN DYKE, THOMAS,
BEARD, HILL, NORMEN, ASHLY; res VA; pub MBR 1:53.
C222 John CRUTCHER Bible; eb 1804; em 1828; on BEARD, HENRY; pub MBR 1:55.
C223 James B. CRUTCHER Bible; eb 1830; em 1853; on MATTON; res Bedford Co., VA;
KY; pub MBR 1:56.
C224 CULLEN Bible; pd 1855; em 1934; on DIXON; res Dor. Co., MD; dep MHS/FCA
C225 CULLY Bible; eb 1907; em 1905; on BECK, CLAYTON, MARSHALL, COALE,
FERGUSON, BARTLEY; res Frenchtown, Balto., Kingsville, MD; VA; DE;
dep BCGS (512).
C226 CUMMINS-BARTLEY Bible; pd 1812; eb 1788; em 1791; on GRIFFIN, HICKEY,
THORNTON, HINSON; res Cecil Co., MD; Wilmington, DE; dep MHS/FCA.
C227 CUMMINS Bible; pd 1812; eb 1793; em 1791; on THORNTON, HICKEY; res DE;
dep MHS/FCA (35).
C228 John Barton CURRY Bible; eb 1793; em 1824; on RILEY; res Harf. Co., MD;
dep BCHS (transcript); dep BCGS (copy).
C229 CURRY Bible; pd 1792; eb 1736; em 1818; on CLARK, BIDDLE; res Harf. Co.,
MD; pub DAR (in MdGRC 9:106-107).
C230 CURTIS Bible; eb 1764; em 1754; on DENNIS, WATERS, UPSHUR, BALLARD,
LOOCKERMAN; dep MHS/FCA (35).
C231 CUSHING Bible; pd 1791; eb 1752; on MACKENZIE, PINKERTON, LEAVETT, MORRIS,
WILEY, PITCHER; res Balto., MD; MA; dep MHS/FCA (35).

D001 DAIL Bible; pd 1810; eb 1786; em 1785; on BARNS, SMITH, ROBINSON,
HARRINGTON; res Dor. Co., MD; pub DOBR,14.
D002 DALE, Thomas Bible; eb 1744; res Som. and Worc. Cos., MD;
pub DAR Mag Nov. 1984 p.640.
D003 DALE Bible; eb 1764; em 1849; res Som. and Worc. Cos., MD;
pub DAR Mag Nov. 1984 p.640.

D004 DALE Bible; eb 1779; em 1823; on BRATTEN, MUMFORD, TOWNSEND; dep MHS/FCA.
D005 DALE Bible; eb 1799; em 1823; on BRATTEN, MUMFORD, TOWNSEND, WARREN,
  HEARNS, WIMBROW; POWELL, HASTINGS, JONES, WHALEY; dep MHS/FCA.
D006 DALE Bible; eb 1804; em 1800; on JOHNSON; dep MHS/FCA.
D007 DALEY Bible; eb 1818; em 1872; on ROWLES, DELANY; res QA Co., Balto., MD;
  NE; pub BMGS 13:212.
D008 DALLAM Bible; eb 1785; on WORTHINGTON; res Harf. Co., MD; dep HCGS.
D009 DALLAM Bible; eb 1829; em 1827; on MURPHY, YATES; dep MHS/FCA.
D010 James DANIEL Bible; eb 1780; em 1779; pub MBR 1:78.
D011 DANIELS Bible; eb 1801; em 1831; on WARNER, ALLEN, CONNER, MORROW, MASON,
  VAN VALKENBERG, HEVALON; res NH; IL; dep MHS/FCA;
  dep BCHS (typed copy).
D012 DANNER Bible; eb 1761; em 1760; on ALBAUGH, LINDSAY, WILSON, HARD, COX;
  res Unionville, Fred. Co., MD; dep CCGS (no.51).
D013 Asa DARLY Bible; eb 1756; em 1779; on GOORE; res AA Co., MD; SC;
  pub Lester,97.
D014 DARBY-BROWN-PEDDICORD Bibles (3); pd 1812; eb 1943; on HARTMAN, RIGGS,
  SHAW; res MD; dep VSL (#776,acc.#28126).
D015 DARLY-HACKETT Bible; pd 1744; eb 1777; em 1775; on TURFORD, VICKERS,
  GENKINS; res Dor. Co., MD; MO; CA; pub DOBR,23.
D016 D'ARCY Bible; eb 1819; em 1818; on DIDIER; res Balto., MD; dep MHS/FCA.
D017 DARNALL-JONES Bible; eb 1760; em 1782; res PG Co., MD; pub Ardery 2:195.
D018 DARNALL Bible;rs 1801-1851; on BROWN, KELLY; res Chas. Co., MD;
  Champaign Co., OH; dep NGS.
D019 John DARWIN Bible; eb 1755; em 1783; on BLAND, HARRINGTON, KENDRICK,
  POWELL, SANDLEN, SMARR, BERRY, SUMMERFORD, WILKINSON, JAMES, HOPE;
  res MD; SC; pub Lester,98.
D020 DASHIELDS Bible; pd 1864; eb 1833; em 1860; on WHITE, KELLY, McDORMAN;
  dep MHS/FCA.
D021 DASHIELL-JONES Bible; pd 1815; eb 1783; em 1805; on JONES, WAINWRIGHT,
  MAYSE, DISAROON; dep MHS/FCA.
D022 DASHIELL Bible; eb 1809; em 1833; on JONES; res Wico. Co., MD;
  pub DAR (in MdGRC 11:138).
D023 DASHIELL Bible; eb 1848; em 1846; on NOBLE, CHANDLER; dep MHS/FCA.
D024 Levin W. DASHIELL; ins 1850; eb 1848; em 1846; on NOBLE, POWELL;
  pub DAR (in MdGRC 25:93).
D025 DAUGHERTY Bible; pd 1850; eb 1848; em 1847; on JESSOP, REESE, McDANIELS,
  WRIGHTSON, GOLDY, MORRISON, HIGGINS; dep MHS/FCA.
D026 DAVENPORT Bible; eb 1714; dep MHS/FCA.
D027 DAVENPORT Bible; eb 1758; em 1792; on LABRITT, ROSS, BOWEN, TRISLER;
  dep MHS/FCA.
D028 DAVENPORT Bible; rs 1790-1931; dep MSA (G-236:59).
D029 DAVIDSON Bible; eb 1750; em 1770; on CLEMENT, KENNARD, CARTER;
  pub MBR 1:76.
D030 William DAVIS Bible; eb 1750; em 1783; on SPENCE; pub MBR 1:74.
D031 Solomon DAVIS; eb 1752; em 1787; on BYRD, CRESWELL, HOLLINGSWORTH;
  res Worc. Co., MD; SC; pub Lester,101.
D032 Ignatius DAVIS Bible; eb 1754; em 1752; on CLAGETT, PERRY, BRISCOE,
  WILLSON, LACKLAND, WOOTEN, BURGESS; pub MGB 8:17.
D033 Ignatius DAVIS Record; ins 1830; eb 1759; em 1781; on BRISCOE, WILLSON,
  WOOTEN; pub MGB 8:19,29,41.
D034 DAVIS Bible; eb 1769; em 1791; on ROBERTSON; pub MRB 2:57; dep BCGS.
D035 DAVIS Bible; eb 1786; em 1809; on TOWNSEND; MHS/FCA.
D036 DAVIS Bible; eb 1799; dep BCHS (typed copy).
D037 DAVIS Bible; eb 1806; em 1829; res Worc. & Chas. Cos., MD; pub MGB 2:12.
D038 DAVIS Bible; eb 1827; em 1828; on VICKARS, MEDFORD; pub DOBR,15.

D039 DAVIS Bible; rs 1831-1948; dep MSA (D-272:5).
D040 DAVIS Bible; rb 1836; on STREETT, RUFF, GLADDEN, SCARBOROUGH, WALLACE,
     MARRY, WILSON; res Harf. Co., MD; dep HCGS.
D041 DAVIS James Wilson Bible; eb 1836; em 1865; on GLADDEN,
     STRATT, SCARBOROUGH, WALLCE; dep BCHS (typed copy).
D042 DAVIS Bible; rs 1845-1959; res Mont. Co., MD; dep MSA (G-560:80).
D043 DAVIS Bible; pd 1873; eb 1848; em 1875; on BREWER; res Fred. Co., MD;
     dep MHS/FCA.
D044 DAVIS Bible; rs 1853-1943; dep MSA (G-223:43).
D045 DAVIS Bible; pd 1872; eb 1857; em 1884; on SPICER; res Harf. Co.; dep BCGS.
D046 DAVIS Bible; rb 1857; res Harf. Co., MD; dep HCGS.
D047 George A. DAVIS Bible; ins 1866; eb 1866; em 1865; on WALLACE, HARRY,
     GLADDEN, WILSON, STREET, SCARBOROUGH; dep MHS (HBFR,6).
D048 DAVIS Bible; eb 1879; em 1877; on RAMEY, NICHOLSON, RODRICK, VAN VALEN,
     FAY, GOEBEL; res Fred. Co., VA; dep MHS/FCA.
D049 DAVIS Bible; rs 1892-1948; dep MSA (D-272:6).
D050 Isaac DAVISSON Bible; eb 1746; em 1779; on ANDERSON; pub MBR 1:79.
D051 DAWSON Bible; rs 1800-1864; res Balto. and AA Cos., MD; dep MSA (G-938:1).
D052 DAY Family Record; ins 1772; eb 1749; em 1772; on CRUIKSHANK, CRANE,
     DUDLEY; res Balto. & Harf. Cos., MD; pub DAR (in MdGRC 5:66).
D053 Edward DAY Bible; eb 1759; em 1787; on PRESBURY, BROWN, TUCKER, WESTON,
     JOHNSON, McGHEE, RIDDLE;res Balto. & Harf. Cos., MD; dep MHS/FCA.
D054 DAY Bible; rb 1829; on JOHNSON, BARNES, FORD, MARTIN, SHERMAN;
     res Havre de Grace, MD; dep HCGS.
D055 DE ALBA Bible; pd 1877; eb 1880; em 1879; on KRAMER; res Balto.; dep AAGS.
D056 DEAN Bible; pd 1872; eb 1798; em 1817; on REESE, DYKMAN, GANNON,
     CARPENTER, CAMBURN, HILLIS, KADILAC, ANDREWS; res Balto. Co., MD;
     Medford, OR; dep BCGS.
D057 DEAN-McNISH; rs 1795-1833 Bible; on McNISH; dep HCGS.
D058 DEAN Bible; pd 1890; eb 1882; em 1880; on CROMWELL, PARLEE, HARRISON;
     res New Brunswick, Canada; dep AAGS.
D059 DEAVER Family Records; eb 1787; em 1777; on BLUNT; pub NGSQ 23-2:52.
D060 DEAVER Bible; rs 1842-1902; dep MSA (G-503:3).
D061 DEAVER Bible; eb 1844; em 1875; on WILSON, FEATHERSTON, BABCOX, WYCHE;
     pub MBR I:84.
D062 Barney DeCORSE Bible; pd 1825; eb 1820; em 1819; on PRICE, BAKER, FRANCE;
     res Kent Co., MD; pub DAR (in MdGRC 7:315).
D063 De JARNETTE Bible; eb 1748; em 1769; on OWEN, PICKETT; pub MBR 1:86.
D064 DELAROCHE Bible; em 1787; on MERKUS, DANGIRARD, KOECHLIN, McNULTY, BELT,
     FRAILEY, PATTERSON; res MD; Amsterdam; dep MHS/FCA.
D065 DELAWTER Bible; pd 1877; eb 1806; em 1895; on GALL, BROWN, SCHROYER,
     BORCHERDING, BIRLEY; res Fred. Co., MD; dep MHS/FCA.
D066 DELCHER Bible; eb 1788; em 1865; on WILSON, BOWEN, BOWMAN, KEMP,
     GOLDSMITH, GEBHARD; res Balto. MD; dep MHS/FCA.
D067 DELONG Bible; pd 1870; eb 1869; res Whitehall, PA; dep CCGS (#43).
D068 de MARCELLIN Bible; eb 1805; em 1830; on SLOCUM, BUDD, FROST; dep MHS/FCA.
D069 DEMMY-STONER Bible; rs 1844-1915; pd 1875; eb 1844; em 1878; on STONER;
     res Lane and Cumberland Cos., PA; pub HCMR 5:69,dep HCGS.
D070 DENMEAD; rs 1796-1855 Bible; dep MSA (G-236:57).
D071 DENNIS Bible; pd 1754; eb 1756; em 1754; on UPSHUR;
     res Northampton Co., VA; dep MHS/FCA.
D072 DENNIS Bible; eb 1821; em 1825; on ROBERTSON, JOYNER, HOOE, PITTS,
     ROBERTS, JOHNSON, MURDOCK, MOORE, BRATTEN, DASHIELL; dep MHS/FCA.
D073 DENNY-ROBERTS Bible; pd 1783; eb 1779; em 1780; on BRUFF, ROBERTS;
     res Balto., MD; dep MHS/FCA.
D074 DENT-PERRY Bible; pd 1764; eb 1737; em 1763; pub NGSQ 52-2:104.

BIBLES

D075 DENT Bible; rs 1848-1927; dep MSA (G-560:81).
D076 George DERN Bible; eb 1818; em 1847; on SNOOK, FORREST, REINSWALD,
     BAUMGARDNER, DUTTERA, TROXELL, MEHRING, LAUBLE;
     pub DAR (in MdGRC 7:61).
D077 DEROCHBRUNE Bible; eb 1820; em 1820; on DOWNES, ORRELL, LEAVERTON,
     MULLIKEN, WILKINSON, SAULSBERY, WILSON; res QA Co., MD;
     dep MHS/FCA; dep MSA (G-560:82).
D078 DETWILER Bible; pd 1873; eb 1846; em 1902; on GRUNDEN, STONE, OWENS,
     KELLY; dep BCGS (from DAR).
D079 DE VAUGHN Bible; rs 1772-1881; pd 1815; on HACKNEY, HEADON, HURDLE,
     MYERS, PASQUAL; res MD; VA; dep VSL (#823, acc. #29741).
D080 DEVILBISS-KOLB Bible; eb 1793; em 1815; on CASTON, KOLB; res Creagerstown,
     MD; pub MDG 12-4:89; dep MHS/FCA.
D081 Charles DEVILBISS Bible; eb 1828; em 1851; on ENGLE, SNADER, ENGLER,
     SHUEY; res New Windsor, MD; dep MHS/FCA.
D082 George W. DEVILBISS Bible; pd 1861; eb 1830; em 1857; on BAILE, ROOP,
     GORSUCH, NUSBAUM, BARNES, STERN, FISHER, GAULT;
     dep BCGS (from Yingling).
D083 DICKERSON Bible; rs 1778-1914; res Mont. Co., MD; dep MSA (G-560:83).
D084 Thomas DICKINSON Bible; eb 1737; em 1760; on STEVENS; pub MBR 1:81.
D084A DICKINSON Bible; pd 1803; eb 1778; em 1802; on STEVENS,
     WILLARD, SCHNAUFFER; dep MHS/FCA.
D085 DICKINSON Bible; pd 1850; eb 1837; em 1751; on MERRILL, ADAMS, BURNETT,
     PORTER, WALLER, SAVAGE, LAMBDEN, PRIMROSE, WOOLVERTON, LLOYD;
     dep MHS/FCA.
D086 DICKINSON Bible; pd 1824; eb 1829; em 1828; dep MHS/FCA.
D087 DIFFENDERFER Bible; eb 1744; em 1773; on ROGERS, WILLIAM; res MD; MO; CA;
     pub MGB 14:41,53 and 15:4,18.
D088 DIGGES Bible; eb 1838; em 1875; on INGLEHART; res PG Co., MD; TX;
     dep MHS/FCA.
D089 DIGGES Bible; pd 1867; eb 1793; em 1821; on SPARK, LANE, OLDNER;
     res Westmoreland and Fauquier Cos., VA; dep MHS/FCA.
D090 Joseph DILL; eb 1788; em 1787; on WRIGHT; res TN; pub MBR 1:91.
D091 DISNEY Bible; pd 1852; eb 1829; em 1851; on WEEAT, BOWEN;
     res Balto. Co., MD; dep MHS/FCA; dep BCHS (typed copy).
D092 William Thomas DISNEY Bible; pd 1834; eb 1771; em 1794; pub NGSQ 20:115.
D093 DISNEY Bible; eb 1831; em 1854; pub MG 2:277.
D094 DITTO Family Record; eb 1865; em 1864; on MILLER; res Wash. Co., MD;
     dep MHS/FCA.
D095 DIUGUID Bible; pd 1892; eb 1863; em 1931; on ZIRKLE, POWELL, SWEENE,
     HACEDY, McLIN, HEANY, NEFF, KING; res Balto., MD; dep CCGS.
D096 DIUQUID Bible; pd 1924; dep CCGS.
D097 DIUQUID Bible; pd 1815; eb 1795; em 1817; on PALTISON; dep CCGS.
D098 DIUQUID Bible; pd 1815; eb 1809; em 1808; dep CCGS.
D099 DIUQUID Bible; pd 1882; eb 1858; em 1853; on CADE, McNAMEE, ZIRKLE,
     SPENCER, HORN, FOY, NALLS, SIMMONS, MYERS; dep CCGS.
D100 DIX Bible; pd 1874; eb 1830; em 1865; on MILSOS, ADAMS, BLOXOM;
     dep BCHS (typed copy), dep MHS/FCA (poor photocopy).
D101 DIXON Bible; pd 1802; eb 170(?); em 1703; on REID, PATTISON, MANNING,
     McKEEL; res Harf. Co., MD; Sussex Co., DE;
     dep MSA (G-475); dep MHS.
D102 DOBBINS Bible; eb 1734; dep MHS/FCA.
D103 DOBBINS Bible; eb 1756; em 1754; on JONES, SHUTE, MURRELL;
     dep MHS/FCA (Dobbins, Budd, etc.).
D104 DOBBINS-BUDD Bible; eb 1816; em 1844; on BISBEE, MOFFETT, STRYKER, BUDD,
     DeMARCELLIN; res Balto., MD; Mt. Holly, NJ; dep MHS/FCA.

25

INVENTORY OF MARYLAND BIBLE RECORDS

D105 DOCWRA Bible; pd 1845; eb 1819; em 1852; on GRISWOLD, TAYLOR, TARR, HORN, ROGERS; res MD; VA; England; dep MHS/FCA.
D106 DONALDSON Bible; eb 1784; em 1808; on HAMMOND, CLAPHAM; res Balto., MD; dep MHS/FCA.
D107 DODD Bible; pd 1880; eb 1861; dep AAGS; dep MHS/FCA.
D108 DONALDSON Bible; pd 1841; eb 1812; em 1837; on MADEN, OWENS, WOODS, HALL, BUFFINGTON, BUTLER; KEITH, STEELE, NEWCOMBE, HILL; dep MHS/FCA.
D109 DONALDSON Bible; rs 1888-1952; dep MSA (in G-536).
D110 DONAT Bible; pd 1844; eb 1839; em 1867; on ROTHROCK; res DC; Germany; dep MHS/FCA.
D111 DONE Bible; pd 1815; eb 1840; em 1814; on WATERS, HAYNIE, MORTON, BISCOE, KERR, GALE, STEWART, MASLIN, PADDOCK; dep MHS/FCA.
D112 DONNELL Bible; eb 1839; em 1795; on KYLE, PATTERSON, KNOX, DOWELL; dep MHS/FCA.
D113 DONNOH Family Record; eb 1768; res Dor. Co., MD; pub DOBR,15.
D114 DONSIFE Bible; eb 1851; em 1893; on AINSWORTH; dep CCGS (14),(fragments).
D115 DONSIFE Bible; pd 1885; eb 1800; em 1826; on STAUP, BISHOP, SHANK, AINSWORTH, KIDDER; res Fred. amd Carr. Cos., MD; dep CCGS (7).
D116 DORSEY Bible; rs 1659-1947; dep MSA (in G-570).
D117 DORSEY Bible; pd 1714; eb 1708; em 1751; on OWINGS, GILLIS; res AA & Balto. Cos., MD; dep MHS/FCA.
D118 DORSEY Bible; eb 1745; on STIMSON, FITZSIMMONS, STRAUGHN, JOHNSON, WRIGHT; res AA, Caro. Cos., MD; DE; dep MSA (in OBR p.87).
D119 DORSEY Bible; eb 1751; em 1772; on WORTHINGTON, BROOKS, MERRIWEATHER, HOWARD, BAER, HAMMOND, WARRING, BROWN; pub BMGS 51-4:65; pub DAR (in MdGRC 35:3).
D120 DORSEY Bible; pd 1815; eb 1760; em 1806; on BROWN, PUE, BOWEN, GRUNDY, CARPENTER; pub DAR (in MdGRC 10:176).
D121 DORSEY Bible; eb 1762; em 1759; pub NGSQ 5-3:46.
D122 Joshua W. DORSEY Bible; eb 1783; em 1840; on LUMMER, WARFIELD, WALLING; res Mont. Co., MD; pub DAR (in MdGRC 33:55).
D123 Harry Woodward DORSEY Bible; eb 1786; dep MHS/FCA.
D124 DORSEY Bible; eb 1790; em 1790; on JOHNSON, LYNN; dep MHS/FCA (Hammond-Dorsey Bible).
D125 William Hammond DORSEY Bible; pd 1788; eb 1790; em 1790; on JOHNSON, LYNN; dep MHS/FCA.
D126 John DORSEY Bible; eb 1809; res Calv. Co., MD; pub O'Brien, p.300.
D127 DORSEY Bible; pd 1831; eb 1809; on CRANFORD, CROMWELL, CHAVANNES; res Huntingtown, Calv. Co., MD; dep MHS/FCA.
D128 DORSEY-LEWIS Bible; pd 1850; eb 1813; on BOSS, BINGHAM, LEWIS; res Carr. Co., MD; DC; pub BMGS 19-3:180; 26-1:81.
D129 Philip Hammond DORSEY Bible; eb 1816; em 1815; on HAMMOND, MACKEY; pub DAR (in MdGRC 25:4).
D130 Stephen B. DORSEY Bible; pd 1842; eb 1818; em 1842; pub DAR (in MdGRC 33:47).
D131 Elizabeth DORSEY Bible; pd 1850; eb 1823; em 1847; pub BMGS 26-1:81.
D132 DORSEY RECORD Bible; em 1831; pub MDG 3-1:10; 15-1:5.
D133 William DORSEY Bible; pd 1845; eb 1845; em 1844; on ANDERSON, CALVERT; res How. Co., MD; pub DAR (in MdGRC 35:82).
D134 Clement DORSEY Bible; pd 1854; eb 1850; em 1849; on OWENS, CRANFORD, WILSON, WILLIAMS, BOWEN, WARD; LYONS, res Calv. Co., MD; pub O'Brien, p.298; dep MHS/FCA.
D135 DORSEY-REHMEYER Bible; pd 1872; eb 1850; em 1851; on CHENOWETH, REHMEYER; dep MHS/FCA.

BIBLES

D136 DORSEY Bible; eb 1861; em 1887; on TAYLOR, HALL, KELLY, BOARDLEY, CARTER, MYERS; res How. Co., MD; dep MHS/FCA.
D137 DOSH Bible; pd 1827; eb 1837; dep BCGS (transcription).
D138 DOTY Bible; pd 1801; eb 1760; em 1786; on MILLENS; dep MHS/FCA.
D139 Abraham DOTY Bible; eb 1779; em 1801; on BARR, KING, HOWEY; pub MBR 1:79.
D140 DOUGHTY Bible; pd 1714; pub MGB 2:6.
D141 DOUGLAS-SMOOT Bible; eb 1790; em 1812; on TURPIN, GIBBONS, SMOOT; res Dor. Co., MD; pub DAR Magazine 66:673.
D142 Stephen Elbert DOUGLASS Bible; rs 1832-1942; pd 1881; on CLARK, FATHERLY, GAREY, GRAFF, KREINER, PHILLIPS, RHOE, WILLIS; res Dor. & Caro. Cos., MD; dep VSL (#875, acc. 30453).
D143 DOUTY Bible; pd 1848; eb 1847; em 1846; on BYERS, TAYLOR, THOMAS, LOUNSBERRY; res Balto. City, Allegany & Carr. Cos., MD; dep MHS/FCA.
D144 DOVE Bible; em 1854; on PERRY, SMITH, HARDY, DESHAROON, JENKINS; dep MHS/FCA (copied from Bible).
D145 DOWDEN Bible; pd 1879; eb 1826; em 1849; res Harf. & Mont. Cos., MD; pub MDG 11-3:40.
D146 DOWNES Bible; eb 1844; em 1820; on ROSSE, GUDLER, MEDLEY; res Centreville, MD; dep MHS.
D147 DOWNES Bible, rs 1820-1932 Bible; dep MSA (in G-552:2).
D148 Samuel DOWNES Bible; eb 1778; em 1800; on EDWARDS, EUBANKS, BELL, PAYNE, HALL, BURGESS, BLACKWELL; pub MBR 1:87.
D149 Frederick DOWNING Bible; eb 1814; em 1841; on BURGESS, KIRK; res VA; pub MBR 1:89.
D150 DOWNING Bible; eb 1885; em 1884; on FORD; dep MHS/FCA.
D151 James DOWNS Bible; pd 1816; eb 1791; em 1816; res MD; IN; pub MBR 4:27.
D152 Thomas DOWNS Bible; eb 1765; em 1788; res MD; Phila. PA; KY; IN; pub MGB 4:19.
D153 DOWSON Bible; pd 1809; eb 1732; em 1808; on SAVAGE; res Balto.MD; Eastern Shore, MD; England; pub MDG 11-1:5; 23-4:112; dep MHS.
D154 DRAGO Bible; pd 1871; eb 1828; em 1849; on BENSON, HIGGINS, SAMES, BROWN, WILKINS, CUBBAGE; dep MHS/FCA.
D155 Albritton DRAKE Bible; pd 1775; em 1735; pub MBR 1:85.
D156 DRAKE-FERGUSON Bible; pd 1866; eb 1780; em 1862; on FERGUSON, GUNN, BIRDWELL, GILLILAND; dep MHS/FCA.
D157 DRIVER Bible; eb 1707; em 1762; pub MDG 18-1:16.
D158 Benjamin DRUMMOND Bible; pd 1832; eb 1775; em 1797; on KERNS, McLINTOCH, WELCH, COX, ROWELL, GRAVEN, VEAL, RANDALL, HITCHCOCK; res OH; pub BMGS 13:20.
D159 DRURY Bible; pd 1863; eb 1883; em 1880; on RAILEY; dep MHS/FCA.
D160 DRYDEN Bible; pd 1814; eb 1792; em 1806; on ROBERTS, OWINGS, HARRIS, APPOLD, HURST, KEIRL, SWINTON; res Worc. & Balto. Cos., Snow Hill, MD; dep MHS/FCA.
D161 DRYDEN Bible; pd 1846; eb 1840; em 1840; on DAVIS, LARKIN, GIVANS, TWILLEY; dep WCFL (Md. Room).
D162 DUBOURG Bible; pd 1875; eb 1849; em 1867; on HOWE; res Louisville, KY; pub BMGS 20-4:342; dep MHS/FCA.
D163 DUER Bible; pd 1807; eb 1812; em 1811; res Balto. MD; PA; pub GPF/PGM p.857.
D164 DUCKETT Bible; rs 1743-1891; dep MSA (in G-598).
D165 DUDROW Bible; dep FCHS (original Bible, in German).
D166 DUKE Bible; eb 1765; em 1786; on SOMERVELL, BROOME, MORSELL, DOWELL; res Calv. Co., MD; dep MHS/FCA (with Wilkinson Bible Record.
D167 DUKE Bible; pd 1803; eb 1788; on MOLER, TOWN, ENGLE, McGARRY, CHISWELL; res Jefferson County VA (now WVA); pub BMGS 24-2:142.

27

D168 DUKE Bible; pd 1849; eb 1847; em 1821; on DENT, COPPAGE, HAMMETT, DURENT, WATHEM; res St.M. Co., MD; pub BMGS 11-3:17.
D169 Matthew DUNAWAY Bible; eb 1777; em 1800; on TUCKER; pub MBR 1:83.
D170 DUNCAN Bible; rs 1861-1912; pd 1881; res Southern MD; dep VSL (#903, acc. 29741).
D171 DUNLAP Bible; pd 1857; eb 1802; em 1808; on HAVNER, HILLSON, KOHR, ANDERSON, HEFFNER, WILLSON, FERLL, BARR, CORE, NEWCOMMER, HOFF; res Balto.Co., MD; York Co., PA; dep MHS/FCA; dep BCGS.
D172 William T. DUNTON Bible; rs 1786-1976; pd 1876; VSL (#909, acc. 3043).
D173 DUPUY Bible; eb 1738; on WINTER; res VA; KY; pub MBR 1:75.
D174 DURHAM Bible; eb 1775; em 1817; dep BCGS (photocopy).
D175 DURHAM Bible; rb 1857; on GLADDEN, LOWE, RICHARDSON, BULL, NORRIS; res Harf. Co., MD; dep HCGS.
D176 DUSHANE Bible; pd 1772; eb 1774; em 1776; on DUTTON, DORAN, dep MHS/FCA.
D177 DUSHANE Bible; pd 1700; eb 1744; em 1776; on WILSON, JONES, BLACKLOCH, PENNEMAN, DUKE; dep MHS/FCA.
D178 DUSHANE Bible; pd 1826; eb 1810; em 1832; on EVANS, CALDWELL, BRUNT, REYNOLDS, TIPPY; dep MHS/FCA.
D179 DUTROW Bible; pd 1880; eb 1855; em 1878; on HOWARD, YASTE, res Fred. & Balto. Cos. MD; DC; dep MHS/FCA.
D180 DUVALL Bible; pd 1803; eb 1747; em 1774; on KEMP, SMITH, DAWSON, HAWKINS, DORSEY, GREEN, HARRISON, CLAGETT; res MD; MI; dep MHS/FCA.
D181 Daniel DUVALL Bible; eb 1750; em 1793; on HERRING, MASON, RUSSELL, DULANY, BATES, JEFFRIES, MANSEN, SETTLE, COVINGTON; pub MBR 1:82.
D182 DUVALL Bible; pd 1833; eb 1755; em 1785; on GARDENER, KNIGHTON, CARR, TUCK, DAVIS, STOCKETT; dep MHS/FCA.
D183 DUVALL Bible; eb 1811; em 1841; on TURNER, LAWRENCE, JAMES, LEE; res Balto. MD; OH; pub MGB 18:27.
D184 DUVALL Bible; pd 1846; eb 1818; em 1855; pub NGSQ 29-2:71.
D185 DYKES Bible; pd 1851; on CONWAY; res Balto., MD; pub PGCGS Bulletin 18-4: Dec. 1986.
D186 DYOTT Bible; pd 1852; eb 1791; em 1803; on LAYTON, DOWNES, ROSZELL, STUBBLEFIELD, COOK; dep MHS/FCA.
D187 DYOTT Bible; pub CC 9-1:6.

E001 EAGON Bible; on WINDSOR, WHEATLEY; pub DOBR,15.
E002 EAGON Bible; eb 1849; em 1896; on COLLINS, WHEATLEY; pub DOBR,16.
E003 EAMS Bible; pd 1816; eb 1798; em 1823; on BALL, OAKLEY, SLATER, YATES; res VA; dep MHS/FCA.
E004 EARLE Bible; pd 1867; eb 1844; em 1873; res Clinton Co., NY; MA; RI; CT; on BURNETT; dep BCGS; dep DAR.
E005 EARLE Bible; eb 1849; em 1848; on GOLDSBOROUGH; dep MHS/FCA.
E006 EARP Bible; pd 1872; eb 1884; em 1882; on LAYNOR; res Elk Ridge, MD; Newark, NJ; dep MHS/FCA.
E007 EASON Bible; eb 1847; res Talb. Co., MD; dep MHS/FCA.
E008 EASON Bible; pd 1885; eb 1887; em 1880; on PRICE, BARNES, ALLISON; res Balto. Co., MD; NC; dep MHS/FCA.
E009 EATON Bible; pd 1893; eb 1847; em 1844; on MAYLER, WELD, dep MHS/FCA.
E010 EBAUGH Bible; pd 1892; eb 1864; em 1917; on GONSO, GROVE, SHAVER, HERRMANN, HAINES, HULL, FRUSH, MARVIN, VAN DYKE, BAUBLITZ; dep BCGS (Yingling).
E011 EBBERT Bible; eb 1753; on SWENDNER; dep FCHS (original Bible).
E012 ECKER Bible; pd 1872; eb 1845; em 1870; on IZER, WRIGHT, ENGLER, BEECHLEY, DICKEY, HELDERBRIDLE, GILBERT, WILLARD; res Carr. Co., MD; dep BCGS (from DAR).

E013 ECKER Bible; eb 1807; em 1833; on HAINES; dep MHS/FCA.
E014 ECKHARDT Bible; eb 1825; on VON GUNTER; res Balto., MD; Germany;
     dep BCHS (typed page).
E015 EDGELL Bible; eb 1843; em 1859; on COLLISON, COATES, RAUGHLEY, OCHELTREE,
     KINDER, PRATT; dep MHS/FCA.
E016 EDWARDS-FARIS Bible; eb 1703; em 1785; on PATTERSON, BOULDIN, FARIS;
     pub DAR (in MdGRC 6:201).
E017 Anna Pickett EDWARDS Bible; eb 1818; em 1857; on BIBB, NEAL, TALIAFERRO,
     CARY, WINSTON; res Balto., MD; AL; pub MBR 1:95.
E018 John EDWARDS Bible; eb 1759; em 1786; on RAINY; res VA; GA; England;
     pub MBR 1:183.
E019 EGERTON Bible; pd 1866; eb 1839; em 1866; res Balto., MD; dep BCGS.
E020 EICHELBERGER, ins 1656 Bible; eb 1782; em 1781; on WELSH;
     dep MHS/FCA (translation from German).
E021 EICHELBERGER Bible; pd 1848; eb 1827; em 1849; on SCHALL;
     dep MHS/FCA (also contains clippings).
E022 EICHELBERGER Bible; eb 1827; em 1849; on SCHALL, DUNCAN;
     dep BCHS (typed copy).
E023 EICHELBERGER Bible; pd 1816; em 1833; on TONHBAUGH; dep DAR
     (in MdGRC 33:93).
E024 EICHELBERGER Bible; pd 1881; eb 1839; em 1802; on WEANT, FAVORITE;
     res Fred. Co., MD; dep BCGS (in Yingling).
E025 ELDER Bible; eb 1707; em 1781; on SNOWDEN, BALDURN, JENKINS, SCOTT,
     WINCHESTER, BLANCHARD; dep MHS/FCA.
E026 James ELKIN Bible; eb 1755; em 1782; on JACKSON, OSBORN; pub MBR 1:93.
E027 ELLENDER Bible; pd 1801; on BOWEN, LAUGHLIN; res Balto. MD;
     dep BCGS (The Notebook, 23:4, Mar.1984).
E028 ELLIOTT Bible; pd 1833; eb 1832; em 1857; on MELCHOIR, SHORT, STRUTHOFF;
     dep MHS/FCA.
E029 ELLIOTT Bible; rs 1862-1954; dep MSA (in G-814:15).
E030 ELLIS Bible; eb 1806; em 1833; on DAUGHTERS, MITCHELL, PHIPPS, REIGHARDT,
     MUMFORD, KREUTZER, PARKER, MILLER, DATTON; res Snow Hill, MD;
     dep WCFL (MD Room).
E031 EMMART Bible; eb 1709; dep MHS/FCA (Gore).
E032 EMMART Bible; eb 1815; em 1791; on BROWN, WORDEN, ZIMMERMAN, CODLING,
     INGLEHART, ALLEN, LYETH, TUNANUS; res Balto. Co., MD;
     dep BCHS (typed copy).
E033 EMMART Bible; pd 1872; eb 1815; em 1797; on CODLING, PEIRPONT, ALVERDA;
     res Balto. Co., MD; dep CCGS.
E034 EMMART Bible; eb 1769; em 1846; on LILLY; dep BCHS (typed copy).
E035 EMMERT Bible; pd 1876; eb 1811; em 1875; on NEWCOMER, WINGERT, LAMBERT,
     PENNINGTON; dep WaHS; dep WaCFL.
E036 EMMORD Bible; eb 1879; em 1911; on FORWOOD, BOESHAL, LANTZ; res Harf. Co.,
     MD; Germany; dep MHS (HBFR,44).
E037 EMORY Bible; pd 1728; eb 1751; em 1756; res Balto. Co., MD; pub MG 1:430.
E038 EMORY Bible; pd 1784; eb 1758; em 1786; on RUTTER, STERLING, MARQUETTE;
     res QA Co., MD; Phila., PA; dep MHS/FCA.
E039 John ENGLAND Bible; eb 1755; em 1782; on MUSSELMAN, BECK, TRUSLOW, BAKER,
     BROOKS; res Bucks Co., PA; Stafford Co., VA; pub MBR 1:99.
E040 Joseph ENGLE Bible; pd 1820; eb 1800; em 1822; dep BCGS (in Yingling).
E041 ENGLAR Bible; eb 1814; on ROYER; res Carr. Co., MD;
     dep BCGS (in Yingling).
E042 Hiram ENGLAR Bible; pd 1863; eb 1823; em 1846; on ENGEL, DEVILLBISS,
     NICODEMUS, BUCKEY, SHUNICK; dep BCGS (in Yingling); dep MHS/FCA.
E043 Elhanan ENGLAR Bible; eb 1833; em 1858; on BUCKEY, NUSBAUM, SNADER;
     res Fred. Co., MD; dep MHS/FCA.

E044 ENGLAR Bible; pd 1879; eb 1852; em 1879; on ROOP, BAILE, NORRIS, SENSENEY; res Carr. Co., MD; dep BCGS (in Yingling); dep MHS/FCA.

E045 Nathan ENGLAR Bible; eb 1853; em 1884; on SMITH, BARNES; res Carr. Co., MD; dep MHS/FCA.

E046 Josiah ENGLAR Bible; eb 1809; em 1840; on HAINES, WRIGHT, FEAGO, BENSON, CREAGER, WALKER, ROUZER, MYERS, BUFFINGTON; res Carr. Co., MD; dep MHS/FCA.

E047 ENSEY Bible; eb 1757; em 1775; on JACOBS, WEST, FAHNESTOCK, DEARDORFF, RICHARDSON, NORRIS, BROCKENBROUGH, HARTWELL; dep MHS/FCA.

E048 Jeremiah ENLOW Bible; pd 1812; eb 1825; em 1813; res Balto. Co., MD; pub MGB 3:30.

E049 ENSEY Bible; pd 1878; eb 1880; em 1819; on BROCKENBROUGH, HARTWELL, LOWE, GORMAN; res Balto., MD; dep MHS (photocopy).

E050 Joseph ENSOR Bible; pd 1752; eb 1758; em 1757; pub DAR (in MdGRC 33:36).

E051 ENSOR Bible; pd 1775; eb 1758; em 1757; on OLDHAM, BIDDLE, BOUCHELLE; dep MHS/FCA.

E052 ENSOR Bible; eb 1788; res Balto. Co., MD; dep MHS/FCA.

E053 ENSOR Bible; eb 1788; em 1787; dep BCGS.

E054 ENSOR Bible; pd 1884; eb 1796; dep BCGS.

E055 ENSOR Bible; eb 1883; em 1910; on MAYS; res Balto. Co., MD; dep BCGS.

E056 William EPPERSON Bible; eb 1806; em 1829; on RICHARDSON, PERKINS, ASH; res TN; IN; IL; CO; pub MBR 1:97.

E057 EPPES Bible; pd 1850; eb 1843; em 1888; on COLEMAN, POWELL, GRIGG, ARCHER, GLIDEWELL, SPENCER; dep BCGS (typed copy).

E058 EPPS Bible; eb 1842; em 1861; on POWELL, COLEMAN, ARCHER, BRIGG, GLIDEWELL; dep MHS/FCA (filed with Dix Bible).

E059 Peter ERB Bible; pd 1852; eb 1789; em 1813; on WIKERT, BROWN, BYERS; dep BCGS (in Yingling p.78).

E060 ESEISI Bible; pd 1765; eb 1762; dep BCGS (typed copy).

E061 ESTEP Bible; rs 1770-1887; on WALL, WHEATLEY; dep MSA (G-544).

E062 ESTEP Bible; rs 1788-1921; dep MSA (G-570:4).

E063 ESTEP-WILEY Bible; eb 1802; on WILEY, KEECH; dep MHS/FCA (photostat hard to read).

E064 ETTER-KISTER Bible; eb 1802; em 1826; on BURGES, BOYERMAN, WILLES, ORT, GIST, WISTER; dep MHS/FCA; dep BCGS(typed copy).

E065 EVANS Bible; pd 1736; eb 1718; on LUCUS, HUGHES, SWAN, CARLE, WILLIAMS; dep MHS.

E066 John EVANS Diary; eb 1705; em 1795; res Balto. and Carr. Cos., MD; dep Methodist Hist. Soc. (#1675), Balto., MD..

E067 EVANS Bible; pd 1828; eb 1773; em 1808; on COARD; res Sussex Co., DE; MD; pub DAR (in MdGRC 7:321).

E068 EVANS Bible; rs 1824-1929; res Kent Co., MD; dep MSA (G-187:5).

E069 John EVANS Bible; pd 1832; dep MHS/FCA (poor photostat).

E070 EVERETT Bible; eb 1716; em 1718; on BEAL, LIRNER, COLLIER, COUNTERS; dep MHS/FCA (under Hancock).

E071 EVERSFIELD Bible; pd 1718; dep MHS/FCA (incl. coat of arms).

E072 EWING Bible; pd 1762; eb 1758; em 1787; on COOKER, DORSEY; dep MHS/FCA.

E073 H. Gorden EWING Bible; eb 1753; em 1788; on ROBINSON, OLIVER, MASON, COURTNEY, WRAY, ANTHONY, REDDIN, BARTON, MITCHELL; dep MHS/FCA.

E074 EYSTER Bible; pd 1874; eb 1866; em 1866; dep MHS/FCA (Bible Records Collection).

F001 FAIRBAIRN Bible; pd 1750; eb 1810; em 1809; on TILGHMAN, HENRY, BREWER, HIGGINS; pub MGB 21:19.

F002 FALLON Bible; pd 1875; eb 1876; em 1875; on REILLY; res CA; Dublin; dep BCGS.

F003 Stephen H. FALLS Bible; rs 1870-1975; pd 1870; on ADAMS, BRAUER, CARR,
        DAVIS, DAY, DENLY; res Bowie, MD; VA; NC; SC;
        dep VSL (#994, acc. 30434).
F004 FARIS Bible; pd 1842; eb 1728; em 1761; on WOODWARD, PITT, KERR, WILLIAMS,
        CHAPPELL, CHAMPLAIN; res AA Co., MD; London; Bermuda; dep MHS/FCA.
F005 FASNACHT Bible; pd 1832; eb 1811; on SANDS; dep BCGS (522).
F006 FASSETT Bible; pd 1860; eb 1777; em 1849; on WEST, HOLLOWAY, CAMBELL,
        McGREGOR; res Wico. Co., MD; pub DAR (in MdGRC 11:140).
F007 FASSETT Bible; pd 1825; on BOWEN, HALL;
        pub DAR (in MdGRC 11:139),(deaths only).
F008 FAULK Bible; pd 1850; eb 1867; dep MHS/FCA.
F009 FAUNTLEROY Bible; rs 1664-1774; on GWYN, TAYLOR, CORBIN, GRIFFIN, PAGE,
        PLATER; res MD; dep VSL (#1002, acc. 21043).
F010 FELDMEYER Bible; pd 1888; eb 1855; em 1839; on WOOLLEY, PALMER, NEWNAM,
        JONES, REIDENBACH; res Annapolis, Balto., Port Deposit, MD;
        dep MHS/FCA.
F011 FENDALL Bible; eb 1875; em 1874; on STREETT; res Harf. Co., MD.;
        dep BCHS (typed copy).
F012 FENLEY Bible; eb 1791; em 1819; on JOHNSTON, BLACKMORE, HOPE;
        dep MHS/FCA.
F013 FENLEY Bible; eb 1830; em 1860; dep MHS/FCA.
F014 FENWICK Bible; rs 1780-1870; dep MSA (G-570:1).
F015 FERGUSON Bible; pd 1792; eb 1801; on HARPER; MHS/FCA.
F016 FERGUSON Family Records; eb 1870; res Baltimore; dep MHS/FCA.
F017 James M. FERRILL Bible; eb 1814; em 1849; on FONVILLE, PICKETT;
        pub MBR 1:107.
F018 John W. FERRILL Bible; eb 1850; em 1881; on PICKETT, BLOCK, HAMILTON;
        res NC,AL,AR; pub MBR 1:108.
F019 FIELD Bible; pd 1837; eb 1754; em 1796; on TARBELL, WILSON, DAGGETT,
        ADEMS, EARLE, BEARD, SPAULDEN, STOWELL, LANDON, ALLBEE, ELLIOT,
        WHIPPLE; dep BCGS.
F020 FILBEY Bible; eb 1833; em 1858; on ABLE; res Wrightsville, Columbia PA;
        dep MHS/FCA.
F021 FILBOY Bible; eb 1807; em 1830; on RODGERS, KLINE; dep MHS/FCA.
F022 Samuel B. FINCH Bible; pd 1831; eb 1823; on PETERS; dep MGS (typed copy).
F023 Finch Bible; eb 1900; on JAMESON; dep MGS (typed copy).
F024 FISH Bible; pd 1867; eb 1873; em 1846; on BOHANON, SANNER, JOHNS;
        dep MHS/FCA.
F025 FISHER Bible; rs 1780-1870; dep MSA (G-570:1).
F026 FISHER Bible; ins 1846; eb 1834; em 1869; on McCULLOH;
        pub DAR (in MdGRC 12:107).
F027 FISHPAW Bible; pd 1820; eb 1775; em 1837; on THOMAS, MUSE;
        pub BMGS 21-1:258; dep BCHS; dep MHS.
F028 FITE Bible; eb 1722; em 1791; on REINECKER, GIST, DUER, WATERS;
        res Hesse,Cassel,Germany; Balto. MD; dep MHS/FCA.
F029 FITZELL Bible; pd 1880; eb 1882; em 1881; on KRAUK, GOETZE, CHAPMAN,
        GORDON, KNACHEL; res Balto. Co.,MD; dep AAHS.
F030 FITZGERALD Bible; eb 1799; em 1798; on SAVAGE, CURRY; res Balto., MD;
        dep MHS/FCA (under Dowson).
F031 FITZGERALD Bible; eb 1906; em 1870; on LITTLE, CLOSE;
        dep BCHS and MHS/FCA (typed copies).
F032 FITZGERALD Bible; eb 1801; em 1834; on CAPITO, SMITH, BORDLEY, LAURENSON,
        JACKSON, TUCKERMAN; res Balto. MD; dep MHS/FCA (under Dowson).
F033 Richard FITZGERALD Bible; pd 1807; em 1834; res MD,NY,MA;
        pub MDG 23-4:112.

F034 FITZGERALD Bible; ed 1933; res Balto., MD; NY; London, England;
     dep MHS/FCA (under Dowson).
F035 FITZGERALD Bible; pd 1854; eb 1816; em 1854; on CREGAN; res Balto., MD;
     Tierkelly, Drumballroney,Ire; dep MHS/FCA; dep BCHS (typed copy).
F036 FLAHERTY Bible; em 1832; on NICHOLSON, HOPKINS, BUIER, HARTLEY, GILBERT,
     CUFF, McLAUGHLEN; res Balto., MD; dep MHS/FCA; dep BCHS (typed copy).
F037 FLEMING Bible; eb 1868; em 1899; on BRACH; res Balto. MD;
     dep BCHS (typed copy).
F038 FLENNER-WINEBERGER Bible; eb 1778; em 1833; on WINEBERGER;
     pub NGSQ 36:114 (abstracted).
F039 FLETCHER Bible; pd 1849; eb 1823; em 1848; on CARROLL; pub DOBR,16.
F040 FLEWELLYN-ALEXANDER Bible; eb 1762; em 1797; on PEOPLES, ALEXANDER;
     pub MBR 1:104.
F041 Charles Tilden FOARD Bible; eb 1795; em 1799; pub NGSQ 32-2:72.
F042 FOLGER Bible; eb 1783; em 1782; pub MG 2:302.
F043 John Adam FOLK Bible; eb 1797; on HENTY; pub MBR 1:110.
F044 FOLTZ Family Record; eb 1757; on ZIMMERMAN, LOWMAN, HUFFER, ROWLAND, LINE,
     CROSS, GROVE, MAY, PETRE, SNAVELY; res Lancaster Co. PA; Wash. Co.
     MD; pub MGB 20:12.
F045 FOOKS Bible; rs 1828-1834; dep MSA (G-307).
F046 FOOKS Bible; rs 1778-1921, on CAUSEY; dep MSA (G-305:1).
F047 FORBES Bible; ed 1847; on FLETCHER, LARMOUR, MANN, MOFFOTT, SLASMAN;
     dep MHS/FCA.
F048 FORD Bible; eb 1770; em 1793; on FOSTER, CAZIER, ALDRIDGE, INSHIP,
     ROBINSON, ONION; dep MHS/FCA.
F049 FORD Bible; eb 1774; em 1799; on MAULDEN, WRIGHT, MEARNS, WILMER;
     pub DAR (in MdGRC 12:114).
F050 John FORD Bible; pd 1850; eb 1805; em 1827; res Cecil Co., MD;
     pub NGSQ 33-1:40.
F051 Alfred FORD; pd 1871; eb 1844; em 1871; res Cecil Co.. MD; pub NGSQ 33-1:40.
F052 FOREMAN Bible; eb 1774; em 1829; on DYER; res Fred. Co. MD;
     dep BCHS (typed copy).
F053 FORMAN Records; eb 1704; em 1732; on LEE, THOMPSON, MARSH, PORTER,
     HEMSLEY; res Kent Co., MD; pub Kent BTR; pub DAR (in MGRC 12:100).
F054 FORREST Bible; pd 1816; eb 1786; em 1809; on FENWICK, CLARKE, FREEMAN;
     res St.M. Co., MD; pub MDG 9-4:77.
F055 FORSYTH Bible; pd 1804; eb 1846; on CUMMING; dep BCGS #547.
F056 FORT Bible; pd 1874; eb 1829; em 1855; on CLARKE; res Ellicott Mills, MD;
     dep BCGS.
F057 John and Hannah FORWOOD Bible; pd 1815; eb 1762; em 1785; on SMITHSON,
     RIGDON, CUMMINS, FRANK; dep BCGS.
F058 FORWOOD Bible; rb 1787; on WATTERS; res Harf. Co., MD; dep HCGS.
F059 William and Sarah FORWOOD Bible; pd 1851; eb 1787; em 1818; res Harf. Co.,
     MD; York Co., PA; dep BCGS.
F060 FOSTER Bible; pd 1804; eb 1727; em 1817; on BATTEN, STREET, ROSE, ELIASON;
     pub Kent BGR 2:64; pub DAR (in MdGRC 7:325).
F061 FOSTER Bible; pd 1834; eb 1748; em 1785; on PLOWMAN, STARNES, WHEELER;
     res Carr. Co. and Balto. Cos., MD; dep CCGS #20.
F062 J.F. FOSTER Bible; pd 1886; eb 1846; em 1908; on BROWNLEY, WEBNAM;
     res Mathews Co.,VA; dep AAGS; dep MHS/FCA.
F063 FOULER Bible; pd 1840; eb 1816; em 1814; on BARBER, BACHER, FOWLER, HAGAN;
     dep FCHS (original Bible).
F064 FOWLER Bible; rs 1751-1840; dep MSA (G-560).
F065 FOWLER Bible; pd 1812; res West Chester, PA.; dep MHS/FCA;
     dep AAGS. (Contains no vital records.)

F066 Gilbert FOWLER Bible; eb 1825; em 1825; res Calv. Co., MD;
    pub O'Brien p.300.
F067 Arthur FOX Bible; eb 1761; em 1786; on YOUNG; pub MBR 1:105.
F068 FOX Bible; eb 1780; on LANCASTER, LEMDIN, HUGG, SINCLARE, TITTON, STROBLE,
    KNAPP; dep BCHS (typed copy).
F069 FOXWELL Bible; eb 1818; em 1846; on WILLEY, CANNON, MORRIS; res Dor. Co.,
    MD; dep BCHS (typed copy).
F070 FRALEY Bible; eb 1857; em 1865; on HARGET, ADAMSON, CLAGETT, MARSHALL,
    BRAKE, ALLNUTT, JOHNSON, SINYARD, HOLLAND, DUVALL, ZIMMERMAN;
    dep MHS/FCA (box 49).
F071 Robert FRANKLIN Account Book; eb 1739; em 1776; on ALLEIN, WATERS,
    HARRIS, JACOB, MACHUHN; dep MHS/FCA (#2).
F072 FRANKLIN Account Book; eb 1741; em 1774; on ALLEIN, MACHUHN, TONGUE,
    HARRIS, MURRAY, MURDOUGH, BALLES; dep MHS/FCA (Box #49).
F073 Joel FRANKLIN Bible; eb 1757; em 1793; on LEWIS; pub MBR 1:109.
F074 FRAZIER Bible; eb 1750; em 1788; on MITCHELL, BENSON, HUBBARD, OREM,
    WHITNEY, KENT, PERRY; pub DOBR,17.
F075 FRAZIER Bible; pd 1856; eb 1750; em 1788; on MITCHELL, BRYAN, FAIRBANK,
    COCKRAN, SEWARD, BARNES, NORTH, HARPER; pub DOBR,18.
F076 FRAZIER Bible; eb 1849; em 1848; on MASON, KILLEN, HEARN, COOK, ROGERS;
    res DE; dep MHS/FCA (box 49).
F077 FRAZIER Bible; rs 1848-1949; dep MSA (G-560).
F078 Ethelbert FREELAND Bible; eb 1765; em 1780; res Calv. Co., MD;
    pub O'Brien p.301.
F079 George Thomas FREELAND Bible; eb 1827; em 1860; on LYLES, CRANFORD,
    SCHAFFER, BYRD, DALRYMPLE, RAWLINGS; pub O'Brien pg.302.
F080 FREW Bible; rs 1819-1950; pub HCMR 5:90.
F081 FRICK Bible; pd 1819; eb 1754; em 1793; on PEIFER; dep MHS/FCA (50).
F082 FRICK Family Records; eb 1752; on BREIDENHART; res Wertheim, Germany;
    dep MHS/FCA (50) (German script).
F083 FRICK Bible; eb 1734; em 1770; on BREIDENHARDT, ALVAN; res Germany;
    Balto., MD; dep MHS/FCA (50).
F084 FRINGER Bible; pd 1830; eb 1831; em 1830; on HOFF, GARDINER, JONES,
    UHLER; res Carr. and Balto. Cos., MD; dep CCGS (#4).
F085 FRITZ Bible; pd 1888; eb 1855; em 1879; on KAUFFMAN, POWELL, YOUNG,
    CARTZENDOFNER, HOOVER, LITTLE, FISHER, DORSEY; res New Windsor,
    Carr. Co., MD; dep CCGS.
F086 FRY Bible; rs 1768-1908; on FOX, FREY; res Mont. Co., MD;
    dep NGS Bible Records Collection.
F087 FRYE Bible; pd 1793; eb 1811; em 1807; on JOHNSON, BUCHANAN; dep MHS/FCA.
F088 FULFORD Bible; pd 1802; em 1840; on MITCHELL; res Harf. Co., MD;
    dep MHS (HBFR,1); dep BCGS.
F089 FULKERSON Bible; eb 1737; em 1763; on VAN HOOK, CRAIG, SHARP, HUGHES,
    NEILL, BRADLEY, HENLEY, VANCE; pub MBR 1:106.
F090 FUNK Bible; pd 1839; eb 1816; em 1841; on DOUB, BOVEY;
    pub DAR (in MdGRC 33:107).

G001 Gaither Bible; rs 1854-1888; dep MSA (G-494:69).
G002 GAITHER-WORTHINGTON Bible; eb 1778; em 1812; on WORTHINGTON, DORSEY,
    MAYNARD; dep MHA/FCA (box 50).
G003 GALE Bible; eb 1815; on SHREVE, DORSEY; dep MHS/FCA.
G004 GALLOWAY Bible; eb 1742; em 1762; on SMITH, LITTLE, LEWIS, ARCHER,
    HOPKINS, MAPES, JACOBUS, DAVIS, FITZGERALD; pub MBR 1:119.
G005 GALLOWAY Birth Records; rs 1720-1755; dep MSA (D633).
G006 GALLOWAY Bible; eb 1806; em 1805; on BRIAN, REVEN, VANDERFORD, SMITH,

Continued on next page

G006 GALLOWAY Bible, contd.;
   STEWARD, KLINGHORN, KNAUFF, LEMMON, McILVAIN, NICOL, ROYSTON;
   res Baltimore, MD.; pub BMGS 27-4:483; dep BCGS.
G007 GALLUP Bible; pd 1852; eb 1822; em 1820; on HOLLOWAY, MARTIN, STEVENS,
   NELSON, DEVOE; res Talb. and Harf. Cos., MD.; dep BCGS.
G008 John GAMBRILL Bible; eb 1808; em 1804; on JACOB, GREEN, HOOK, HEACOCK,
   BAKER, THOMPSON, MILLS; dep BCHS (typed copy).
G009 GAMBRILL Bible; ins 1890; eb 1842; em 1866; on MYRESS, MOORE, BROWN,
   PARLETT; res Balto. Co., MD; dep BCHS (typed copy).
G010 GAND-(?) WELGEN (?) Bible; dep FCHS (original Bible).
G011 Daniel GARBER Bible; pd 1829; eb 1825; em 1851; on GROVES, BOWERS,
   LANDES, McCARY, PATTERSON; dep BCGS #493.
G012 GARNER-WILKERSON Bible; eb 1773; em 1834; res St.M. Co., MD;
   pub MDG 21-4:114.
G013 GARNER Bible; rs 1886-1961; dep MSA (G-597).
G014 GARRETT Bible; eb 1733; on OUSELEY; dep MBR 1:130.
G015 GARRETT Bible; eb 1796; pub MGB 19:39.
G016 George S. GARRISON Bible; pd 1903; rs 1713-1976; on CRANDALL, EVANS,
   HARDESTY, HART, KELLAM, NUTWELL, PHIPPS, RUEHL, SMITH;
   res Balto., Sudley MD; FL; dep VSL (#1144, acc. 30453).
G017 Joseph GARRISH Bible; eb 1874; em 1873; on ARDINGER; res Williamsport, MD.;
   dep MGS/FCA.
G018 GARTRELL Bible; eb 1777; em 1806; on MUSGROVE, MOREHEAD, GAITHER, HINTON,
   WATKINS; dep MHS/FCA.
G019 GASSAWAY Bible; eb 1807; em 1825; on CALDWELL, BURNS; res IN;
   dep MHS.
G020 GASSAWAY Bible; eb 1822; em 1847; on MILLER, ARMSTRONG, BRISCOE;
   res Mont. Co., MD; WVA; OH; PA, WA; pub DAR (in MdGRC 33:73).
G021 GATCHELL Bible; rs 1734-1926; res Cecil Co., MD;
   dep MSA (G-236:58 with D-150).
G022 GATRELL Bible; pd 1910; eb 1909; on HAND, LEY, HOLBERT, TROLLINGER, PRIM;
   res MD; WVA; dep CCGS (#32).
G023 GEOGHEGAN Bible; pd 1772; eb 1733; em 1803; pub DOBR,19.
G024 John GEORGE Bible; pd 1749; eb 1749; em 1835; pub NGSQ 32-2:70;
   dep MSA (D-181).
G025 Stephen GEORGE Bible; eb 1787; res Cecil Co., MD; pub NGSQ 33-1:41.
G026 GEORGE Bible; em 1797; on HEART, ELLIOTT, NEAL, POWELL;
   pub DAR (MdGRC 6:216).
G027 GEORGE Bible; eb 1818; em 1817; on STEWART, MAYDWELL, DOOMES, JERMAN,
   BOND, SANDERS, on FRANCIS, STEVENS, BOSLEY, RIDGELY, BUFFINGTON;
   pub MGB 10:39; 11-1:17.
G028 GEORGE Bible; pd 1838; eb 1835; res Gettysburg, PA area; dep CCGS (#6).
G029 William Thomas GERARD Bible; eb 1837; em 1856; on WALLER, ARMOR, LANE,
   HUMBER; pub MBR 1:113.
G030 Jacob GERRARD Bible; eb 1763; em 1786; on BENSON, THOMAS; res Duplin Co.,
   NC; pub MBR 1:111.
G031 William Barron GERRARD Bible; eb 1791; em 1822; on ALLEN, CLEMENS, MAHONE,
   IRBY, PERRY, WALLER; pub MBR 1:112.
G032 GETTY Bible; eb 1777; on LILLESON, TILESON, DUKHART, BIRELY, HAINES;
   res New Windsor and Balto. Co., MD; pub DAR (in MdGRC 7:57).
G033 GETTY Bible; eb 1780; on LAUB, JOHNS, BROOKE, STEVENSON, WILMOT,
   MARBURY; res Annapolis, MD; VA; Ireland; pub DAR (in MdGRC 25:21).
G034 GHARLIEZ Bible; eb 1806; em 1830; res Allegany Co., MD; pub NGSQ 63-1:57.
G035 Rev. John GIBSON Bible; eb 1759; em 1798; on HARVEY, BUSH, SMITH, MORRIS,
   ESTES, COLLINS; res Calv. Co., MD; VA; Lester,137.

G036 GILBERT Bible; eb 1707; em 1728; res Balto. and Harf. Cos., MD; pub MDG 19-1:18.
G037 GILBERT Bible; pd 1860; on ONRON, KENNARD, GORSUCH, WALTERS, WALSH; dep BCGS (MMAF p.2, typescript).
G038 GILLESPIE Bible; eb 1829; em 1853; on EVANS, HUGHES, CAMPBELL, STANSBURY; res Balto. Co., MD; dep BCGS.
G039 GILLIS Bible; pd 1725; eb 1835; on HILL, SHIPLEY; res Som., AA, Carr. Cos., MD; dep CCGS (#28).
G040 Samuel GILLIS Bible; pd 1867; eb 1846; on ROBINSON; res Barren Creek, Mardella Springs, MD; dep WCFL.
G041 GILMOR Bible; eb 1748; em 1771; on AIREY, COOKE, LADSON, SHERLOCK, SMITH, DORSEY, GRANT, SWANN; res Dor. Co., MD; Charleston, SC; VA; Liverpool; dep MHS/FCA (Gilmor notes).
G042 GIST Bible; pd 1839; res Carr. Co., MD; dep CCGS.
G043 Mordecai GIST Bible; pd 1858; eb 1712; em 1735; on COCKEY, HARVEY, HAMMOND, JONES, BEATY, DORSEY; dep BCGS (from Yingling).
G044 GIST Bible; eb 1687; on COCKEY, SLADE, HAMMOND; res Balto. Co., MD; pub DAR Mag. 70:458.
G045 Thomas GIST Bible; eb 1712; em 1735; on COCKEY; res Balto. & Carr. Cos., MD; dep MSA (G-130, D-452); pub DAR (in MdGRC 5:24).
G046 GIST Bible; pd 1791; eb 1738; em 1759; on MURRAY, TRIPPE, DORSEY, REINECKER; res Balto. Co., MD; pub MGB 15:35.
G047 GIST Bible; eb 1751; em 1773; on BREEDON, WOO, MITCHELL, BATTLE; res Arkansas; pub MBR 1:116.
G048 Joshua Thomas GIST Bible; eb 1839; em 1837; on NORRIS; res Carr. Co., MD; pub DAR Mag 70:457.
G049 GITTINGS Bible; eb 1858; on SELLMAN, BROGDEN; res Balto. City, Balto. & AA Cos., MD; dep MHS/FCA.
G050 GLADDING Bible; eb 1825; em 1849; on GREEN, WARDWELL, LYONS, MARROLDT, MASSEY; pub MBR 1:124.
G051 John B. GODWIN Bible; eb 1783; em 1813; on HALL, ROCHESTER; res QA Co., MD; pub DAR (in MdGRC 7:25); dep MHS/FCA (typed copy).
G052 GODWIN Bible; pd 1769; eb 1776; em 1796; on RUTH, CORRIE, PRICE, HACKETT; res QA Co., MD; pub DAR (in MdGRC 7:23).
G053 GOLDSBOROUGH Bible; eb 1640; em 1659; pub DOBR,20; dep MSA (G-542).
G054 GOLDSBOROUGH Bible; eb 1690; em 1721; on THOMAS, ROBINS; dep MHS/FCA.
G055 GOLDSBOROUGH Bible; eb 1714; on ROBINS; dep MHS/FCA.
G056 GOLDSBOROUGH Bible; pd 1712; eb 1722; em 1721; on TURBUT; dep MHS/FCA.
G057 GOLDSBOROUGH-PASCAULT Bible; pd 1752; eb 1755; em 1755; on YERBURY, PASCAULT; dep MHS/FCA.
G058 GOLDSBOROUGH Bible; rs 1768-1888; dep MSA (G-542).
G059 GOLDSBOROUGH Family Record; eb 1770; em 1792; on WORTHINGTON, SCHLEY, DUCKETT; pub MGB 10:15.
G060 Robert H. GOLDSBOROUGH; eb 1879; em 1898; on KELLY, COULBOURNE; res Sussex Co., DE; Som. Co.,MD; dep WCFL (Maryland Room).
G061 GOLDY Bible; eb 1847; em 1835; dep MHS/FCA.
G062 GOLLADAY-HARE-PIERSON Bible; rs 1809-1839; on JOHNSON, McINTURFF, MUNCH, TRACEY; res Balto., MD; PA; VA; dep VSL (#1209, acc. 30418); see also VSL (#1209).
G063 Lyde GOODWIN Bible; pd 1829; eb 1802; em 1801; on WORTHINGTON, WILSON, SWOOPE, SOLLERS, HOGG, BEATTY; dep MHS/FCA.
G064 GOOTEE Bible; eb 1892; em 1894; on CUSICK, TALL, WALLACE, PAUL, PARKS, RIGGINS; pub DOBR,21.
G065 Enich GORDON Bible; eb 1745; em 1767; on CARTER, LADD, EASTMAN; pub MBR 1:120.

G066 Thomas GORDON Bible; eb 1758; em 1777; on BUFFINGTON; res VA; SC; PA;
     pub MBR 1:121.
G067 GORDON Bible; em 1912; on BURK, WINTERODE, WATTS, GROSS;
     res Havre de Grace and Glyndon, MD; dep BCGS.
G068 GORDY Bible; eb 1796; em 1793; on INSLEY, HACKETT, ELLIOTT, WALLACE,
     WHATLEY, CANNON; res Dor. Co., MD; pub DOBR,24.
G069 GORE Bible; pd 1859; eb 1812; em 1834; dep BCGS (typed copy).
G070 GORE Bible; eb 1813; em 1834; on CAPLES; dep MHS/FCA.
G071 GORSUCH Bible; pd 1807; eb 1769; em 1803; on EMICH; dep MHS/FCA.
G072 GORSUCH Bible; pd 1813; eb 1779; dep MHS/FCA.
G073 GORSUCH Bible; pd 1859; eb 1827; em 1856; on GARDNER; res Carr. Co., MD;
     dep MHS/FCA (contains clippings).
G074 GORSUCH Bible; eb 1835; em 1834; on SMITH, COVINGTON, WILKINS, WILBOURNE;
     res Kingston, MD; dep MHS/FCA.
G075 GORSUCH Bible; pd 1887; eb 1855; em 1879; on RIDDLE, HERGENRATHER,
     BEADENKOPF, HARRISON; res Balto. Co., MD; dep MHS/FCA.
G076 GORSUCH Bible; pd 1887; eb 1883; em 1879; on HERGENRATHER; res Balto. Co.,
     MD; dep MHS/FCA.
G077 Clarence M. GOTT Bible; eb 1875; em 1898; on BUCKLER, BOWEN, MARROW;
     pub O'Brien p.303.
G078 James Boyd GOTT Bible; eb 1853; em 1939; on HAIGHT, CULLEMBER,
     WHITTINGTON, RAWLINGS, BUCKLER, DEVERS, PRICE, SNEDEN;
     pub O'Brien p.304.
G079 Milton Boyd GOTT Bible; eb 1872; em 1909; on RAWLINGS, HAIGHT, CULLEMBER,
     WHITTINGTON, DRESSER, GARNER; pub O'Brien p.304.
G080 GOUGH-CARROLL Bible; eb 1745; res Balto. Co., MD; pub MG 2:23.
G081 GOULD Bible; pd 1750; eb 1751; em 1770; on NELSON, BREMMER; dep MHS/FCA.
G082 GRACEY Bible; pd 1830; eb 1763; em 1792; on ARCHIBALD, HALL, WADDLETON,
     BRATTON, CARNES, ADAMS, DICKERSON, BENSON, WOOD, CALHOUN, WARNACK;
     res NC; dep MHS/FCA.
G083 GRAFFLIN Bible; pd 1680; eb 1769; em 179(?); on FRYMILLER, HARDESTY,
     HERRING; dep MHS/FCA (old German bible).
G084 GRAFFLIN Bible; pd 1798; eb 1769; em 1793; on CLARK, COMEGYS, KALBFUS,
     PHILIPE, COOK, HOOPER, STANSBURY, LYNCH, KEENER, MASON, FRYMILLER,
     HERRING; res Balto. MD.; dep MHS/FCA.
G085 GRAFTON Bible; eb 1760; em 1820; on HULL, KURTZ, DAVID, FAHNESTOCK,
     FRAZIER, TONGE, FORBES, BUMBAUGH; dep MHS/FCA (photocopy).
G086 GRAHAM Bible; eb 1792; em 1761; on RIGIN, MORRIS; dep MHS/FCA.
G087 GRANBERRY Bible; rs 1834-1927; res Som. Co., MD;
     dep MSA (G-560:101 with D-150).
G088 GRAPE Bible; ins 1859; eb 1839; em 1839; on CLINE, HINDES; res Balto. MD;
     pub BMGS 13:277; dep BCGS.
G089 GRAVES Bible; eb 1713; em 1841; on STANSBURY, BOYD, COLGATE, MERRITT;
     res Balto. Co., MD; dep MHS/FCA; dep BCHS.
G090 GRAVES Bible; eb 1749; on THOMPSON, JONES, BAKER; res Westmoreland,
     Wales; Baltimore, MD; dep MHS/FCA.
G091 GRAY Bible; eb 1755; em 1800; on POWELL, ELZEY; res Winchester, VA;
     dep MHS/FCA (photocopy).
G092 GRAY Bible; eb 1755; em 1800; on GLASS, ELLZEY, SMITH, BROWN; res VA;
     dep MHS/FCA (photocopy).
G093 GRAY Bible; pd 1814; eb 1764; em 1789; on LOWES, BOND, HITCH, ALLEN,
     DASHIELD, ABBOT, BROOKE, WILKINSON, SOMERVELL; res MD.; dep MHS/FCA.
G094 Laurence R. GRAY Bible; eb 1869; em 1899; on HARNNETT, BOWEN, COX, NOLL,
     KOPP, SIBLEY; pub O'Brien p.305.
G095 Shadrach GREEN Bible; pd 1792; eb 1747; dep MHS/FCA.

G096 GREEN Bible; pd 1792; eb 1747; em 1875; on SPARKS, MAYS, COOPER, GRUNER;
     res Balto. Co., MD; dep MHS/FCA.
G097 GREEN Bible; pd 1815; eb 1776; em 1794; on LANTERMAN, BERRY, YATES;
     dep MHS/FCA.
G098 GREEN Bible; eb 1835; on CARROLL, TAYLOR, DOUCH, DALEY, NEWMAN, SMITH,
     McHENRY, CRAUMER, WISE; res Balto. Co., MD; dep HCGS.
G099 John Adlum GREEN Bible; pd 1843; eb 1841; em 1840; on CAMERON, JONES,
     HOUSE, LITTLE; res PA; dep MHS/FCA.
G100 S.G. GREENAWALT Bible; pd 1882; eb 1860; em 1884; on MILLER, AUGHENBAUGH,
     ADAMS, CUMP, DERBYSHIRE, BURGNER, HOLLIS, MURPHY; res PA; MA;
     pub DAR (in MdGRC 33:122).
G101 GRENBERRY Bible; eb 1669; dep MHS/FCA.
G102 GREENBERRY Bible; pd 1628; eb 1734; on STIMPSON, FREEBORNE, HOMEWOOD,
     DORSEY, HAMMOND, BENSON, INGRAMS, MARRIOT;
     dep MHS/FCA (photostat copy).
G103 GREENFIELD Bible; pd 1747; eb 1762; em 1818; on WALTHAM, GARRETTSON,
     OSBORN, EVERIST, CREVENSTEN; res Balto. Co., MD;
     dep MHS (HBFR,45); dep BCGS.
G104 GREENFIELD Bible; pd 1892; eb 1859; em 1856; on SANDERS, BLACK, RAY,
     ZEIGLER, RILEY, SESSA; dep BCHS (typed copy).
G105 GREENWAY Bible; pd 1830; eb 1844; dep MHS/FCA.
G106 GREENWOOD Bible; pd 1828; eb 1778; on GOWING, POWERS;
     pub DAR (in MdGRC 11:127).
G107 GREENWOOD Bible; pd 1846; eb 1783; em 1813; on DEVILBISS, ECKER, BARNES,
     SHUNK; dep BCGS (from Yingling).
G108 GREENWOOD Bible; eb 1821; em 1848; on SHRINER, MAINES, GOSNELL, NUSBAUM,
     FRITZ, GAVER, BLACK, MYERS, STATON; dep MHS/FCA.
G109 GREER Bible; on JONES, PIERCE; res Harf. Co., MD; NC; dep HCGS, dep MHS.
G110 GREGORY Bible; eb 1784; dep MHS/FCA.
G111 GRIEL Bible; pd 1827; eb 1804; on FARVEL; res Phila., PA; Germany;
     dep MHS/FCA (Bible in German).
G112 GRIFFIN Bible; res Balto. Co.,MD;
     pub NGSQ 70-2:102 (incl. pension application).
G113 GRIFFIN Bible; eb 1705; em 1731; on ROUT, LEE, COLEMEN, ADAMS;
     pub MBR 1:115.
G114 GRIFFIN Bible; eb 1789; em 1816; on MARSH, BROADAWAY, COVINGTON, FOXWELL,
     WILDES, CARTY, BLACKSHIRE; res Cecil Co., MD; Del.;
     dep BCGS (from DAR).
G115 GRIFFIN Bible; eb 1810; em 1811; on HAYS, FAIRBAIRN, DAW, CARRIS, STOAKES,
     O'LAUGHLIN, WEIMER, MARRETEN, SEYMOUR, McKCECHNIE;
     res Dor. Co., MA; pub MGB 18:39.
G116 GRIFFIN Bible; pd 1846; eb 1843; em 1842; on MORRIS; dep MHS/FCA.
G117 GRIFFITH Record Book; bought 1716; eb 1715; em 1717; on DEVALL, WILLIAMS,
     MERCER, MARTEN, WORTHINGTON, JOHNSON; dep MHS/FCA.
G118 GRIFFITH Bible; eb 1727; em 1752; res Mont. Co., MD; pub NGSQ 17-3:51.
G119 GRIFFITH Family Register; eb 1745; em 1797; on MERRIWEATHER, DORSEY,
     HOWARD, RIDGELY, HOOD, TILTON, BROWN, JUPENLATZ, RIGGS, MacGILL,
     BREWER, STANSBURY, COOKSON; res MD; PA; KY; OH; pub BMGS 18-3:169.
G120 GRIFFITH Bible; eb 1767; em 1819; on MAGILL, OWINGS, OBER, MERIWEATHER,
     ARMAT, TILTON, BREWER; dep MHS/FCA.
G121 GRIFFITH Bible; eb 1797; dep MHS/FCA.
G122 GRIFFITH Bible; pd 1833; eb 1805; em 1829; on OBER, GAITHER, CARROLL,
     WARFIELD, DORSEY, SARGENT, WEBB, CHURCH; pub DAR (in MdGRC 33:50).
G123 GRIFFITH Bible; pd 1856; eb 1819; em 1786; on PLUMMER, JACOB;
     dep MHS/FCA (includes clippings).

G124 GRIFFITH-DUVALL Bible; eb 1827; em 1817; on DUVALL, HOWARD, PLUMMER;
      res PG Co., MD; dep MHS/FCA.
G125 GRIFFITH Bible; pd 1874; eb 1856; em 1884; on CORSON, POOLEY, POWELL,
      CAULDER; res Millville, NJ; dep AAGS.
G126 GRIFFITH Bible; eb 1873; em 1870; on POOLE, MARKS, MARSHALL, STEVENSON,
      MASON, MEARS; dep MHS/FCA (Griffith).
G127 GRIFFITH Bible; eb 1887; res Balto. and AA Cos., MD; dep AAGS.
G128 GRIGGS Bible; pd 1825; eb 1788; em 1826; on GRAY, JONES, LANGDON, FULLER,
      SACKETT, PEMBER; res NY; CT; WS; dep MHS/FCA; dep BCHS (typed copy).
G129 GRILLO Bible; eb 1884; em 1930; on ALLUISI, HANNON, DALY; res CT; Italy;
      dep BCHS (typed copy).
G130 Nicholas GRIMES Bible; eb 1766; em 1803; on COE, WILSON, HARRISON, YOCUM,
      LOWRY; pub MBR 1:117.
G131 GROENDYCKE Bible; pd 1833; eb 1807; em 1833; on CURRIER; res NC; NY;
      dep MHS/FCA.
G132 GROSSNICKEL Bible; eb 1786; em 1810; on BARNHISER, BECKER, MANNER;
      res MD; Indiana, PA; dep MHS/FCA.
G133 GRUBBS Bible; eb 1775; on BYELL; res MD, OH; pub DAR (in MdGRC 35:27).
G134 GUEST Bible; pd 1810; eb 1793; em 1792; on HALL, JITE, SEMMES, GROVER;
      res Harf. Co.,MD; Cumberland, MD; PA; dep MHS/FCA.
G135 GUION Bible; on NICHOLS, BRADFORD, NUNN, GARRETT, YOUNG, DRAKE; res LA;
      dep MHS/FCA.
G136 GUNBY Bible; pd 1831; eb 1736; em 1829; on SUMMERS, JONES, McCLELLEN,
      LENK, LAWS, NOBLE, COLLINS, MORRIS, BRINKLEY, DISHAROON, LAIRD,
      FULLER; res Wico. Co.,MD; pub DAR (in MdGRC 11:142).
G137 GURNEY Bible; rs 1826-1927; on PERKINS, LANGE, CORKREN, CUNNINGHAM,
      GEORGE, WHITE; dep MHS/FCA; dep AAGS.
G138 GURNEY-WHITE Bible; pd 1892; eb 1862; on WHITE, GRANT, ZIMMERMAN, MARSHALL;
      res Wilmington, DE; dep AAGS.
G139 GURNEY Bible; pd 1938; eb 1891; em 1943; on MARSHALL, NAGY, GEORGE,
      ABBOTT, ZIMMERMAN; res Balto., MD; dep AAGS.
G140 GUTHRIE-GUTRY Bible; pd 1827; eb 1828; em 1827; on HUTT, TAYLOR;
      res Balto., MD; dep AAGS.
G141 GUYTON Bible; eb 1761; em 1789; res Balto. Co., MD; SC; pub NGSQ 21:49.
G142 GWINN-TOLLEY Bible; eb 1771; on TOLLEY, BALDWIN, SCARFF; dep MHS/FCA.
G143 GWYN Bible; eb 1829; em 1832; on SANGSTON, THRUSTON, TALIAFERRO, SCOTT,
      BARRETT, OGLE; res Balto., MD; VA; dep MHS/FCA.
G144 GWYN Bible; rs 1832-1892; res Balto., MD; Alexandria, VA;
      dep MSA (G-560:106 with D-150).

H001 HACKETT-GODWIN Bible; pd 1769; eb 1776; em 1796; on RUTH, COOPER, GODWIN;
      res QA Co., MD; dep MHS/FCA (Godwin).
H002 Benjamin D. HACKETT Bible; eb 1798; em 1855; on TAYLOR, WILSON, WEST,
      PHILLIPS, MEEKENS, SHAW; res Dor.Co., MD; pub DOBR,22.
H003 James M. HACKETT Bible; eb 1839; em 1838; on INSLEY, SHEHIE; res Dor. Co.,
      MD; TX; pub DOBR,28.
H004 Luke HACKETT Bible; eb 1779; em 1804; on DARLY, VICKERS, WHEATLEY, ADAMS,
      TULL, SMOOT, WRIGHT; res Dor. Co., MD; pub DOBR,25.
H005 Luke K. HACKETT Bible; eb 1863; em 1887; on PHILLIPS; res Dor.Co., MD;
      pub DOBR,26.
H006 Perry Greensbury HACKETT Bible; eb 1818; em 1851; on TULL, PHILLIPS,
      BRILEY; res Dor. Co.,MD; pub DOBR,26.
H007 Tilghman HACKETT Bible; eb 1814; em 1843; on BRINSFIELD, WHEATLEY;
      res Dor. Co.,MD; pub DOBR,26.
H008 HACKETT Bible; eb 1828; em 1855; on WRIGHT, HOWETH, TAYLOR, WILSON, WEST,
      PHILIPS, MEEKINS, SHAW; pub DOBR,22.

BIBLES

H009 HADAWAY Bible; eb 1837; em 1867; on KENDALL, WILLSON, WALBERT, RINGGOLD,
        TOWNSEND; res Kent Co., MD; pub MDG 25:83.
H010 HADDAWAY Bible; eb 1828; em 1875; on NEWMAN, LLOYD, KEMP, BOHANNON,
        HEINKE, DAWSON, DOCKERY, FARMER, TOMPKINS, BLACKBURN, BRADLEY,
        HENNESSEY; DOZIER, SANDS, JOHNSON, WEEDMAN, BEATTY, HARRIS, EVANS;
        res Talb. Co., MD; KY; pub BMGS 16-4:181.
H011 HAGER Bible; pd 1850; eb 1825; em 1846; on PRITCHARD;
        pub DAR (in MdGRC 33:94).
H012 HAGER-HALL Bible; eb 1850; on SPIELMAN; res Wash.Co., MD; Trumble Co., OH;
        pub DAR (in MdGRC 33:93).
H013 HAGNER Bible; rs 1720-1947; dep MSA (G-252:22).
H014 HAINES Bible; eb 1834; em 1857; on DENNINGS, NISER, GREENWOOD;
        dep MHS/FCA (under Greenwood).
H015 HALE Bible; eb 1759; on HAILE; res Balto. Co., MD; TN; pub NGSQ 23-2:55,
        (incl. pension application of Arnon and Mary Haile).
H016 HALL Bible; on HARWOOD, STOCKETT; dep MHS/FCA.
H017 HALL Bible; rs 1689-1875; dep MSA (G-258:17 & 56).
H018 HALL Bible; rs 1689-1957; dep MSA (G-569).
H019 HALL Bible; pd 1707; eb 1694; em 1726; on STODDART, GREENFIELD, DENT,
        MACCUBBIN, CLAGETT, HARDESTY, POTTS, LYLES; res Marshall Hall,
        Chas.Co., MD; dep MHS/FCA.
H020 HALL Bible; eb 1738; em 1794; on HAWKINS, MASSY; res Chambersburg, PA;
        dep MHS/FCA.
H021 Elihu HALL Bible; rs 1757-1778; on ORRICK; dep VSL (#1328, acc. 30435).
H022 HALL Bible; pd 1723; eb 1774; em 1792; on CATTELL, CALHOUN; dep MHS/FCA.
H023 HALL; Bibles (3); rs 1780-1870; 1825-1854; 1770-1937; dep MSA (G-570).
H024 HALL Bible; eb 1795; em 1795; on HILL, SNOWDEN, CLAGETT, ARTHUR;
        dep MHS.
H025 HALL Bible; pd 1826; eb 1806; em 1838; on WISSMAN; res Beltsville, PG
        Co., MD; pub PGCGS 16-7:83, March 1985.
H026 James Alexander HALL Bible; pd 1834; eb 1808; em 1847; on WILLEY, KIELEY,
        BONSELL, SWEET, RASH, MACKEY, EWING, RICH; res Cecil Co., MD; DE;
        pub DBR p.65.
H027 HALL Bible; pd 1855; eb 1811; dep MHS/FCA.
H028 HALL Bible; rs 1821-1842; res Balto. Co., MD;
        dep MSA (G-214:29, with D-250).
H029 HALL Bible; pd 1860; eb 1839; em 1860; on DUNCAN, BROADWATER, PHILLIPS,
        INSLEY, FAIRCLOTH; res Cecil Co., MD; dep MHS/FCA (Beaver).
H030 Joseph W. HALL Bible; pd 1841; em 1839; on ROBINSON; pub O'Brien p.306.
H031 HALL-FARN Bible; eb 1853; em 1852; on FARN; res Pocomoke City; MD;
        pub DAR Mag, Nov.1960, p.660.
H032 HALL Bible; pd 1892; eb 1887; em 1887; on CATTERTON, STEVENS, MARCELLUS;
        res Calv. Co., MD; dep AAGS.
H033 HALLEY Bible; pd 1824; eb 1767; em 1791; on SANDERS; res CT; dep LDS
        Library,Columbia, MD.
H034 HAMANN Bible; pd 1781; eb 1779; dep MHS/FCA (in German).
H035 HAMBLIN Bible; eb 1828; em 1826; on DALE, CARY; res Worc. Co., MD;
        pub BMGS 24-3:252.
H036 HAMILTON Bible; eb 1779; em 1807; on NEWELL, GEMMILL, RITCHIE; dep MHS/FCA.
H037 HAMILTON Bible; rs 1812-1888; res NJ; NY; IA; MA;
        dep MSA (G-560:107 with D-150).
H038 HAMILTON Bible; eb 1848; em 1875; on WOOLSEY; res NY; IA; NJ; CT;
        dep MHS/FCA.
H039 T.W. HAMILTON Bible; pd 1900; rs Records 1886-1966; on FITZGERALD, LAMB,
        LEWIS, SMITH; res Balto., MD; VA; NC; DC;
        dep VSL (#1330, acc. 30435).

39

H040 HAMMETT Bible; rs 1819-1926; res St.M. Co., MD;
          dep MSA (G-236:64 with D-150).
H041 HAMMOND Bible; pd 1704; eb 1765; on WRIGHT; dep MHS/FCA.
H042 HAMMOND Bible; pd 1851; eb 1786; dep MHS/FCA.
H043 HAMMOND Bible; pd 1870; eb 1801; em 1891; on GILBER, DAVIS, SMITH, HALLER,
          WILLIS, KLUTS; res Woodsboro, NJ; dep MHS/FCA.
H044 HAMMOND Bible; eb 1824; em 1823; on VICTOR, TOADVINE, HOPKINS, FLEMING,
          DICKERSON; dep MHS/FCA.
H045 HAMMOND Bible; ins 1848; eb 1846; em 1845; on WILSON, DOWNEY, STONE,
          WILLIS, FRAZIER; res Fred. Co., MD; dep MHS/FCA.
H046 HAMNER Record; eb 1773; em 1797; dep MHS/FCA.
H047 HANCOCK Bible; eb 1799; em 1825; on WILKINSON; res Balto. & AA Cos. MD;
          dep MHS/FCA.
H048 HANCOCK Bible; eb 1811; em 1820; on FOREMAN, GRAY, ARMIGER; dep MHS/FCA.
H049 HANDLEY Bible; eb 1808; em 1834; on WRIGHTSON, PHILLIPS; res Dor. Co., MD;
          pub DOBR,29.
H050 HANDY Bible; pd 1793; eb 1703; on WINDER; dep MHS/FCA.
H051 HANDY Bible; eb 1734; em 1748; on MARTIN, WILAN, GLASGOW, MORRIS;
          res Som. Co., MD; dep MHS/FCA.
H052 HANNA Bible; eb 1822; em 1851; dep BCGS.
H053 HANNA Bible; rb 1859; on MECHEM, DURHAM, KOONS, KARG, KEAN, TAYLOR,
          KULLMER, SPENCER, FENDER, SATTERFIELD, YINGLING, SAVIN, BULL, TODD,
          STOLL, LANCASTER, QUINN, DEMARCO, HOPKINS; res Harf. Co., MD;
          dep HCGS.
H054 HANSHEW Bible; eb 1766; em 1870; on BENNETT, KOLB, NEIDHARDT, FRITCHIE,
          DeGRANGE; res Fred. Co., MD; dep FCHS (original Bible).
H055 HANSHEW Bible; pd 1822; dep FCHS (original Bible).
H056 John HANSON Bible; eb 1744; em 1743; on GARRETTSON, COURTNEY, OSBORNE,
          THOMPSON, COLE; res Harf. Co., MD; pub BMGS 3-3:26;
          dep MSA (G-560:84).
H057 HANSON Bible; pd 1798; eb 1749; em 1778; on HOWARD, DORSEY, RIDGELY;
          dep MHS/FCA.
H058 HANSON Bible; eb 1764; on POULTNEY, ROBINSON; dep MHS/FCA.
H059 HANWAY Bible; pd 1891; eb 1884; em 1910; on THOMPSON, MICHAEL, HARLAN;
          res Harf. Co., MD; dep BCGS.
H060 HARBAUGH Bible; eb 1782; em 1851; on WILLIARD; res Fred. Co., MD;
          dep MHS/FCA; dep BCHS (typed copy).
H061 John HARDCASTLE Bible; ins 1802; eb 1757; em 1781; on CULBRETH, POTTER,
          COSTIN, ORRELL; pub GPF/PGM 3:713; dep MHS/FCA.
H062 Thomas HARDCASTLE Account Book; eb 1757; em 1756; pub GPF/PGM 3:716.
H063 HARDEN Bible; pd 1896; eb 1873; em 1898; on NAYLOR, LEWIS,
          BOONE; res Carr. and Balto. Cos., MD; dep CCGS #46.
H064 HARDESTER Bible; eb 1800; em 1833; on HARDESTY, MITCHELL, HOYT;
          pub MGB 13:34.
H065 HARDING Bible; eb 1815; em 1837; on ANDERTON, IRVING, TAYLOR;
          res Cumberland, England; NY; WI; dep MHS/FCA; dep BCGS (typed copy).
H066 HARDING Bible; pd 1892; eb 1870; em 1869; on TUCKER, MULLICAN;
          res Mont. Co., MD; dep MHS/FCA.
H067 HARDINGER Bible; pd 1881; eb 1857; em 1909; on EPPERLY, WALLERS, YOUNG,
          BRUNER; res Allegany Co., MD; OH; IA; pub BMGS 21-1:74.
H068 HARDON-HARDING Bible; pd 1812; eb 1770; em 1846; on MOORE, JACKSON,
          WHEELER, TUCKER, HARDING; dep MHS/FCA (Harding).
H069 HARE Bible; eb 1868; em 1892; on TRACEY, JOHNSON, PIERSON, PERSON;
          res Balto., MD; PA; Prince Wm. Co., VA; dep BCGS #527.
H071 HARKINS Bible; eb 1787; em 1785; on POTTS; dep MHS/FCA.

H072 Enos HARMAN Bible; eb 1817; em 1826; on FISHER, LILLY, DENNIS, CARTER,
     CROMWELL, WELSH, GRAY; dep MHS/FCA.
H073 HARMAN Bible; res AA Co., MD; dep MHS/FCA (in German).
H074 HARP Bible; rb 1845; on COLLIFLOWER, GLENN; res Fred, Co., MD; dep HCGS.
H075 HARRIS Bible; pd 1798; rs 1650-1914; res Chas. Co., MD; dep MSA (G-157).
H076 Nathan HARRIS Bible; eb 1726; em 1759; on DORSEY, OWINGS, LAURENCE, OFFUTT,
     AITKEN, STEVENSON, IJARIES, DRYDEN; dep MHS/FCA.
H077 Isaac HARRIS Bible; pd 1799; eb 1725; em 1786; on TULL; dep MHS/FCA.
H078 HARRIS Bible; eb 1786; dep MHS/FCA (Blaine).
H079 HARRIS Bible; eb 1806; em 1803; on VICKERS, HOPKINS, FOWLER, CATHELL,
     ANDERSON, WILBORN; dep MHS/FCA.
H080 HARRIS Bible; pd 1872; eb 1835; res Sussex Co., VA; dep AAGS.
H081 HARRIS Bible; pd 1873; eb 1847; em 1873; on WINKLER, MITCHELL, LEAGUE;
     dep BCGS.
H082 HARRIS Bible; pd 1872; rs 1835-1878; res Sussex, Greensville,
     Southampton Cos., VA; dep AAGS.
H083 HARRISON Bible; rs 1733-1951; dep MSA (G-464).
H084 HARRISON Family Record; eb 1787; em 1812; on COOPER, JOHNSON, FILLISON,
     FANNING, AULD; dep MHS/FCA (59).
H085 HARRISON Bible; pd 1834; eb 1788; em 1800; on LEITCH, MITCHELL, JONES,
     TALBOTT, SPICKNALL, WOOD, BRICE; res Calv. Co., MD; pub MDG 25:92.
H086 HARRISON Bible; eb 1799; em 1798; res Caro. Co., MD; pub MG 2:39.
H087 William T. HARRISON Bible; eb 1834; em 1834; on HALL, PRICE, EAMES, REID,
     MILLER; res Balto. Co., MD; dep WCFL (Md.Rm).
H088 HARRISON Bible; eb 1841; dep MHS/FCA.
H089 HARRISON Bible; em 1841; pub BMGS 19-1:24.
H090 HARRISON-ATHEY Bible; eb 1848; em 1874; on ATHEY, TURNER, ROBEY, BURTON,
     SCHOOLEY, HOLLEY, DISNEY; dep MHS/FCA (59).
H091 HARRISON Bible; pd 1885; eb 1875; em 1874; on ATHEY, TURNER, ROBEY,
     BURTON, SCHOOLEY, LUSBY, HOLLEY, DISNEY, CORNEL; dep MHS/FCA.
H092 HARRISON Bible; eb 1927; on LESTER, ATHEY, SNOWDEN, HORACE, MELVIN;
     dep MHS/FCA.
H093 HARROLD Bible; rs 1862-1934; on BORING, KELLEY, LEE, MARSH; res MD; NC;
     FL; dep VSL (#1414).
H094 HARRY Bible; pd 1809; eb 1780; em 1805; on NEVITT, WILLISS, WOODWARD,
     BURROUGHS, FRELINGHUYSEN, LIGHTFOOT; res Georgetown, DC; dep AAGS.
H095 HARRYMAN Bible; eb 1781; em 1804; on WHEELER, CHOATE, PRICE;
     dep BCHS (photocopy).
H096 Robert HART Bible; eb 1778; em 1780; res Cecil Co., MD; pub NGSQ 44:78.
H097 HART Bible; rs 1802-1941; res Kent Co., MD; dep MSA (G-560:102 with D-150).
H098 HART Bible; eb 1814; em 1835; on SMITH, GOODWIN, VERES;
     res Fredericksburg, VA; NE; dep MHS/FCA (Hart).
H099 HARTAN Bible; rb 1855; dep HCGS.
H100 HARTMAN Bible; eb 1788; on LEITER; res Leitersburg, MD; pub MMG 2-1:21.
H101 HARTT Bible; eb 1754; em 1803; on EUSTIS, CAMP, PRATT, JUSTICE;
     res Boston, MA; dep BCGS #494.
H102 HARVER Bible; eb 1845; em 1872; on SPIED, MINNERT; res Westminster
     and Balto., Harf. Co., MD; dep BCGS (from Yingling).
H103 HARVEY-HARVYE Bible; pd 1599; eb 1724; em 1682; on HARVYE, HARNINGTO,
     JACKSON, BRITTON, HORBIS; res PA; London, England;
     dep MHS/FCA (Harvey).
H104 HARVEY Bible; pd 1829; eb 1761; em 1829; res Cecil Co., MD;
     pub NGSQ 42-1:51.
H105 HARVEY-BURWELL Bible; eb 1808; em 1807; on BURWELL, SIMMONS, KOINER;
     res Roanoke Co., VA; dep MHS/FCA (Harvey).

H106 HARVEY-RORER Bible; eb 1818; em 1845; on SMITH, BOOKER, INGLES, TROLINGER,
SHELBURNE, RORER; res Mont. Co., VA; dep MHS/FCA (Harvey).

H107 HARVEY Bible; pd 1852; eb 1820; em 1846; on WARNER, MARKS, RUTLEDGE,
MATTHEWS, EARICKSON; dep CGS.

H108 HARVEY-HELMS Bible; eb 1853; em 1879; on LANCASTER, LEWIS, HURT, McCLUNG,
SHELBURNE, HELMS, PARROTT; res Franklin Co., VA; CA;
dep MHS/FCA (Harvey).

H109 HARVEY Bible; eb 1875; em 1873; dep CGS.

H110 HARVEY Bible; pd 1881; eb 1883; em 1882; on WHITEHOUSE, WHITMAN, BREED,
CAMPBELL, ONDERDONK, HOPKINS, CROMWELL; res Balto., MD; TN;
dep MHS/FCA (Harvey).

H111 HARWOOD Bible; rs 1689-1875 Bible; dep MSA (G-258:17).

H111A HARWOOD Bible; rs 1677-1875 Bible; dep MSA (G-258:19).

H111B HARWOOD Notes; dep MSA (G-258:56).

H112 HARWOOD Bible; rs 1689-1957; dep MSA (G-569).

H112A HASELTINE Bible; rs 1753-1890; on ANES, PEABODY, RUTLEDGE, FIFE,
WARREN, WARNER, MANNING, BARNS, WYMAN, BAILEY; res Balto. & How.
Cos., MD; VT; dep HOGS.

H113 HASTINGS Bible; eb 1797; em 1831; on POWELSON, HOFFMAN; res NJ; IL;
England; dep MHS/FCA (Hastings).

H114 HAUER Bible; dep MHS/FCA (Hauer).

H115 HAUSKINS Bible; pd 1855; eb 1817; em 1816; on McDONALD, CLARK, BALDWIN,
ABBOTT; dep BOGS.

H116 HAWKINS Family Record; eb 1725; on STEELE, BROWN; res Balto., MD; England;
dep MHS/FCA (Hawkins).

H117 HAWKINS Bible; pd 1615; eb 1729; em 1795; on FRY, DORSEY; res Balto., MD;
dep MHS/FCA (Hawkins of Fells Pt.).

H118 HAWKINS-DOWNS Bible; eb 1791; em 1826; on DOWNS, FAIRALL, CROMWELL,
YEADHALL, SMITH, SEDWICK, WELLHAM, WIDGEON, WOODWARD, PUMPHREY,
WESLEY, HODGES, JONES, DAUGHTERY, WILLIAMS, JUNKINS, EVANS, KAISER,
FLAYHARDT, CLARK, OWENS; res AA Co., MD; MI; VA; CA; dep MHS/FCA.

H119 HAWKINS Bible; rb 1834; on FORWARD, FORWOOD; res Harf. Co., MD; dep HOGS.

H120 HAY Bible; eb 1764; em 1791; on MAYER, BARGER; res Balto., MD; PA;
pub MDG 9-4:79; dep MHS/FCA.

H121 James HAYES Bible; eb 1705; on SPENCE, CAULFIELD, GEDDES;
res Liverpool, England; dep MHS/FCA.

H122 HAYES Bible; pd 1814; eb 1793; em 1816; on SALISBURY, BLACKWELL, CALLOWAY,
GALLAHER; res Kent and Cecil Cos., MD; pub OBR,136.

H123 Reverdy HAYES Bible; pd 1811; eb 1812; em 1811; on FAIRLAWN, GRIFFIN,
GOULD; res Balto., MD; pub NEHGR 108:230; dep MHS/FCA.

H124 HAYMAN-CROCKETT-FITZGERALD Bible; eb 1787; em 1846; on REDDEN, PARADEE,
McGRATH, FITZGERALD, CROCKETT;
dep MHS/FCA (Hayman-Crockett-Fitzgerald).

H125 HAYMAN Bible; eb 1815; em 1847; on BENSON, ADAMS, BOWLAND, HAWKES, WILEY,
KERNAN, WILSON; res MD; dep MHS/FCA (Hayman,etc.-Turner Coll.).

H126 HAYNIE Bible; pd 1797; eb 1760; em 1786; on BAYLY, POLK, DONE;
res Worc. Co., MD; Princess Ann, MD; VA; dep MHS/FCA.

H127 HAYS Bible; eb 1764; em 1792; on BERRY, WATSON, LINDSAY, FLADGER, ADAMS,
DUPRE, MEEKINS, MILES, JACKSON, GREENWOOD; dep MHS/FCA.

H128 HAYS Bible; eb 1783; em 1825; res Mont. Co., MD; pub MGB 4:5;and 8:1.

H129 HAYS Bible; eb 1783; em 1782; on SIMMONS, TILLARD, CHANDLER, RAWLINGS,
TRAIL, HOWARD, POOLE, HARDY, WILLSON, WARD, NICHOLS, DAVIS, TRUNDLE;
res Mont. and Fred. Cos., MD; pub MDG 3-2:38.

H130 HAYS Bible; pd 1816; eb 1823; res Harf. Co., MD; pub MGB 1-3:17.

H131 HAYS Bible; pd 1830; eb 1838; em 1834; on FULFORD, MITCHELL; res Balto.
and Bel Air, MD; dep BOGS; dep MHS/FCA (HBFR typescript).

BIBLES

H132 HAYWARD Bible; rs 1733-1951; dep MSA (G-464).
H133 HAYWARD Bible; eb 1813; em 1812; on WATERS, DUER, BOWEN, SPENCE, ROBINS;
      dep MHS/FCA.
H134 HEARD Bible; eb 1823; em 1851; on SCHLERCH, OVERTON, DUNLAP; res Fred.,
      MD; York, PA; England; pub BMGS 14:19.
H135 HEATH Bible; pd 1799; eb 1725; em 1749; on BANNISTER;
      pub DAR (in MdGRC 11:148).
H136 HEATH Bible; eb 1759; em 1758; pub MMG 2-2:84.
H137 Josiah Wilson HEATH Bible; eb 1792; on HARRIS; res Som. Co., MD;
      dep MHS/FCA.
H138 HEBRON-BURLEY-ROBINSON Bible; eb 1825; em 1867; on BURLEY, ROBINSON,
      TYSON; res Laurel, MD; pub BMGS 26-1:80.
H139 HEATH Bible; pd 1831; eb 1828; em 1854; res Wico. Co., MD;
      pub DAR (in MdGRC 11:147).
H140 HECKMAN Bible; res Germany; Russia; dep AAGS.
H141 HECKMAN Bible; pd 1907; eb 1894; em 1919; on ASMUS, BIANCAVILLA, PENTICO;
      res Saline Co. NB; dep AAGS.
H142 HEETER Bible; rb 1853; on STUDYBAKER, COOK, HECKMAN, WEAVER, SCHWARTZ,
      WORKMAN; res IN; dep HCGS.
H143 HEINTZ Family Bible; rs 1803-1968; dep MSA (G-857-2, microfilm M 1247.
H144 HELMING-BINNANZER-SMITH Bible; pd 1832; rb 1828, on BENNANZER, BINNANZER,
      SMITH, HEMLING; dep MHS/FCA (photocopy, in German).
H145 HELTIBRIDLE Bible; eb 1883; res Carr. Co., MD; dep CCGS.
H146 HELTIBRIDLE Bible; eb 1893; em 1898; on WOLF, WELK; res Carr. Co., MD;
      dep CCGS (contains clippings).
H147 HELTIBRIDLE Bible; pd 1883; res Carr. Co.,MD; dep CCGS.
H148 HENDERSON Bible; pd 1810; eb 1779; em 1806; on BROWN, McCORILL, ELLIOTT,
      ANDERSON, WATTS, IRELAND, PARRISH, GUYTON, SHAW; res Harf. Co., MD;
      dep MHS/FCA.
H149 HENDERSON-HICKMAN Bible; pd 1819; eb 1778; em 1809; on HICKMAN, DOUGLASS,
      WILBOURN, MELVIN, JOHNSON, BLOXSOME; res Worc. Co., MD; VA;
      dep MHS/FCA.
H150 HENKLE Bible; pd 1773; eb 1787; em 1812; res Balto. Co., MD; VA;
      pub MGB 6:2.
H151 HENNESBERGER Bible; pd 1862; eb 1832; em 1858; on BITZBERGER, WAMPLER;
      res Wash. Co. and Balto., MD; dep MHS/FCA (photocopy in MdSAR 2699).
H152 HENNING Bible; rb 1766; pd 1787; dep MHS/FCA (in German).
H153 HENSHAW Bible; pd 1815; eb 1784; em 1815; on SANFORD, THOMAS;
      res Bethany, PA; dep MHS/VCA.
H154 HENSHAW Bible; rs 1784-1910; res MA; dep MSA (G-560:108, with D-150).
H155 HENTHORN Bible; rs 1905-1963; on BULLOCK, HAYWELL, LOWDENSLAGER, RAWLINGS;
      res MD; dep NGS (Bible Records Collection).
H156 HENYE Bible; eb 1825; em 1845; on HARVEY, HULSE; dep BCGS (no.528).
H157 HERBERT Bible; eb 1778; em 1811; on FISHER, ZELLINGER, CURLLEY;
      dep MHS/FCA.
H158 HERDMAN Bible; eb 1776; em 1739; dep MHS/FCA (MdSAR #2330).
H159 HERRERA Bible; pd 1856; eb 1874; em 1873; dep BCGS (typed copy).
H160 HERRING Bible; eb 1820; em 1842; on GILBERTHORP, WILD, TURNER, WEIL, COBB,
      HAMILTON, KLAUSMAN; pub BMGS 21-1:71; dep GPL (original).
H161 Not assigned.
H162 HESS Bible; rb 1820; on THOMPSON, BOOKMAN, EVELER, ZARBAUGH, WHITE,
      HOLLAND, LONG, GORDON, SCOTT, LOUDENSLAGER; res OH; dep HCGS.
H163 HESS Bible; eb 1877; on NORTHAMER, CROSSGI; res Balto. & Harf. Cos.,
      MD; Alsace; dep BCGS.
H164 HESSELIUS-WOODWARD Bible; pd 1807; eb 1682; em 1737; on YOUNG, ADDISON,
      ROGERS, MURRAY; res DE; MD; Sweden; dep MHS/FCA.

43

H165 HESSON Bible; pd 1841; eb 1811; em 1841; on DEVILBISS; res Uniontown, MD;
    dep CCGS (no.10).
H166 HETRICK Bible; em 1889; on WALKER; res Havre de Grace, MD; dep BCGS.
H167 HIGDON Record; pd 1786; eb 1772; em 1771; on PEERCE;
    dep MHS/FCA (in old Catechism).
H168 Jesse HIGGINS Bible; pd 1834; eb 1812; em 1837; on WATERS, DAVIS,
    FITCHETT, HALL, OULD, WHITE, STUART; res Cumberland & Poolesville,
    MD; Lincoln, IL; dep MHS/FCA.
H169 HIGGINS Bible; pd 1865; eb 1851; em 1869; on WHITE, WILLIS, ZEPP;
    res Balto., MD; dep CCGS(#40-B).
H170 HIGGINS Bible; eb 1851; em 1912; on TALBOT, MERYDITH, LIPSCOMB, BROWN,
    DAILEY, McDANIEL; res MD; VA; WVA; OH; pub DAR (in MdGRC 33:62).
H171 HIGH Bible; pd 1819; eb 1839; em 1860; on HYMES, RAY;
    dep MHS/FCA (contains clippings).
H172 HILL Bible; rs 1689-1957; dep MSA (G-569).
H173 HILLE Register; eb 1723; on MILES, HAMILTON, HADSKIN, CALHOUN, TURNER,
    PAYTON, ADAMS, HAYDON, MATTINGLY, SPAULDING, WHEATLEY, DALY, COOPER,
    HOCKIN, INGRAHAM, HOSKINS; res P.G. Co., MD; KY; dep MHS/FCA.
H174 HILL Bible; pd 1842; eb 1792; em 1816; on BRYANT, SLUBEY; res Phila., PA;
    dep MHS/FGCA.
H175 HILL Bible; rs 1798-1865; dep MSA (G-499).
H176 HILL Bible; eb 1877; em 1911; on LOCKARD; res Carr. Co., MD;
    dep CCGS (no.45).
H177 HILLEARY Bible; rb 1785; res Fred. Co., MD; dep HCGS.
H178 Tilghman HILLEARY Bible; eb 1752; em 1782; pub BMORS 1:53.
H179 HILTABIDLE-FOWBLE Bible; eb 1800; em 1836; on FOWBLE, SENSENEY,
    TROWBRIDGE, STONER, COOK, LANDIS; res Carr. Co., MD;
    dep MHS/FCA (original).
H180 HILT Bible; pd 1874; eb 1849; em 1873; on HOFFMAN, MURPHY, WORTHINGTON;
    dep BCGS (no.523).
H181 HILTON-NICHOLSON Bible; pd 1794; rs 1752-1842; on GREGORY, HENDON, NOULD,
    JACKSON, STREET, NICHOLSON; res Balto. MD;
    dep VSL (#1511, acc. 31122).
H182 HOBBS Bible; rs 1831-1933; dep MSA (D-272:4).
H183 HOBBS-DAVIS Bible; rs 1831-1948; dep MSA (D-272:5).
H184 HOBBS Bible; rs 1892-1948; on DAVIS, LOOMIS; dep MSA (D-272:6).
H185 HODGKIN Bible; pd 1825; eb 1728; em 1747; on PAGE, HODGKISS, STONE;
    dep MHS/FCA.
H186 HOBRON Bible; pd 1825; eb 1803; em 1822; on WOLCOTT, DARROW, ROGERS, PAIN,
    DAVIS; res New London, CT area; dep AAHS.
H187 HOERSTER Bible; pd 1736; eb 1776; on STROEHLER; dep MHS/FCA.
H188 John HOFF Family Record; pd 1896; eb 1870; em 1896; on FROCK, BROWN,
    LAMBERT, KITY, WARNER, ZIMMERMAN, PURDOM; res New Windsor, MD area;
    dep BCGS (from Yingling); MHS/FCA (Hoff).
H189 Samuel HOFF Bible; eb 1842; em 1869; on MYERS, FROCK, LAMBER, BROWN,
    KINTZ, WARNER, PURDUM, MAXWELL; res Black Rock, PA;
    dep BCGS (from Yingling); see H188.
H190 HOHF Bible; pd 1776; eb 1813; on McMASTER; dep BCGS (from Yingling).
H191 Frederick William HOFFMAN Bible; pd 1742; eb 1772;
    dep MHS/FCA (in German).
H192 William Davis HOFFMAN Bible; eb 1823; on DANDY; res Balto. Co., MD;
    dep MHS/FCA.
H193 H. HOHF Bible; eb 1813; em 1869; on MYERS, STARMER, BUDD; res New Windsor,
    MD; PA; dep MHS/FCA.
H194 HOLDERBY Bible; pd 1873; eb 1831; em 1853; on MILLS; res Reidsville, NC;
    dep AAGS.

H195 HOLLAND Bible; pd 1842; eb 1773; em 1852; on HARRIS, WANN; dep MHS/FCA.
H196 HOLLIFIELD Bible; pd 1834; eb 1807; em 1829; on WILSON, NELSON, VERNAY, BOLTON, HULTS; dep MHS/FCA.
H197 HOLLINGER Bible; pd 1874; eb 1860; em 1843; on DIEHL, CLUTZ, HARTMAN, NELSON, REIFSNYDER, BAKER; res Adams Co.,PA; dep MHS/FCA.
H198 HOLLINGSWORTH Bible; eb 1760; on YELLOTT, WILLIS, CARROLL; res MD; MO; NY; dep MHS/FCA.
H199 HOLLINGSWORTH Bible; pd 1870; eb 1862; em 1860; on PRICE; res Carr. & Balto. Cos., MD; dep CCGS (no.12).
H200 HOLLINGSWORTH Bible; eb 1913; em 1912; on BANDEL; res Balto. Co., MD; dep CCGS.
H201 HOLLINGSWORTH Bible; pd 1891; eb 1872; em 1913; on PARRY; res Balto. Co., MD; dep CCGS.
H202 HOLLIS Bible; rs 1746-1837; dep MSA (G-132).
H203 Frisby HOLLIS Bible; pd 1830; eb 1822; em 1854; on MURPHY, EDGELL, LLOYD; res DE; dep MHS/FCA.
H204 HOLLOWAY Bible; pd 1813; eb 174(?); em 1775; res Worc. Co., MD; pub DAR (in MdGRC vol.4, 1952); dep MDSAR.
H205 HOLLOWAY-CAREY Bible; pd 1805; eb 1799; em 1797; on WATTERS, CAREY; dep MHS/FCA.
H206 HOLLOWAY Bible; pd 1813; eb 1804; em 1802; on FOOKS, HEARVE, FURLOW, LYNCH, TRUIT, PARSONS, HAYMAN; pub DAR (in MdGRC 11:150).
H207 John HOLLOWAY Bible; eb 1829; em 1855; on BAILEY, HEARN, WRIGHT, RUMBOLD, BOUNDS; res Worc. Co., MD; dep MHS/FCA.
H207A HOLLOWAY Bible; eb 1859; em 1885; res Wico. Co., MD; dep MdSAR #2211 (typed copy).
H208 HOLLOWAY Bible; eb 1696; em 1721; res Easton, MD; pub MGB 1-2:9.
H209 HOLLOWAY-WARING Bible; pd 1843; eb 1788; em 1876; on WARING, HALL, STONE, YOUNG, BEALL, GREENFIELD, LANE, CRAWFORD, WALLIS; res Kent & PG Cos., MD; Washington, DC; dep MHS/FCA.
H210 HOLLYDAY Bible; pd 1834; eb 1826; em 1825; on CARVILL, HARPER, CHAMBERLAIN; dep MHS/FCA.
H211 HOLMEAD Bible; eb 1724; em 1742; res MD; County Devon, England; dep MHS/FCA.
H212 HOLMES Bible; eb 1725; em 1759; on WELLS, BROWN; dep BCGS (photocopy).
H213 HOLTER Bible; eb 1776; em 1776; pub NGSQ 23-1:20.
H214 HOLTZ Bible; eb 1717; em 1741; on BOSSEN; res Fred. Co., MD; Germany; dep MHS/FCA (typed copy).
H215 HOLTZ Bible; pd 1892; eb 1801; dep MHS/FCA.
H216 HOLTZ Bible; rs 1812-1953; pd 1885; eb 1865; em 1892; on MINNICK, WEBB, BULL, SEIBOLD, HOBBS, WALTON, NULL, MABEN, RUSSELL; res BALTO., MD; pub HCMR 5:75; dep HOGS.
H217 HOMER Bible; pd 1825; em 1828; on DeWOLD, BEDLOW, PEGRAM, AUSTIN, LYNCH; res Bristol, RI; IL; Canada; dep MHS/FCA.
H218 HOOD-OWINGS Family Record; ins 1866; eb 1714; em 1771; on BAINES, HOWARD, GAITHER, WORTHINGTON, WAYMAN, MERRIWEATHER, LAWRANCE, BOYLE, JENNINGS, WARFIELD, DORSEY, HARPER, CLARK, WICKERT; dep MHS/FCA; dep BCGS.
H219 HOOD Bible; pd 1814; eb 1771; em 1774; res AA Co., MD; pub MGB 2:10.
H220 Sarah Smith HOOD Bible; pd 1805; eb 1775; em 1806; on HOWARD, HOPLINS, MEEDS, WORTHINGTON, CIPRIANI; dep MHS/FCA.
H221 HOOD-OWINGS Bible; rs 1780-1973; on COOK, OWINGS, STEWART, DORSEY, KEYS, ROSE; res How. Co., MD; dep HOGS.
H222 HOOK Bible; pd 1874; eb 1784; on BOWEN, SOLLARS, WATTS, ELDER, MERCERONI; dep MHS/FCA.
H223 HOOK Bible; pd 1799; eb 1785; em 1784; on CAMPBELL; pub BMGS 20-4:344.

H224 HOOK Bible; pd 1799; eb 1785; em 1784; on CAMPBELL; dep MHS/FCA.
      Note: Probably duplication of H223 above.
H225 HOOK Bible; pd 1870; eb 1830; em 1872; on EASTON, SAYLOR, MYERLY, POOL,
      SHIPLEY, STRINE; dep CCGS no.44.
H226 HOOPER-KILLOUGH Bible; eb 1748; em 1769; on BANE, RICHARD, GRIENDFIELD,
      LAMBORN; dep MHS/FCA.
H227 HOOPER Bible; eb 1776; em 1806; on STANFORD, TROTH, ENNALLY, SEWARD,
      WILLIAMS, WHITTINGTON, WHEELER, PENNINGTON, GORE; dep MHS/FCA.
H228 HOOPER-KILLOUGH Bible; pd 1824; eb 1791; em 1815; on MOORE, WRIGHT, WAY,
      GATCHELL, WHITE, KILLOUGH; res Chester Co., PA; dep MHS/FCA.
H229 HOOPER-KILLOUGH Bible; eb 1802; on CLAYTON, GILPIN, WAY, BROOMELL,
      KILLOUGH; res Chester Co., PA; dep MHS/FCA (contains clippigs).
H230 HOOPER-KILLOUGH Bible; eb 1839; em 1837; on WRIGHT, CLAYTON; dep MHS/FCA.
H231 HOOPER Bible; eb 1856; em 1855; on COBLE, CHILTON, WILLIS, SWAINE, RATHELL,
      RHODES, DAVIS; res Talb. Co., MD; dep AAGS.
H232 HOOPES Bible; eb 1748; em 1769; on BANE;
      dep MHS/FCA (with Hoopes-Killough).
H233 HOOPES-KILLOUGH Bible; pd 1824; eb 1791; em 1815; on MOORE, WRIGHT, WHITE;
      res Cecil Co., MD; Chester & Lancaster Cos, PA; dep MHS/FCA.
H234 HOOVER Bible; pd 1846; eb 1798; dep MHS/FCA.
H235 HOOVER Bible; eb 1843; res PA; dep MHS/FCA.
H236 HOOVER Bible; eb 1850; em 1872; on WOLF; res PA; dep MHS/FCA.
H237 HOPE Bible; eb 1732; em 1766; on DeMOSS, BARRON, POWELL, DARWIN;
      res Harf. Co., MD; York Co., PA; NC; SC; England;
      pub DAR Mag 84:770 (1950).
H238 HOPEWELL Bible; eb 1838; em 1837; on CULBRETH; dep MHS/FCA.
H239 HOPKINS Bible; pd 1831; eb 1742; em 1797; on BRYAN, HALL, McELDERY;
      res Phila., PA; pub DAR (in MdGRC 4:67 (1929)).
H240 HOPKINS Bible; pd 1839; eb 1774; em 1842; on SEPNCER, WALKER, HOOPMAN,
      HANNA, HETRICH; res Harf. Co., MD; dep BCGS.
H241 HOPKINS Bible; rs 1794-1945; res Talb. & QA. Cos., MD;
      dep MSA (G-560:97, with D-150).
H242 HOPKINS Bible; rb 1801(?); dep HCGS.
H243 HOPKINS-HARRIS Bible; eb 1824; em 1852; on HARNES; dep MHS/FCA; dep BCHS.
H244 Solomon S. HOPKINS Bible; pd 1837; eb 1835; em 1834; res Talb. Co., MD;
      pub MDG 24-1:28.
H245 HOOPER Bible; pd 1753; eb 1733; em 1731; on NICHOLSON, LLOYD, HINDMAN,
      NOEL, CHAMBERS, EMERSON, BARNEY, INGRAHAM, PATTERSON, NICOLS;
      dep MHS/FCA.
H246 HOPPER Bible; eb 1812; em 1840; on ALER, ALLEN; dep MHS/FCA.
H247 HOPPER Bible; pd 1880; eb 1860; em 1842; on MASSEY, PERKINS, McCOLLISTER;
      res VA; dep MHS/FCA.
H248 HORINE Bible; pd 1876; rs 1800-1880; on ROUTYON; res MD;
      dep VSL (#1563, acc. 29741).
H249 HORINE Bible; pd 1870; rs 1841-1972; on CAMPBELL, GAVER; res MD;
      dep VSL (#1564, acc. 29741).
H250 HORNER Bible; eb 1792; em 1776; on PATTERSON, LeCOMPTE, NORTH, LEONHARDT,
      McLAUGHLIN; dep MHS/FCA.
H251 HORNER Bible; pd 1871; eb 1854; em 1875; on LEVENGOOD, UPHOUSE, GNAGEY;
      dep MHS/FCA; dep AAGS.
H252 HORSEY Bible; eb 1777; em 1804; on SKINNER, RENCHER, CUSTIS, WISE;
      dep MHS/FCA.
H253 HORSEY Bible; rs 1763-1878; on BELL, KEANE; dep MSA (G-503:4).
H254 HORSEY Bible; rs 1819-1925; dep MSA (G-506).
H255 HORSMON Bible; eb 1863; em 1859; on HUGHES, WILLEY; res Dor. Co., MD;
      pub DCGS 2-6:18.

BIBLES

H256 HOSHAL Bible; eb 1780; em 1852; on ROWBLE, KEITH; dep MHS/FCA; dep BCHS.
H257 HOUGHTON Bible; pd 1817; eb 1796; on RUTLEDGE, DORSEY; res Balto. Co., MD;
      Liverpool, England; pub QMF 1:32 (typescript in BCGS).
H258 HOULTEN Bible; pd 1816; em 1811; on MURTS, GORSUCH, BANKS;
      dep MHS/FCA (poor photocopy).
H259 HOUSELL Bible; eb 1842; em 1861; on STEVENSON; res NJ; dep MdSAR (#2698).
H260 HOUSTON Bible; pd 1831; eb 1779; em 1794; on THOROUGHGOOD, WHARTON,
      MILLER, LAWS, BELL, AYDELOTT, BURTON, HITCHENS; dep MHS/FCA.
H261 HOUX Bible; pd 1770; eb 1782; on MORNINGSTAR, HOLTZ, MORGENSTERN, MOLL,
      LEGESTER, TRAUTMAN; dep MHS/FCA.
H262 Benjamin HOWARD, Sr. Bible; eb 1755; em 1792; res Fred. Co., MD;
      pub GKF 2:693.
H263 HOWARD Bible; pd 1836; eb 1776; em 1800; on MASON, MYERS; pub WMG 1-2:90.
H264 HOWARD Bible; eb 1779; em 1826; res Eastern Shore; pub MGB 2:18.
H265 HOWARD Bible; eb 1785; em 1819; res Zanesville, OH; on GIST, BECKWITH,
      COLE, FULTON, WILLIS; Registration incomplete.
H266 HOWARD Bible; pd 1793; eb 1788; em 1787; on READ, McHENRY, RIDGLEY,
      GILMOR, CHEW, EAGER; res Balto. Co., MD; dep MHS/FCA.
H267 HOWARD Bible; eb 1788; em 1787; on READ, GILMOR, McHENRY, RIDGLEY, CHEW,
      KEY; dep MHS/FCA.
H268 HOWARD Bible; pd 1850; eb 1792; em 1839; res Zanesville, OH; on GIST,
      SCOTT, BRACKEN; Registration incomplete.
H269 HOWARD Family Record; eb 1793; em 1867; dep MdSAR (no.2589).
H270 John HOWARD Bible; pd 1805; eb 1848; em 1795; on NEWBERRY, PAYNE, DARROW,
      HOBRON; res New London, CT; dep AAHS.
H271 HOWARD-GOVANE-LAW Bible; eb 1839; em 1798; on GOVANE, HOOD, BRICE,
      WOODYEAR, MURDOCK, LAW, DALLAM; res Phila., PA; dep MHS/FCA.
H272 HOWARD Bible; eb 1799; em 1826; on TAYLOR, TULL, STEVENSON; res Rehoboth,
      DE; dep MHS/FCA.
H273 James Varley HOWARD Bible; eb 1799; em 1852; on HASLEM, SUTTON, RILEY;
      res Ely, England; Balto. MD; dep BCHS (typed copy).
H274 HOWARD Bible; eb 1801; em 1811; on JONES, BIDDLE, ASH, WALMSLEY, CASHO;
      res Cecil Co., MD; Lancaster. PA; dep MHS/FCA.
H275 HOWARD Bible; pd 1802; em 1825; on KEY, LLOYD, MORRIS, WINDER, MORGAN,
      COLEMAN; res Balto. Co., MD; dep MHS/FCA.
H276 HOWARD Bible; pd 1816; eb 1802; em 1825; on KEY, LLOYD, MORRIS, WINDER,
      MORGAN, COLEMAN; res Balto. Co., MD; dep MHS/FCA.
H277 HOWARD Bible; pd 1803; eb 1846; em 1802; on STEELE, HARWOOD, KEY, LLOYD,
      TURNER, BLUNT, PENDLETON, SWAN; dep MHS/FCA.
H278 HOWARD-HAYS Bible; eb 1816; em 1815; on HAYS, CHAPMAN; res Balto. City &
      Co., MD; dep MHS/FCA.
H279 HOWARD Bible; eb 1826; em 1892; on TOWNSEND, HASLEM, HILL, SUTTON, HUNTER;
      res Relay, Balto. Co., MD; dep MHS/FCA.
H280 John W. HOWARD Bible; eb 1874; em 1871; on PITCHER; pub O'Brien,306.
H281 HOWELL Bible; eb 1759; em 1755; on CARROLL, WILLIAMS, HILL, EDMONDSON,
      PALMER, SMITH, ROGERS, MILES, BARRY; dep MHS/FCA.
H282 HOWWELL Bible; pd 1895; eb 1896; em 1895; on BIDDLE, BOYD, LONGBREY,
      BROWN; res Cecil Co., MD; pub DBR 12:64.
H283 HOWLETT Family Records; eb 1764; em 1815; on ADAMS, MITCHELL, YEANEY,
      MILLIGAN, BARRATT, LEE; res Aberdeen, MD; dep MHS/FCA.
H284 HOYLE Bible; pd 1826; eb 1835; em 1834; on WALLS, EASTBORN, FORCAN;
      pub DAR (in MdGRC 11:121).
H285 HOYLE Bible; eb 1869; em 190(?); on HARRISON; pub DAR (in MdGRC 11:120).
H286 HOYT Bible; eb 1833; em 1855; on LACEY, WALKINS, HOWARD, GROMAN, DURHAM,
      WRIGHTSON, WRIGHT, COCKEY, NOVAK, WINDSOR, HEINMILLER, CARRICO,
                    (continued on next page)

47

H286 HOYT Bible; on SEWELL, BUCKEL, BEAMAN, FOGERTY, YOUNG, PIERCE;
     res QA Co., MD; CT; PA; dep MHS/FCA.
H287 HUBBARD Bible; eb 1812; em 1846; on SMITH, MYERS; dep BCGS (#514).
H288 HUFF Bible; pd 1867; eb 1847; em 1844; on PRESTON, AMOSS, GRYMES, STREETT,
     BYURGEON, DRIVER, DAVIS; res Harf. Co., MD; dep BCGS.
H289 HUFF Bible; pd 1882; eb 1847; em 1883; on PYLE, JOHNSON, BROTHERTON,
     LINEBURG, CHILTUM; res Harf. Co., MD; dep BCGS.
H290 HUFFER Bible; eb 1741; on BAUCHTEL, HUSH, NEWCOMER, LINE, CRAMPTON,
     MILLER, FOLTZ; dep MHS/FCA (filed with Chrisman).
H291 Christopher HUGHES Bible; pd 1610; eb 1815; em 1835; on ABELL, BULL,
     PHELPS, COOK, STITCHER, CHILDS; dep MHS/FCA.
H292 HUGHES Bible; rs 1739-1896; dep MSA (G-890:1).
H293 HUGHES Bible; pd 1822; eb 1772; em 1796; on ADAMS, MITCHELL, COOLEY,
     HOPKINS, KNIGHT; res Harf. Co., MD; dep MHS (HBFR,46).
H294 HUGHES Bible; pd 1858; eb 1815; em 1835; on ABELL, BULL, PHELPS, STITCHER,
     GARRETT; res MD; VA; dep MHS/FCA.
H295 HUGHES Bible; eb 1817; em 1850; on BENSON, WILSON, LANKFORD; res Westover,
     MD; dep MHS/FCA (from Turner Collection).
H296 HUGHES Bible; eb 1881; em 1882; on SCRIVENOR; res Carr. Co., MD;
     dep CCGS (#1).
H297 HULL Bible; eb 1792; on COVER, HAHN, MAUSE; res Carr. Co.,MD; dep MHS/FCA.
H298 HULL Bible; eb 1818; em 1842; on HAHN, COVER, MAUSE; res Carr. Co., MD;
     pub BMGS 27-1:125.
H299 HULL Bible; pd 1885; eb 1894; em 1893; on MYERS, ENGLER, GRAHAM, MINKER,
     SHOEMAKER, EBAUGH, LOGUE; res Carr. Co., MD; dep BCGS (from Yingling).
H300 Washington HUNT Bible; pd 1854; rs 1855-1910; on COFER, GOFFIGON, McKOWN,
     TANKARD, WILKINS; res Balto., MD; dep VSL (#1622, acc. 30453).
H301 Rev. William HUNT Bible; pd 1859; eb 1801; em 1823; on KELLER, GILBERT,
     WILLHIDE, SILL, MULLIN, DIEHL, VOLK; res PA; Western MD;
     pub BRP 1:47.
H302 HUNTING Bible; pd 1856; eb 1807; dep MHS/FCA;
     dep BCHS (has newspaper obituaries).
H303 Joshua HURLEY Bible; eb 1849; em 1871; res Dor. Co., MD; pub DCGM 3-5:16.
H304 HURLEY Bible; pd 1843; eb 1865; on BRADLEY; res Dor. Co.,MD;
     pub DCGM 3-4:18.
H305 HURST Bible; on BERRY; res Balto. Co., MD; dep MHS/FCA.
H306 HURST Bible; pd 1816; eb 1804; em 1802; on MARSHALL, LITTLE; res MD; OH;
     IN; pub MGB 21:45.
H307 HUSBAND-PRICE Bible; eb 1722; em 1765; on PRICE; res Cecil Co., MD;
     pub GPF/B p.449.
H308 HUSBANDS-PRICE Bible; pd 1754; eb 1766; em 1765; on PRICE, HAINES;
     res Cecil Co., MD; dep MHS/FCA (photocopy, hard to read);
     dep Somerset Co., PA Hist.Soc. (original).
H309 Allen Harry HUTCHENS Bible; eb 1893; em 1924; on WOOD, BOWEN;
     pub O'Brien,307.
H310 Thomas Love HUTCHINS Bible; eb 1872; em 1871; on BOWEN, KING, WARD,
     NORTHAM, DULANEY, MILLER, SUNDERLAND; pub O'Brien,307.
H311 HUTCHINS-HAWKINS Bible; pd 187(?); eb 1848; em 1873;
     dep BCGS (transcription).
H312 HUTSON Bible; pd 1739; eb 1790; em 1789; on ODELL, BAKER, HOOPER;
     pub MGB 17:68.

I001 IGLEHART Bible; rs 1752-1934; dep MSA (G-412 with G-258).
I002 IGLEHART Bible; rs 1760-1934; dep MSA (G-258:20).
I003 INGLEHART Bible; pd 1828; eb 1781; on BURNS; dep MHS/FCA.

I004 INGLE Bible; eb 1799; em 1825; on PECHIN, EDWARDS; res Alexandria, VA;
  Baltimore, MD; DC; dep MHS/FCA.
I005 IRELAND Bible; pd 1832; eb 1807; em 1803; on WILSON, GIBSON, LAVEILLE,
  BASFORD, FREELAND, COX, YOUNG, FALK; res Calv. Co., MD; dep MHS/FCA.
I006 INGMAN Record; eb 1807; pub BMGS 26:392.
I007 IRELAND Bible; rs 1803-1947; dep MSA (G-653).
I008 John M. IRELAND Bible; em 1820; on MILLS, SEDWICK, DUKE, GOVE, HELLEN,
  PETERSON, KENT, LATIMER; pub O'Brien p.308.

J001 JACKSON Bible; eb 1729; em 1791; on WEBSTER, BUCKEY, COOPER; dep MHS/FCA.
J002 JACKSON Bible; pd 1880; eb 1812; em 1848; on LITTLE, COOPER, BARNES,
  PIERSON, ALDERMAN, CONRAD; res Cecil Co., MD; dep MHS/FCA.
J003 JACKSON Bible; ins 1881; eb 1822; em 1847; res Principio Furnace and
  Woodlawn, MD; dep BCGS (from DAR).
J004 JACKSON Bible; eb 1885; em 1888; on MATTHEWS, McCORD, SMITH, BROWN,
  EICHORN, ROSE, WEBB; res Balto., MD; OH; VA; WV; KY; dep MHS/FCA;
  dep BCHS (typed copy).
J005 JACOB Bible; eb 1766; em 1789; on HACH, BOWDOIN, EVANS, DORSEY, KILLAM,
  RENDALL; dep MHS/FCA.
J006 JACOBS Bible; rs 1753-1854; dep MSA (G-890:2).
J007 JACOBS Bible; rs 1753-1854; pd 1828; eb 1811; em 1809; on BECK, STRAYER,
  MUMMONERT, GEIB; res Adams and York Cos., PA; IL;
  dep BCGS (from DAR).
J008 JAMES Bible; eb 1767; em 1829; on WHITE, WILLOUGHBY, EVELINE; res IN;
  dep MHS/FCA.
J009 Charles JAMISON Bible; pd 1862; eb 1856; em 1855; on DOUGLASS;
  res Phila., PA; dep MGS (vertical file).
J010 Stewart JAMISON Bible; eb 1842; on DENDLER;
  dep MGS (vertical file, typed copy).
J011 JEFFERS Bible; pd 1846; eb 1811; em 1838; on WOODELL, COLQUITT, WATTS;
  res Balto., MD; dep CCGS (no.15).
J012 JEFFERS Bible; res Balto., MD; dep CCGS (no.15).
J013 JEFFERSON Bible; eb 1794; on VICKERS, WAPLES, MARVEL; dep MHS/FCA.
J014 JENKINS Bible; pd 1805; eb 1774; em 1803; on DEVEREUX, HICKLEY, FORD,
  KERNAN, GARLAND; res Balto. & Chas. Cos., MD; WV;
  dep BCGS (photocopy).
J015 JENKINS Bible; pd 1805; eb 1774; em 1803; on PLOWDEN, O'DONNELL, PLATT,
  PROCTOR, DALLAM, DAVIS, SIMMS, SANDERS, TAYLOR, BRADY, MORTON, MILES,
  GARDINER, JAMESON, BRAWNER, FERGUSON, PERKINS, HAMILTON, SPALDING,
  LILLY, HICKLEY, FORD, DEVEREUX, KERNAN, LOWE, BONSAL, BOONE, GARLAND,
  LYON; res MD; DE; DC; PA; NY; dep MHS/FCA.
J016 JENKINS Bible; pd 1855; eb 1808; em 1841; on GREELEY, ARNOLD, CLARK, LINE,
  KRANTZ, BROWN, INGERSOLL; res Hyattsville, MD;
  pub PGCGS 16-8:94 (April 1985).
J017 JENNINGS Bible; ins 1803; eb 1721; em 1793; on OWINMGS, COX, HYNSON,
  MARRAST, HOOD, FRENCH; dep MHS/FCA.
J018 JENNINGS Bible; pd 1802; eb 1794; em 1793; pub MGB 2:9.
J019 Kensay JOHNS Bible; eb 1785; on STEWART, STOCKTON, JOHNSON;
  res West River, MD; DE; dep MHS/FCA; dep VSL (#1690).
J020 David JOHNSON Bible; pd 1863; eb 1744; em 1773; on STANDEFORD, JARRETT,
  PAINE; res Harf. Co., MD; pub DAR (MdGRC 35:70).
J021 JOHNSON Birth and Death Records; rs 1771-1848; dep MSA (D-186).
J022 Roger JOHNSON Bible; eb 1781; em 1781; on THOMAS, MACTIER, DORSEY, NEWMAN,
  ARMSTRONG, SEDGEWICK; dep MHS/FCA.
J023 JOHNSON Bible; pd 1815; eb 1812; em 1812; on NORRIS, HALE, HAYWARD,
  HOLLIS; dep MHS/FCA.

J024 JOHNSON Bible; rs 1818-1943; dep MSA (G-341).
J025 JOHNSON Bible; eb 1864; on NABB; res Dor. Co., MD; pub DCGM 3-4:10.
J026 JOHNSTON Bible; eb 1799; em 1829; on TAYLOR, JOHNSON, MICHAEL;
   res Harf. Co., MD; dep MHS (HBFR,48).
J027 JOHNSTON Birth and Deaths Records; rs 1809-1822; dep MSA (G-518:1).
J028 JOHNSTON Bible; rs 1818-1833; on BERESFLOYD, FLOYD, HANDY, JONES, LEE;
   res MD; VA; NY; TX; dep VSL (#1709, acc. 20645).
J029 JONES Bible; res AA Co., MD; pub MG 2:106.
J030 JONES Bible; pd 1727; eb 1704; em 1712; on FORMAN, LEE, CHAMBERS, GIBBONS,
   SMITH; res MD; PA; dep MHS/FCA (73).
J031 JONES Bible; eb 1716; em 1715; on KOWEL; dep MHS/FCA (73).
J032 JONES Bible; rs 1755-1848; dep MSA (D-185).
J033 JONES Bible; pd 1801; eb 1771; em 1751; on MANNING, HARPER;
   dep BCGS (from DAR).
J034 JONES Bible; rs 1772-1800; on MORRIS; res Taneytown, MD;
   dep NGS Bible records collection.
J035 JONES-LETTON-MATHERS Bible; pd 1807; eb 1772; em 1796; on BURNAN,
   RICHARDS, LETTON, MATHERS; pub MGB 14:19.
J036 JONES Bible; pd 1795; eb 1774; em 1796; on DURBIN, MATTHEWS, SMITH,
   HEWLETT, McCOY, THOMSON; res Cumberland, MD; dep MHS/FCA.
J037 JONES Bible; eb 1777; em 1804; on DOWNEY, POOLE, MAYNARD, HAMMOND,
   GAMBRILL, BROOKE, STANSBURY, ATTEE, SLINGLUFT; res Fred. & Balto.
   Cos., MD; WV; dep MHS/FCA (73).
J038 JONES Bible; eb 1782; em 1811; on GILL, CREIGHTON, ROBBINS, PEOPLES, PAYNE,
   PARMED; pub BMGS 22-2:156.
J039 JONES Bible; pd 1809; eb 1783; em 1782; on BATES, KEMP, SHIELD, WILKINS;
   res Kent Co., MD; pub DAR (MdGRC 8:230).
J040 JONES-DASHIELL Bible; pd 1815; eb 1783; em 1805; on DASHIELL, WAINWRIGHT,
   HAYSE; pub MDG 20-2:66.
J041 JONES Bible; rs 1786-1816; dep MSA (D-272:1).
J042 JONES Bible; rs 1782-1884; res St.M. Co., MD;
   dep MSA (G-520:85 with D-150).
J043 JONES Bible; rb 1791; on EVANS; res Harf. Co., MD; dep HCGS.
J044 JONES Bible; eb 1803; em 1830; res Dor. Co. & Balto., MD; dep CCGS.
J045 JONES Bible; ins 1834; eb 1808; em 1830; on BONNAWILL, HANCOCK, PILCHARD,
   PAYNE, PARADISE; dep BCGS.
J046 JONES Bible; pd 1847; eb 1817; res Allen, MD; pub DAR (MdGRC 11:152).
J047 Elhanan JONES Bible; pd 1842; eb 1818; em 1863; on ANDREW, GORE, TODD,
   NICHOLS, CORKRAN, WICKLEIN, CRAMMER; dep MHS/FCA;
   dep BCHS (typed copy).
J048 JONES Bible; rs 1819-1933; on ARCHER, COLEMAN, JEFFREES, REINS, RICHFORD,
   RIDLEY, ROBERTS, WILLINGHAM; res Balto., MD; VA; NC;
   dep VSL (#1744, acc. 20489).
J049 Thomas C. JONES Bible; on HALL; res QA & Caro. Cos., MD; pub MDG 23-4:114.
J050 JONES Bible; rs 1832-1956; res How. Co., MD; dep MSA (G-713).
J051 Daniel JONES Bible; pd 1835; eb 1837; em 1836; on GASSAWAY, DORSEY,
   CASTLEMAN, GAMBRILL, FRESHOUR; res How. Co., MD;
   pub DAR (MdGRC 35:84).
J052 JONES Bible; eb 1839; em 1837; on LYNCH, POLLARD, SELDEN; res Balto., MD;
   VA; dep MHS/FCA.
J053 JONES Bible; eb 1849; em 1873; on STORY, LOTZ, BURNS, BRINSFIELD;
   res Talb. Co. & Balto., MD; pub BMGS 7-4:111.
J054 William ap Catesby JONES Bible; em 1849; on POLLARD, LYNCH, MYRICH,
   MEREDITH; res Balto., MD; VA; dep BCHS (typed copy).
J055 JONES Bible; pd 1837; eb 1854; em 1852; on VAN BUREN, HARVEY, STUMP,
   BOLVILL, COURTRIGHT, THIELA; dep MHS/FCA.

J056 JONES Bible; rb 1864, on BOYLE, GAITHER, ALLISON, WEBSTER, LOCKHART,
    ASBURY; res Harf. Co., MD; dep HCGS.
J057 Edward B. JONES Bible; pd 1876; eb 1876; em 1876; on WILKINS, MACKEY,
    SIMPERS; res Kent Co., MD; pub KBR.
J058 Jacob C. JONES Bible; eb 1890; em 1889; on WALLEN, GILLIAN, DYKES;
    res VA; dep MdSAR (#2741).
J059 JOY Bible; eb 1884; em 1930; on PARKER, LUSBY; pub O'Brien p.329.
J060 JOYCE Bible; pd 1885; eb 1844; em 1869; on COLLINSON, BRICE, COX, BOLGIANO,
    TYDINGS, KNIGHT, JENKINS, MONROE; res AA Co., MD; dep AAHS (#2516).
J061 JULIAN Bible; rs 1788-1882 Bible; dep MSA (G-344).
J062 JUNGST Bible; eb 1736; em 1828; on KREIDER, STRICKLER, MILLER, DINGES,
    EMRICH; res Phila., PA; Germany; dep BCHS (typed copy).

K001 KEAFAUVER Bible; pd 187(?); eb 1878; em 1877; on REMMELL; res Fred. Co.,
    MD; dep FCHS (original Bible).
K002 KEAN Bible; rs 1803-1910; pd 1754; on KEYSER, VAWTER; res MD; VA; WV;
    dep VSL (#1778, acc. 30433).
K003 KEAN Bible; pd 1840; eb 1803; em 1829; on BUCKLEY, ADY, CAIN; res Balto.,
    MD; pub BMGS 20-3:239; dep BCHS (typed copy).
K004 KECK Bible; pd 1853; eb 1826; em 1853; on HIRSCH; res Balto., MD;
    dep CCGS (#33).
K005 KEECH Bible; rs 1855-1915; dep MSA (G-323:2).
K006 KEENE Bible; rs 1763-1878; dep MSA (G-503:4).
K007 KEENE Bible; eb 1808; em 1843; on BROHANN, DARRS, COFS, LEE, CORNISH,
    TRAVERS, NOBLE, BOSLEY; res Dor. Co., MD; pub DOBR,30.
K008 KEENE Bible; pd 1830; eb 1806; em 1831; on MILES, CRAIG, HOLLINGSWORTH,
    HALL; res Balto., MD; dep MHS/FCA.
K009 KEENER Bible; pd 1685; on BRICE; res Balto., MD; dep MHS/FCA.
K010 KEERL Family Record; pd 1825; eb 1793; em 1825; on MUNDELL; dep MHS/FCA.
K011 KESSLER Bible; pd 1848; eb 1861; dep MHS/FCA (poor photocopies).
K012 KELLER Bible; pd 1842; eb 1817; em 1840; on EADER, HUNT, DIEHL, SINN,
    EICHOLTZ; res Fred. Co. MD; pub BRP 1:57.
K013 Noah T.KELLEY Bible; eb 1848; em 1871; on PARKS, GOLDSBOROUGH, COULBOURNE,
    HOLLAND; res Deale Island, Som. Co., MD; dep WCFL.
K014 KELLY Bible; pd 1873; eb 1849; em 1875; on KIRKER, DONAHUE, BIRD;
    res Ironton, OH; dep BCGS.
K015 KEMP-SHIELDS Bible; eb 1753; em 1782; on WILKINS, JONES, SHIELDS;
    pub MdGRC 7:277.
K016 KEMP Family Record; eb 1782; em 1823; on GREENBURY, HARWOOD, COX, RIGGS,
    RHETT, NOEL, SWAN, DONNELO; res Balto., MD; Charleston, SC;
    dep MHS/FCA.
K017 KEMP Bible; pd 1856; eb 1827; em 1803; on LAMBDEN, COOPER, RIDGEWAY,
    IRVING, ROBY, DAWSON; pub DAR (MdGRC 35:21).
K018 Not assigned.
K019 KENNARD Family Register; eb 1726; pub DAR (MdGRC 13:111).
K020 KENNARD Family Register; eb 1744; em 1769; on OGDEN, MILTON, DIGES,
    SINCLEAR; pub DAR (MdGRC 13:109).
K021 KENNARD Bible; eb 1769; em 1794; res Harf. Co., MD; pub MGB 3-1:2.
K022 KENNEDY Bible; pd 1878; eb 1841; em 1839; on CAMPBELL; res Balto., MD;
    dep MHS/FCA.
K023 KENT Bible; pd 1783; em 1788; on GILDER, ALKIN, KILTRY, SPAIHT, CHALMERS;
    res Balto., MD; dep MHS/FCA.
K024 KERR Bible; eb 1841; on O'LAUGHLIN, BURGESS; res Balto., MD;
    dep MHS/FCA (Kerr-Burgess).
K025 KESSLER Bible; eb 1767; em 1807; on NOTE, JONES, EMMERT; res Ashe Co., NC;
    Berks Co., PA; Wash. Co., MD; dep MHS/FCA.

INVENTORY OF MARYLAND BIBLE RECORDS

K026 KEY Bible; pd 1817; eb 1816; em 1815; on HILL, HAM, HARRIS, ROBERTSON,
     BRISCOE, SMITH; res St.M. Co., MD; VA; dep MHS/FCA.
K027 KEY Bible; eb 1834; em 1833; on SEWALL, BARTON, KLINGERDER, THORNTON,
     JENKINS, DAINGERFIELD; res St.M & PG Cos, MD; LA; MI; VA;
     dep MHS/FCA (Philip Barton Key Bible).
K028 KEYSER Bible; pd 1809; dep MHS/FCA (Keyser).
K029 KIBBLE Family Record; eb 1774; on WHAYLAND; res Salisbury, MD;
     pub DAR (MdGRC 11:153).
K030 James Edward KIDD Bible; eb 1829; em 1890; on EDWARDS, CULVER, CHEELEY,
     DAY, SMITH; res Balto., MD; GA; pub Austin,78.
K031 KIDD Bible; eb 1840; em 1860; on HOWARD; res Fred. Co., MD; dep MHS/FCA.
K032 KIDEL Bible; rs 1840-1934; res Fred. Co., MD;
     dep MSA (G-560:86 with D-150).
K033 KILMON Bible; pd 1888; eb 1816; em 1841; on RIGS, BYRD; res VA;
     dep MHS/FCA.
K034 KIMMEL Bible; eb 1742; dep MHS/FCA (In German).
K035 KING Bible; eb 1752; em 1829; on TAYLOR, AMOS; res Balto., MD;
     pub CMF 1:41.
K036 KING Bible; pd 1791; eb 1790; on TAYLOR, WILSON, REVES; res Balto. Co.,
     MD; MI; dep BCGS.
K037 KING-RITTER Bible; eb 1864; em 1863; on LOCKARD, RITTER; res Balto. Co.,
     MD; dep MHS/FCA.
K038 KING Bible; res Cecil Co. & Balto., MD; dep MHS/FCA.
K039 KING Bible; rb 1872; on ADAMS; res Harf. Co., MD; dep HCGS.
K040 KING Bible; pd 1892; eb 1903; on ELLIS; res Calv. Co., MD;
     pub DAR (MdGRC 35:52).
K041 KINNA Bible; rb 1832; on SULSER, HARP, HOFFMAN; res Fred. & Wash. Cos.,
     MD; HCGS.
K042 KIRK Bible; eb 1777; on BROWN; dep BCGS (#513).
K043 KIRK Bible; pd 1831; eb 1794; em 1793; on DUNGAN, McMULLIN; res NY; NJ;
     dep AAGS; dep MHS/FCA.
K044 KITZMILLER Bible; pd 1840; eb 1806; em 1828; on HARPER, HAYDEN; res VA;
     PA; MI; dep MHS/FCA.
K045 KNIGHT Bible; eb 1747; em 1838; on WYNKOOP, MILNER, KRENSON, CONARD,
     BANKEN, EATON; res Bucks Co., PA; dep BCGS (from Yingling).
K046 KNIGHT Bible; rb 1786; on BARNES, WHITSON, BEARD; res Harf. Co., MD;
     dep HCGS.
K047 KNIGHT Bible; pd 1812; eb 1786; em 1804; on BARNES, WHETSON, TAYLOR,
     PRICE, HUNTER; res Harf. Co., MD; dep MHS/FCA.
K048 KNIGHT Bible; pd 1841; eb 1809; em 1845; on THECKELL, BENTON; dep MHS/FCA.
K049 KNIGHT Bible; rb 1816, on SHECKELL, BENTON, HEIDLER; res Harf. Co., MD;
     dep HCGS.
K050 KNIPPLE Bible; eb 1840; em 1860; on BENTON, WENTZ, WALTER; res PA;
     dep MHS/FCA.
K051 KNOCK Bible; eb 1827; em 1857; on HINEBAUGH, LEWIS, NEAL, GRUBB; res MD;
     VA; dep MHS/FCA.
K052 KNOPP Bible; rb 1860, on FREY, MAR, GARDNER, LEE, JONES, MOORE;
     res Harf. Co., MD; dep HCGS.
K053 KNOPP Bible; rb 1878; on HORN, BALDWIN, SMITH, ILEY, WALTERMEYER, COX,
     AXE, MARTIN, BARE; res Harf. Co., MD; dep HCGS.
K054 KNOTT Bible; eb 1787; em 1828; on HARDING, BOND, MERCER; dep MHS/FCA.
K055 KNOWLES Bible; res Fred. Co., MD; OH; dep NGS Bible Collection.
K056 KNOX Bible; pd 1854; eb 1794; em 1821; on WITHEROW, MARSHALL, CULBERTSON,
     McSHERRY, RINEHART, MASON, RANKIN, BOYD; res Hagerstown, MD;
     pub DAR (MdGRC 33:75); pub MDG 7-2:30.
K057 KOEHM-KAHM Bible; pd 1819; on KAHM; dep AAGS; dep MHS/FCA.

52

BIBLES

K058 KRUSEN Bible; eb 1826; em 1850; on COLLINGSGROVE, WARE, YETTER, HUNT,
      SOUDERS, BURTON, HUGHES, HEADLEY, HOLLOWAY, MYERS, RALEY;
      dep MHS/FCA.
K059 KREBS Bible; pd 1847; eb 1808; em 1831; on WARNER; res Balto., MD;
      dep MHS/FCA.
K060 Solomon KRISE Bible; eb 1804; em 1835; on STEVENSON, BIGGS, CROUSE,
      MORRISON, BUCKEY, CLOSE; res MD; OR; pub DAR (MdGRC 7:62).
K061 KRISE Bible; pd 187(?); eb 1850; em 1878; on STOVER, SAYLOR, HAMMAKER;
      res Fred. Co., MD; York Co., PA; dep FCHS (Original Bible).
K062 KUHN-SLUSER Bible; pd 1847; eb 1818; on SLUSER, SHOEMAKER;
      dep BCGS (from DAR).
K063 KUHN Bible; pd 1871; eb 1841; on INGRAM, SMITH, BREWER; dep BCGS (no.524).
K064 KYLE-SPENCE Bible; pd 1868; eb 1820; em 1840; on SPENCE, ADAMS, LEFEVRE,
      LOVE, WOOD, BARNARD, on McCULLOUGH; res Cecil Co. & Balto., MD; NJ;
      DE; York and Chester Cos., Phila., PA; pub DelBR 12:13.

L001 Daniel LAKIN Bible; eb 1757; em 1787; on SHECKELL, FLENNIKEN, TROWBRIDGE,
      SHRUM; res Fred. Co., MD; pub OSR p.427.
L002 Basil LAMAR Bible; eb 1795; res MD; VA; GA; pub Austin,55.
L003 Thomas LAMAR Bible; eb 1740; em 1794; on POTTINGER, URQUART, BUGG,
      APPLING, KELLY, HARLOW; res MD; GA; France; pub Austin,55.
L004 LAMAR Bible; ins 1861; pd 1816; dep FCHS (Original Bible).
L005 Francis LAMB Bible; pd 1823; eb 1772; em 1818; on PERACE, BECK, FRAY,
      PLUMER, DOWNIE, GROVES; res Kent Co., MD; pub KBR p.13.
L006 LAMBDIN Bible; eb 1726; res Talb. Co., MD; pub MDG 9-1:15.
L007 Daniel LAMBDIN Bible; pd 1765; eb 1750; em 1779; res Talb. Co., MD;
      pub MDG 24-1:25.
L008 LAMBDIN-DORSEY Bible; eb 1854; em 1888; on DEAL, PAULUS, SHUGARS, DORSEY;
      dep MHS/FCA.
L009 LAMDIN Bible; eb 1821; em 1845; on FOX, DUNGAN, DANBY, DAVEY, GRESSILT,
      HUGG, LITTON, GREEN, STROBEL, KNAPP; res Balto., MD; dep MHS/FCA.
L010 LANDERS Bible; eb 1796; em 1824; on CARMACK, RINEDOLLAR; res Fred. Co.,
      MD; Scotland; pub DAR (MdGRC 7:60).
L011 Tidence LANE Pension Application; eb 1786; res Balto. Co., MD; TN;
      pub Austin,419.
L012 LANE Bible; pd 1846; eb 1770; em 1835; on BLAND, WELSH, MUNSON,
      McDONALD, EVANS, FLEMING; pub MGB 17:17.
L013 LANE Bible; eb 1791; on CLARK, PARROTT; dep MHS/FCA (typed copy).
L014 LANE Bible; pd 1843; eb 1791; em 1814; on BUTLER, McDONALD, MUNSON,
      HUMPHREY, DORSEY; pub MGB 17:1.
L015 LANG Bible; eb 1865; em 1890; on WEISBECKER, HUBER, LEITHAUSER; res
      Balto, MD.; dep MHS/FCA; dep BCHS (typed copy).
L016 LANGFORD Bible; eb 1828; em 1854; on LANKFORD; res Dor. Co., MD;
      pub DCGM 1-5:3.
L017 Littleton E. LANKFORD Bible; rs 1794-1887 on BAYLEY, BOUNDS, BROWN,
      MEYRICK, POWELL, SMULLING, TOWNSAND, WILLIS; res MD;
      dep VSL (#1869, acc. 29745).
L018 LANKFORD Bible; eb 1831; em 1851; on MARSHALL, GUNBY, BARNES, FITZSIMMON,
      RIGGIN, PRINCKARD, PORTER, HALL, MILES; dep MHS/FCA.
L019 LANKFORD Bible; rs 1870-1919; on WHEATLEY; res MD;
      dep VSL (#1870, acc. 29741).
L020 LANTZ Bible; pd 1845; eb 1817; em 1846; on OTTO, FORREST, SLINGLUFF,
      OTTO, FORREST, SLINGLUFF, MYERS, MARTIN, PAIN, SAYLOR, MEDFORD;
      dep CCGS (#18).
L021 LARZELERE-SCARBOROUGH Bible; eb 1767; em 1788; on LYNCH, HYRONS, ANTRAM,
      (Continued on next page)

53

L021 LARZELERE-SCARBOROUGH Bible, contd.; on SIMPERS, BOYD, STEEL, SPENCE, NOWLAND, DAVIDSON, SCOTT, SCARBOROUGH; dep MHS/FCA.

L022 LASSITER Bible; eb 1828; res VA; NC; dep MHS/FCA.

L023 LATE-SCHAEFFER Bible; eb 1838; on CHABROUGH, OTIS, SCHAEFFER; dep MHS/FCA.

L024 LATROBE Bible; pd 1838; eb 1833; em 1833; on HEGLEHURST, GAMBLE, WESTON, ONDERDINK, ROBINSON, YEATES; res Balto., MD; NJ; FL; pub DAR (MdGRC 33:102).

L025 LAVEILLE Bible; eb 1827; em 1820; on LOMAX, HARRIS, SEDWICK, FRAIZER, McKENZIE; dep MHS/FCA.

L026 LAVEILLE Bible; rs 1820-1873; res Calv. Co., MD; dep MSA (G-651).

L027 LAW-DAVIES Bible; eb 1768; em 1795; on McLAUGHLIN, CRAWFORD, HOWARD, DOUGLAS, DAVIES; res Balto., MD; TN; England; dep MHS/FCA.

L028 LAWRENCE Bible; pd 1802; eb 1743; em 1766; on WEST, SHRINER; res AA and PG Cos., MD; dep MHS/FCA.

L029 LAWRENCE Bible; eb 1779; on DANIELL, HALL, COUTURIER, MACKALL, BRAILSFORD, GANTT, HUGVELET, GUERARD, WINANT, COLSON, GAGE, LYNCH, MANN; res NY; GA; SC; dep MHS/FCA; pub SCHM 1952.

L030 LAWRENCE Bible; pd 1855; eb 1817; em 1856; on CARTER; dep MHS/FCA.

L031 LAWS Bible; pd 1828; eb 1793; em 1823; on DUNCAN; res Wico. Co., MD;

L032 LAWSON Bible; pd 1876; eb 1891; em 1890; on BAUBLITZ, KERSHNER, HOWARD; res Balto., MD; dep CCGS (no.27).

L033 LEAVERTON Bible; pd 1839; eb 1809; em 1808; on BLACK, BLAKE, BLADES, BRUFF, CORDRAY, VICTOR, QUIGG, IRELAND; res Kent Co., MD; pub DAR (MdGRC 7:311); pub KBGRI p.50.

L034 LEAVERTON Bible; rs 1809-1900; res Kent and QA Cos., MD; dep MSA (G-560:87 with D-150).

L035 LEAVERTON Bible; eb 1809; em 1839; on DEROCHBRUNE, PRATT; res Kent and QA Cos., MD; dep MHS/FCA.

L036 LEEKE Bible; rs 1682-1902; res Mont. Co., MD; dep MSA (G-900:5).

L037 Benedict LEE Bible; eb 1784; em 1854; on FRENCH, BAUER; dep BCGS (typed copy).

L038 LEE Bible; pd 1868; eb 1833; em 1861; on JONES, WARD; dep BCGS.

L039 LEECH Bible; eb 1806; em 1805; on THOMAS, ROSS, STEVENS, ELLIOTT, MORRISON; res Cecil Co. and Balto, MD; pub PGCGS 18-3:50.

L040 LEESE Bible; pd 1875; eb 1763; em 1864; on EARHART, KING, KOONTZ, WAREHIME, RAVER, DALEY, BUSH, ERB, HUMBERT, HANCOCK; dep BCGS (in Yingling).

L041 LEGGETT Bible; eb 1833; em 1890; on BLOUNT, SOMERS, ROBERTSON; res Balto., MD; dep MHS/FCA.

L042 LEIFERT Bible; eb 1821; em 1876; res Germany; dep BCGS (typed copy).

L043 LEIGH Bible; eb 1685; em 1718; on GUYTHER, HOWELL, CHILTON, THOMAS, LEEDS, GARDINER, SPALDING; res St.M. & Talb. Cos., MD; England; dep MHS/FCA.

L044 LEITHISER Bible; eb 1819; em 1874; on BAYARD, JARRELL; dep BCGS.

L045 LEPPO Bible; pd 1858; eb 1872; em 1876; on BEACHTEL; res PA; dep CCGS (#50).

L046 LEPPO Bible; pd 1890; eb 1872; em 1897; on UTZ; res York Co., PA; dep CCGS (#48).

L047 LESTER Bible; eb 1882; em 1881; on KOONTZ, CRUMPECKER; dep BCGS.

L048 LEVERING Bible; rs 1686-1896; res PA; dep MSA (G-205:18 with D-150).

L049 LEVERING Bible; eb 1686; res PA; Germany; dep MHS/FCA.

L050 LEVIS Bible; rs 1765-1882; dep MSA (G-402).

L051 LEVY Family Records; ins 1779; eb 1719; pub MG 2:283.

L052 Levin LEWIS Bible; pd 1832; eb 1583; on MARSHALL, BRANNOCH; res Dor. Co., MD; pub DOBR,31.

L053 LEWIS Bible; eb 1757; em 1779; on DAINGERFIELD; res VA;
     pub DAR (MdGRC 11:108).
L054 LILLARD Bible; eb 1819; em 1842; res KY; dep MHS.
L055 LILLY Bible; rb 1834; res Harf. Co., MD; dep HCGS.
L056 LINDSAY Bible; eb 1799; em 1798; on BEAVANS, SLOCUM, COLLINS, TOWNSEND,
     BISHOP, MEEKINS; res Stockton, MD;
     dep MHS/FCA (Turner General Collection, 58).
L057 LINKENHOGER Bible; pd 1816; eb 1733; em 1848; on LAYNE, BREWBAKER,
     KIZER, MOORE, LINKENHOKER; res Botetourt Co., VA;
     dep BCGS (from Yingling).
L058 LINN Bible; rs 1800-1941; res Balto., MD; PA;
     dep MSA (G-189:7 with D-150).
L059 LINN Bible; pd 1853; eb 1800; em 1918; on LINNA, BYRENS, SMICK,
     SMICKLEY, McILVANE, REIGLE, SMICKLE, EUSTON; res Adams Co., PA;
     Balto., MD; VA; FL; dep MHS/FCA.
L060 LINNANZNER Bible; pd 1832; eb 1828; dep MHS/FCA (Binnanzer)(in German).
L061 LINVILLE Bible; eb 1800; em 1812; on WOLFE, LONG, McALLISTER;
     pub DAR (MdGRC 7:54).
L062 LIPPINCOTT-CASSARD Bible; eb 1782; em 1840; on CASSARD, MILLER, OWENS,
     RESOR, CREIGHTON, McCURLEY, TROUT, EMERSON, WOOD, WHILLDIN,
     BREITENBACH, NICHOLS, REESE; res MD; PA; VA; OH; dep MHS/FCA.
L063 LITTLE Bible; pd 1826; eb 1811; em 1810; on TANEYHILL, BRAGG, YOUNG;
     dep MHS/FCA.
L064 LITTLE Bible; rs 1821-1942; res Cecil Co., MD; dep MSA (G-214:29).
L065 LITTLE Bible; eb 1832; em 1870; on JACKSON, FOUNDDS, DAWSON, OWENS,
     CRAIG, WALKER; res Cecil Co., MD;
     pub DA (MdGRC 35:53); dep MHS/FCA (Beaven).
L066 LLOYD Bible; rs 1703-1947; dep MSA (G-252:22).
L067 LLOYD-BUCHANAN Bible; eb 1775; em 1797; on BUCHANAN, WINDER, MURRAY,
     LOWNDES, McNAIR, GOLDSBOROUGH; dep MHS/FCA.
L068 LLOYD Bible; eb 1795; em 1812; on ERDMAN; res Balto. City and Co., MD;
     Phila., PA; pub BMGS 23-1:20.
L069 LLOYD Bible; eb 1846; em 1871; on ERDMAN; res Balto. Co., MD;
     pub BMGS 19-1:20; dep MHS/FCA; dep BCHS.
L070 LLOYD Bible; eb 1847; em 1872; on BLOODSWORTH, WHEATLEY; res Sussex Co.,
     DE; pub MDG 1-1:19.
L071 LOBACH Bible; ins 1849; eb 1836; em 1835; on TAYLOR, HUGHES, SNYDER,
     PILKEY, KUHNS, LOUGH; dep BCGS.
L072 LOCKERMAN Bible; pd 1809; eb 1771; em 1804; pub MG 2:184.
L073 LOKER Bible; pd 1832; eb 1836; em 1835; on GARDINER, JONES, KILBOURNE,
     HOSTLER; res St.M. Co., MD; dep MHS/FCA.
L074 LOMAX Bible; rs 1716-1828; dep MSA (G-556).
L075 LONG Bible; pd 1816; eb 1790; on ANDERSON; pub DAR (MdGRC 33:97).
L076 LONG-CAULK Bible; rs 1780-1809; on LAWS, ROBERTS, CAULK; res DE; MD;
     dep VSL (#1988, acc. 28933).
L077 Ellis B. LONG Bible; rs 1807-1928; on BALTZELL, CHRISMAN, JACKSON,
     PENDLETON, WARD, WILLIAMS; res Balto., MD; VA;
     dep VSL (#1985, acc. 22500).
L078 LONG Bible; pd 1896; eb 1871; em 1896; on MURDOCK, MYERS, NICODEMUS;
     res Fred. & Wash. Cos., MD; OH; pub DAR (MdGRC 33:88).
L079 John LOOKABAUGH Bible; eb 1790; em 1925; on FERGUSON, CARSON;
     pub DAR (MdGRC 33:113).
L080 LOOMIS Bible; rs 1892-1948; dep MSA (D-272:6).
L081 LOUDERMAN Bible; pd 1802; eb 1791; em 1791; on FICKEY, BARNS, SHAFFER,
     KING, REITER, BELL, MAJOR, DICKSON; res Fred. & Balto., MD;
     pub BMGS 21-3:256.

L082 LOWRY Bible; rs 1790-1931; res Balto. Co., MD;
      dep MSA (G-236:59 with D-150).
L083 LUCKETT Bible; eb 1756; res MD; KY; pub Ardery 2:203.
L084 Rev. George LUCKEY Bible; pd 1792; eb 1789; em 1825; on DREGHORN, LYLTE;
      res Harf. Co., MD; pub DAR (MdGRC 10:274).
L085 LUGENBEEL Bible; rs 1802-1933; on BUCKINGHAM, LINDSAY, PEARCE, SHRINER;
      res Carr. Co., MD; dep NGS (Bible Records Collection).
L086 LUGENBEEL Bible; pd 1871; eb 1802; on SHRINER, REESE; res Carr. Co., MD;
      pub MDG 25:12.
L087 LUKENS Bible; rb 1796; on COOPER; res York Co., PA; dep BOGS.
L088 LYLES Bible; rs 1788-1921; dep MSA (G-570:4).
L089 LYNCH-ROBERTS Bible; eb 1789; on ROBERTS; res Lynchburg, VA;
      pub DAR (MdGRC 1:70).
L090 LYON Bible; ins 1854; pd 1800; on BOWLES, HOWERTON, HALEY; res VA; NC;
      dep BOGS.
L091 LYTLE Bible; eb 1864; dep BOGS.
L092 LYTTLE Bible; eb 1876; em 1875; on LITTLE, PARR, SAYLES, EMORY,
      GWALTNEY, LUNETTE, on NICHOLSON, WILLIS, MANN, KNIGHTLY;
      pub BMGS 22-3:229; dep BOGS.

M001 MACHEM Henry Bible; eb 1745; em 1772; on BELLINGER; pub MBR 2:3.
M002 MACKALL Bible; eb 1790; em 1813; on HOLLINGSWORTH, WHANN; res Cecil Co.,
      MD; VA; MA; dep MHS.
M003 MACKEY Bible; eb 1808; on EVANS, MILLER; pub CMF 3:22.
M004 MACKEY Bible; eb 1812; em 1798; on FRASER, JENNINGS, RICHARDS;
      pub CMF 3:22.
M005 MACOMBER Bible; rb 1820; on KALKMAN, ORR, SCARBOROUGH; res MD; PA;
      dep HOGS.
M006 MADDOX Bible; rs 1804-1927; dep MSA (G-308).
M007 MAGRUDER Bible; rs 1703-1947; dep MSA (G-252:22).
M008 Col. Zadock MAGRUDER Bible; eb 1755; em 1791; on POTTENGER;
      pub DAR Mag. Oct 1980 p.1033.
M009 MAGRUDER Bible; rs 1758-1921; res PG Co., MD;
      dep MSA (G-560:89 with D-150).
M010 Aquilla MAGRUDER Bible; eb 1773; em 1799; on AFFLICK, CARDWELL;
      pub DAR Mag. Oct.1980.
M011 MAGRUDER Bible; eb 1805; em 1831; on RIGGS, WATERS, GRIFFITH;
      pub DAR (MdGRC 33:53).
M012 MAGRUDER Bible; rs 1807-1902; dep MSA (G-560:90 with D-150).
M013 MAGRUDER-SINT Bible; pd 1831; eb 1807; em 1832; on SINT; res St.M. Co.,
      MD; pub NGSQ 66-3:175.
M014 Thomas MAGRUDER Bible; eb 1871; em 1893; on HESSER, HAWKINS, BRAITHWAITE,
      BEALL, SMITH, POTTENGER, WILSON, KEARNEY, CORRELL; res WV; DC;
      pub DAR Mag Oct.1980 p.1033.
M015 MALEY Bible; pd 1848; eb 1843; em 1843; on ROBERTS, DAWSON, STREET,
      MESSICK, EFFORD; res Wico. Co., MD; pub DAR (MdGRC 11:156).
M016 MALLALIEU Bible; rs 1843-1918; dep MSA (G-675:2).
M017 MALLALIEU Bible; rs 1843-1948; res Kent Co., MD; dep MSA (G-716).
M018 MALOTT Family Record; eb 1759; pub MGB 4:21.
M019 MANGER Bible; rs 1819-1926; res St.M. Co., MD;
      dep MSA (G-236:64 in D-150).
M020 MANN Bible; eb 1909; em 1908; on THOMPSON; pub BMGS 22-3:230.
M021 MANSHIP Bible; eb 1778; em 1810; on HARRIS, MILLINGTON;
      dep MHS/FCA (Manship Family).
M022 MARGURGER Bible; pd 1870; eb 1877; em 1824; on ROLKEY, DENNIS, FORD,
      MITCHELL, FARLEY, RESAU; res Balto., MD; dep AAGS; dep MHS/FCA.

BIBLES

M023 MARBURY Bible; rs 1738-1876; res PG Co., MD;
        dep MSA (G-560:92 with D-150).
M024 MARBURY Bible; rs 1791-1916; res PG Co., MD;
        dep MSA (G-560:91 with D-150).
M025 MARINE Bible; pd 1719; eb 1700; em 1769; on de MARIN, WART, PHILLIPS;
        res Worc. Co., MD; pub DAR (MdGRC 3:40).
M026 MARPLE Bible; eb 1796; em 1841; on JENKINS, BOWERS;
        pub DAR (MdGRC 8:157).
M027 Major B. MARSHALL Bible; eb 1857; em 1856; on COVINGTON; res Dor. Co.,
        MD; pub DOBR,34.
M028 Marion H. MARSHALL Bible; ins 1890; eb 1858; em 1856; on HANDLEY,
        PETERS, WEBB, WARRINGTON, SMOOT, GRAY, SHARP, EHLERS, BREWSTER,
        JOURDAN; res Dor., Co., MD; pub DOBR,34.
M029 MARSHALL Bible; pd 1702; eb 1694; em 1726; res Marshall Hall, Chas. Co.,
        MD; pub NGSQ 15-3:36.
M030 MARSHALL-HONEYWELL Bible; eb 1792; em 1813; on ALLEN, GRANT, FRAILEY,
        ALFORD, SMITH, PASSANO, HONEYWELL; res Balto., MD; NY;
        pub DAR (MdGRC 10:172).
M031 Robert MARTIN Bible; pd 1834; eb 1775; em 1775; res Talb. Co., MD;
        pub MDG 21-4:112.
M032 MARTIN Bible; pd 1850; eb 1810; res AA Co., MD; IN; IL; pub MGB 14:4.
M033 MARTIN Bible; eb 1876; em 1902; on MAGRUDER, STEWART, BRYAN;
        pub DAR (MdGRC 33:58).
M034 MARTIN Bible; rs 1786-1862; pd 1814; on BANKS, VADEN, BOUGHAN, JOHNSON,
        WILLIAMS, WREN; res Balto., MD; Chesterfield, VA;
        dep VSL (#2059, acc. 28186).
M035 MARTIN-MATTHEWS Bible; eb 1770; em 1769; on MATTHEWS; res Chas. & Talb.
        Cos., MD; pub MDG 21-4:113.
M036 MARVEL Bible; eb 1735; em 1784; on RODNEY, JONES, HARRIS, TRUITT,
        JEFFERSON, MORRIS, LINDELL, COLLINS, DERECKSON, TINDLE, BOYD,
        ENNIS; res DE; pub MDG 3-4:81 and 4-1:16.
M037 MASON Bible; eb 1855; em 1854; on LYNCH; pub DAR (MdGRC 12:112).
M038 MASON Bible; eb 1919; em 1918; on SPATH, BROWN, SCHLERF, STONESIFER,
        HYMILLER, BIDDINGER; res Carr. Co. & Balto., MD;
        dep BCGS (from Yingling).
M039 MASSEY Bible; rs 1790-1922; on CREACY, EDGE, HOLLADAY, KABLE, LLEWELLYN,
        NOEL, SMITH, THOMAS; res Mont. Co., MD; VA;
        dep VSL (#2068, acc. 30414).
M040 MATHAWSON Bible; eb 1848; on FURMAN, ROBINSON, HOLLINGSWORTH;
        res Wash., D.C.; Asheville. NC; dep MHS.
M041 MATHIAS Bible; pd 1844; eb 1821; em 1851; on LEE; res Carr. Co., MD;
        Danville, VA; pub DAR (MdGRC 35:30).
M042 John MATTHEWS Bible; eb 1742; em 1769; on THOMAS; pub MBR 2:4.
M043 MATTHEWS Bible; eb 1839; em 1838; on THOMPSON, SMITH, LANE; res
        Gettysburg, PA; pub DAR (MdGRC 13:182).
M044 MATTHEWS Bible; eb 1865; em 1864; on CULVAN, MILLER, STERN, TOWNSEND,
        GARRETTSON; res Carr. Co. and Pocomoke City, MD;
        pub DAR (MdGRC 13:184).
M045 MATTHEWS Bible; eb 1865; em 1831; on NEALE, BRENT, JONES, HOOPER, LYON,
        MOHLERS; dep MHS.
M046 MAULDIN Bible; rs 1684-1827; res Cecil Co., MD;
        dep MSA (G-223:46 with D-150).
M047 MAULDIN Bible; eb 1791; em 1813; on THOMAS, HYLAND; res Cecil Co., MD;
        dep MHA/FCA.
M048 MAXWELL Bible; eb 1746; em 1866; pub MBR 2:2.

M049 MAYER Bible; eb 1851; on HUBNER; res Germany; dep MHS/FCA
(photocopy of original German).
M049A MAYES Bible; rs 1812-1941; pd 1873; res TX; dep HOGS.
M049B MAYES Bible; rs 1812-1953; pd 1891; res TX; dep HOGS.
M050 MAYES Bible; pd 1891; eb 1812; on BARMORE, LAUDERBACK, PIERCE, PENN,
MOWELS, FALLEY; pub HCMR 5:83.
M051 D.H. MAYES Bible; pd 1873; eb 1826; em 1871; on MOORE, BARMORE, GOULD,
MOWELS, PENN; pub HCMR 5:92.
M052 MAYNARD Bible; pd 1812; eb 1809; em 1808; on CALLAHAN, NETH, SELLMAN,
JOHNSON, ROACH, INGLEHART; res AA Co., MD; pub DAR (MdGRC 35:5).
M053 Samuel MAYS Bible; eb 1765; em 1793; on GRIGSBY, LIPSCOMB, BUTLER, SMITH,
EARLE, SUMPTER, GLACOCK, JOHNSON, WILLIAMS, HILL, THOMAS, BREVARD,
LINTON; res Halifax Co., VA; SC; pub MBR 2:16.
M054 MAYS Bible; pd 1871; eb 1869; em 1868; on TURNBAUGH, JONES, BURNS,
MILLER, FOSTER, BULL, THOMPSON, RHULE; res Balto., Co., MD;
dep BCGS.
M055 McCARTHY Bible; pd 1882; eb 1883; em 1882; on WHIBELBY, O'BREIN, EGAN,
WINDER, NOEL, WELLS; dep MHS/FCA.
M056 McCAULEY Bible; eb 1835; on BROOKS, WILKINS; pub MGB 9-4:3.
M057 McCAULEY Bible; pd 1837; eb 1823; em 1847; res Cecil Co., MD;
pub NGSQ 42-1:51.
M058 McCLATCHY Bible; eb 1831; em 1852; on SEWELL; res Alexandria, VA;
pub DAR (MdGRC 7:56).
M059 McCLELLAN Bible; eb 1762; dep BCGS (typed copy).
M060 McCLELLAN Bible; eb 1777; em 1801; on EWING, GILLESPIE, RAWLINGS, McVEY;
res Cecil Co., MD; pub DAR Mag Jan.1981 pg.111.
M061 McCLELLAN Bible; pd 1852; eb 1824; em 1850; on de ROULHAC, LEAKE,
PADGETT, GAMBELL, MOSS, RONEY, ROLLINS, ATTEWAY, COKER,
TILLINGHAST, MALONE, DICKINSON, YONGE, DAZEY, DIXON, MILTON;
res VA; dep AAGS; dep MHS/FCA.
M062 McCLINTIC Bible; pd 1849; eb 1818; em 1847; on MANN, ARLUCEL, HAMILTON,
BONNER, HANDLEY, LIGON, GRIFFITH, ROWAN, CONGER; dep BCGS (#495).
M063 McCOLLISTER Bible; eb 1775; em 1794; on HARPER, MINEAR, STINSON,
KIRKPATRICK, BILLINGS, HAYNES, SANDFORD, CHESTNUT, HONNOLD, WRIGHT,
KINDLER; res Dor. Co., MD; OH; pub MDG 5-3:58.
M064 John McCOLLUM Bible; pd 1844; em 1809; dep BCGS (from Yingling).
M065 McCOMAS-GILBERT Bible; eb 1787; em 1834; on GILBERT, MICHAEL, CARSINS,
GOUGH, MITCHELL; res Harf. Co., MD; pub MMAF p.4.
M066 Isaac Taylor McCOMAS Bible; pd 1868; eb 1798; em 1824; on SLICER, HAYNES,
THOMPSON; res Harf. & Carr. Cos., MD; CA; dep BCGS (from DAR).
M067 McCOMAS Bible; pd 1828; eb 1848; em 1846; on TAYLOR, ALLEN, HUDSON,
CUNNINGHAM, WISE; dep BCGS (from DAR).
M068 McCONKEY Bible; pd 1840; eb 1843; em 1866; on COCKEY; res Balto., Co.,
MD; dep MHS/FCA.
M069 McCONNER Bible; rs 1756-1950; res QA Co., MD;
dep MSA (G-560:88 with D-150).
M070 John McCORKILL Bible; eb 1740; em 1767; on RUTH, SCOTT, GOODEN, WYATT,
YOUNG, PATTON, HARRISON, OSBORN, NESSLE, McHARRY, BARKER; res KY;
pub MBR 2:12.
M071 McCORMICK Bible; rb 1799; res Harf. Co., MD; dep HOGS.
M072 McCORMICK Bible; rb 1882; res Harf. Co., MD; dep HOGS.
M073 McCOURTNEY Bible; rb 1865; res Harf. Co., MD; dep HOGS.
M074 McCOY Bible; pd 1873; eb 1873; em 1868; on ARDENGER; res Williamsport, MD;
pub DAR (MdGRC 33:121).
M075 McDERMOTT Bible; rb 1804; res Harf. Co., MD; dep HOGS.
M076 McDOON Bible; rb 1805; on PAIRA; dep HOGS.

BIBLES

M077 McDOWELL-McCOMAS Bible; rb 1836; pd 1904; on BRICKER, HARRISON, McCOMAS;
      res MD; KY; MI; TN; dep VSL (#2117, acc. 28126).
M078 McFADDEN Bible; rb 1806; on STILLINGS, FISHER; dep HCGS.
M079 McGAW-HUTCHINS Bible; pd 1829; eb 1770; em 1792; on SLADE, HOWARD,
      HUTCHINS, PEARCE, RICHARDSON; dep BCHS (photocopy).
M080 McGEE Bible; pd 1830; eb 1786; em 1813; on DORSEY, BAINTER, CULLARS,
      McCOY, SQUIRES, BUTLER, GORSUCH, POSEY; res MD; OH; pub MGB 16:21.
M081 McGRAW Bible; eb 1782; em 1807; on HANBY, WANKOP, MENAFEE, DURRUM, BOWER,
      HALL, PILCHER, ANNEN, CARR, HARRIS, JACKSON; pub MBR 2:8.
M082 McGREGOR Bible; pd 1816; eb 1796; em 1820; on HUDSON; res Wico. Co., MD;
      pub DAR (MdGRC 11:141).
M083 McINTIRE Bible; eb 1856; em 1880; on WHITENECK; dep MHS/FCA.
M084 McKEE-BLACK Bible; eb 1836; em 1835; on ERWIN, JESTER, TORRENCE, GRABLE,
      McDOWELL, FUNK, REMSEYER, GADDIS; dep BCGS (from Yingling).
M085 McKEEN Bible; eb 1796; dep BCHS (typed copy).
M086 McKENNEY Bible; rs 1800-1866; dep MSA (G-503:1).
M087 McKENNEY Bible; rs 1829-1955; dep MSA (G-503:2).
M088 McKENNEY-BUSHEY Bible; pd 1882; eb 1812; em 1836; on KEPNER, HESS, NAIL,
      BERGSGESSER, ENGLAR, MARTIN, BUSHEY, CARPENTER, JOHNSON; res Carr.
      Co., MD; Juniata Co., PA; VA; dep BCGS (from Yingling).
M089 McKITRICK Bible; pd 1881; eb 1867; em 1890; on HOFFMAN, MAXWELL, SNYDER,
      COLE; res Balto., MD; dep CCGS (#13).
M090 McLEAN Bible; eb 1842; em 1872; on COVINGTON, WILSON, GANT, RANKEN,
      PADGETT, HOWLAND, NEUSEL, FISTER; res Winchester, VA; TN; IN; CA;
      dep MHS/FCA.
M091 McMACKEN Bible; pd 1783; eb 1789; em 1817; on RILENGER, REED, STALLING;
      dep BCHS (typed copy).
M092 McMASTER Bible; pd 1792; eb 1782; em 1781; on JOHNSON, FLEMING, MERRILL,
      TOWNSEND, COTTINGHAM, GILLETT, STEVENSON, STAGG, COARD, SLASS;
      res Som. Co., MD; dep WCFL.
M093 McMICHAEL Bible; pd 1850; eb 1830; em 1853; on GAMBRIEL; res Dor. Co.,
      MD; pub DOBR,35.
M094 McNEW Bible; rs 1875-1931; dep MSA (G-532).
M095 William McPHERSON Bible; pd 1816; rs 1817-1889; on DARRS, FITZHUGH,
      HAMMOND, KENNEDY, NETH; res Fred. MD; dep VSL (#2145, acc. 30391).
M096 MARSH Bible; em 1872; res NY; Wash., DC; dep BCHS (photocopy).
M097 MATTHEWS Bible; pd 1826; eb 1771; on TRIMBLE, GILL, BIRDSALL;
      dep BCHS (typed copy).
M098 Edward MEALEY Bible; pd 1824; eb 1789; em 1813; on WINDSOR, PARKS,
      ALLERDICE; pub DAR (MdGRC 33:100).
M099 MEEK Bible; pd 1854; eb 1813; on ORWIG, CAMPBELL; dep AAGS.
M100 Alfred MEEKINS Bible; eb 1908; em 1903; on HOOPER, PARKS; res Dor. Co.,
      MD; pub DOBR,35.
M101 Joseph U. MEEKINS Bible; eb 1816; em 1840; on TRAVERS, PARKER, CREIGHTON;
      res Dor. Co., MD; pub DOBR,36.
M102 Rebecca Simmons MEEKINS Bible; eb 1831; em 1830; on HEWITT, RUARK,
      TRAVERS, SIMMONDS; res Dor. Co., MD; pub DOBR,36.
M103 George MEHN Bible; pd 1772; eb 1746; em 1770; on DERR, YOUTZEY, BRUCHEY,
      WERL; res Fred. Co., MD; dep MHS/FCA.
M104 Solomon MELVIN Bible; eb 1823; em 1848; pub GPF/PGM 3:722.
M105 MERCER Bible; pd 1883; eb 1837; em 1866; on CLELAND, GOSSETT, DENNIS,
      FARLEY, REYNOLDS, SANDERS, REICHERT; res Rulville, MO;
      dep AAGS; dep MHS/FCA.
M106 MEREDITH Bible; eb 1825; on ROWINS; res Dor. Co., MD; pub DOBR,37.
M107 MERRIKEN Bible; eb 1811; em 1832; res Balto., MD; dep BCGS (photocopy).

59

M108 MERRITT Bible; eb 1884; em 1911; on SHANNON, SEIDEL; res Grange, MD;
dep BCHS (typed copy).
M109 MERRITT Bible; eb 1834; em 1856; on PLUMMER, JACOB, VINCENT, BRAY;
dep BCHS (typed copy).
M110 John MESSLER Bible; eb 1759; em 1780; on JONES, DICKENSHUT, WILSON;
dep BCHS (typed copy).
M111 Jacob MICHAEL Bible; eb 1796; em 1795; on EVERIST, CRANE, OSBORN, HANSON,
MURPHY; dep BOGS.
M112 Jacob MICHAEL Bible; pd 1811; eb 1796; em 1795; on EVERIST, CRANE,
OSBORN; dep BOGS.
M113 MICHAEL Bible; eb 1813; em 1853; on IRVIN, COURTNEY, RICHARDSON, WRIGHT,
BAILEY, GILBERT, CRONEN, KELLY; dep BOGS.
M114 MICHAEL Bible; em 1816; res Balto., MD; dep BOGS (transcription).
M115 MICHAEL Bible; eb 1856; em 1825; on MITCHELL, KERWAN; res Harf. Co., MD;
pub MMAF p.7.
M116 Henry Clay MICHAEL Bible; eb 1855; em 1853; on IRVIN, OSBORN, COURTNEY,
RICHARDSON, WRIGHT, BARLEY; res Perryman, MD; PA; dep BOGS.
M117 MICHAEL Record Book; pub MMAF p.27.
M118 MIDDLETON-LAUDERBACH Bible; pd 1855; rs 1806-1943; on LAUDERBACH;
pub HCMR 5:87; dep HOGS.
M119 MILBURN Bible; pd 1828; eb 1839; em 1832; on ROBERTSON; res St.M. Co.,
MD; dep SMGS.
M120 MILES Bible; rs 1815-1847; on FOSTER; res Balto., MD; PA;
dep NGS (Bible Records Collection).
M121 MILLER-JEAN Bible; eb 1760; em 1801; on BAKER, MALONEY, STENCHCOMB, JEAN;
res Balto. Co., MD; pub DAR (MdGRC 7:42).
M122 MILLER Bible; rs 1779-1899; on ALBAUGH, SPURRIER; res Fred. & Carr. Cos.,
MD; dep MSA (G-863:1).
M123 MILLER Bible; pd 1862; eb 1813; em 1864; on LIN; pub MGB 18:4.
M124 Harman MILLER Bible; eb 1813; on SARGENS; res AR; dep BCHS (typed copy).
M125 MILLER Bible; em 1868; on SHUMWAY, PARSONS, CAMPBELL; res Balto., MD; CT;
dep MHS/FCA.
M126 Ida T.N.MILLIGAN Bible; eb 1863; em 1891; on NELSON; res Som. Co., MD;
dep WCFL.
M127 MILLS Bible; pd 1887; eb 1808; em 1832; on COLLINS, PERDUE, COVINGTON,
MADDUX, FREENY; res Wico. Co., MD; pub DAR (MdGRC 11:157).
M128 MILLS Bible; eb 1867; em 1936; on SINCLAIR, HALL; res Dor. Co., MD;
pub DCGM 1-2:6.
M129 MINER-MINNER Bible; pd 1852; eb 1806; em 1827; on BENNETT, VON FOSSEN,
MINNER; res Columbiana Co. & Wellsville, OH; dep CCGS (#3).
M130 Noah MINOR Bible; eb 1781; em 1801; on SOUTH; res Greene Co., PA; NJ;
pub MBR 2:9.
M131 MINOR Bible; rs 1863-1954; res VA; dep MSA (G-560:109 with D-150).
M132 MIRCH Bible; eb 1832; em 1854; on TAYLOR, WEBB; res Phila., PA;
pub DAR (MdGRC 11:77).
M133 Rev. William MITCHELL Bible; eb 1792; em 1813; on SAWYER, MURPHY, SHARP,
PETFORD, ROCKWELL, TINTENS, NIXON; res Talb. Co., MD; IL;
pub NEHGR 90:298.
M134 MITCHELL Bible; rb 1779; res Harf. Co., MD; dep HOGS.
M135 MITCHELL Bible; pd 1875; eb 1845; em 1817; on STREET, MICHAEL, OSBORNE,
BONN, CAIN, ANDERSON, CLARK; dep BOGS.
M136 MITCHELL Bible; eb 1895; em 1894; on DEVILBISS, HARRIS, MORAN, WILCOX,
BEALL, FEDDON, SHELTON, HARDEE, LARSON; res Lewiston, MD; dep
MHS/FCA.
M137 MITTEN Bible; pd 1890; on STAUB; dep CCGS (#53).

BIBLES

M138 MOALE-NORTH Bible; rs 1731-1809; on TODD, NORTH; res MD; England;
     dep VSL (#2198, acc. 30287).
M139 Ann E. MOBRAY Bible; rs 1804-1892; on CLARK, DOUGLAS, GREER, PHILLIPS,
     WILLIS; res Dor. & Caro. Cos., MD; dep VSL (#2199, acc. 30453).
M140 MOFFERT Bible; eb 1768; em 1802; on LISK; res Freehold, NJ; dep MHS/FCA.
M141 MOFFERT Bible; eb 1816; em 1871; on LEONARD, BUDD, de MARCALLIN; res
     Balto., MD; Phila., PA; dep MHS/FCA.
M142 MOKE Bible; pd 1852; eb 1828; em 1827; on JOYCE, WATTS, PETTIBONE,
     SNELLING, FLEMING; res Annapolis, MD; dep AAGS.
M143 Dennis S. MONETT Bible; eb 1835; em 1856; on BOWEN, WILLIAMS, OGDEN,
     HODGES; pub O'Brien p.309.
M144 MONROE Bible; pd 1815; eb 1785; em 1784; on DAILEY, KAIGHN, CRIDLER,
     RICKNER, FADELEY, McCARTY, NORWOOD, HOOPER; res Leesburg, VA;
     Western MD; pub BMGS 25-4:405.
M145 MONTGOMERY Bible; pd 1884; eb 1871; em 1807; on WITHERS, BROOKS, SLACH,
     POOR, WHELAM, SIONS; LEE; res NJ; NY; KY; VA; dep BCGS.
M146 Francis MOORE Bible; pd 1812; eb 1745; em 1774; on ALLNUT, BOVEN, DUKE,
     KEYS, BOTELER, STRIDER; pub DAR Mag. Oct.1968 p.772;
     pub BMGS 24-2:148.
M147 Jesse MOORE Bible; pd 1803; eb 1772; em 1788; on BRENT, WALLACE, INGRAM,
     WILSON, GARRET; res Fairfax Co., VA; IN; pub BMGS 24-2:145.
M148 John Nelson MOORE Bible; pd 1899; eb 1817; em 1883; on KINNAMONT, EAGON;
     res Dor. Co., MD; pub DOBR,39.
M149 MOORE Bible; eb 1851; on HAWTHRONE; res Dor. Co., MD;
     pub DCGM 3-2:6 and 3-3:3.
M150 MOORES Bible; eb 1795; em 1855; on SMITH, WARDON, OLD, HERRICH; res MD;
     VA; dep MHS/FCA.
M151 Nathan MORGAN Bible; eb 1776; em 1775; on WILLIAMS; pub MBR 2:11.
M152 MORGAN Bible; eb 1843; em 1870; on OSBORN; res Aberdeen, MD; dep BCGS.
M153 MORGAN Bible; rs 1885-1956; res QA Co., MD; dep MSA (G-560:93 with D-150).
M154 MORRIS Bible; eb 1802; on CENER, SHREFF; dep MHS/FCA (Cener Family).
M155 MORRIS Bible; rs 1827-1854; res Som. Co., MD;
     dep MSA (G-560:94 with D-150).
M156 MORRIS Bible; pd 1850; eb 1836; dep BCGS.
M157 MORRIS Bible; rs 1853-1922; pd 1886; eb 1853; em 1874; on CASON, SLATER,
     LISTER, WASDEN; res IN, MO; pub HCMR 5:70; dep HOGS.
M158 MORRIS Bible; eb 1885; em 1886; on WATSON, LOUD, HENDRICKSON, WILLSON;
     pub DAR (MdGRC 11:119).
M159 William Bruce MORRISON Bible; eb 1819; em 1843; on JONES;
     pub DAR (MdGRC 7:68).
M160 MORRISON Bible; pd 1827; eb 1804; pub DAR (MdGRC 33:20).
M161 MOSELEY Bible; eb 1715; em 1746; on GREEN, BOULDIN, GOODE, WATKINS,
     COLLIER, HERNDON, PATRICK, JOHNSTON, FINCH; pub MBR 2:5.
M162 MULL Bible; eb 1804; em 1826; on MOREHOUSE, TILLSON, BALKENS, PURCELL,
     WILSON; res VA; NY; CT; dep BCHS (typed copy).
M163 MUMMA Bible; pd 1811; eb 1787; em 1808; on SHAFER, SCHNEBLEY;
     pub WMG 1-3:130.
M164 MUMMAUGH Bible; eb 1831; on ARNOLD, WARD; res Woolery Dist., Carr. Co.,
     MD; dep CCGS (#31).
M165 Abner MUNDEL Bible; pd 1787; eb 1758; em 1782; res Wash. Co., MD;
     pub DAR Mag Aug. 1967 p.658.
M166 MUNROE Bible; eb 1771; em 1789; on WALTER, STANSBURY, WELLS, CHASE;
     res AA Co., MD; dep AAHS.
M167 MURPHY Bible; eb 1830; em 1853; on BRAMBLE, PRITCHETT; res Dor. Co., MD;
     pub DCGM 3-6:18; dep BCGS.

M168 MURPHY Bible; pd 1890; eb 1872; em 1899; on BRAMBLE; res Dor. Co., MD;
      dep BCGS.
M169 MURRAY Bible; pd 1895; eb 1750; em 1842; on CROWTHER, CHILCOAT, COX,
      PEREGOY; res Balto. & Carr. Cos., MD; dep BCHS (photocopy).
M170 Jabez MURRAY Bible, Bible; pd 1815; eb 1771; em 1802; res Balto., &
      Carr. Cos., MD; dep BCGS (transcript).
M171 MURRAY Bible; rs 1830-1942 Bible; res Mont. Co., MD;
      dep MSA (G-223:47 with D-150).
M172 MURRAY Bible; pd 1858; eb 1835; em 1859; on HARP, REID, HOLMES, MONAGHAN,
      MORSE, McCLUNG, TAYLOR; dep BCGS.
M173 MURRAY Bible; eb 1836; em 1863; on HUNT, FRANCIS, KOSKA; res Bryantown,
      MD; pub NEHGR 107:235.
M174 Hudson MUSE Bible; eb 1740; em 1773; on SLURMAN, NEALSON, CORBIN, MURRAY,
      GAINES, QUARLES; pub MBR 2:15.
M175 MUSGRAVE Bible; eb 1905; em 1926; on STANSFIELD, BRANDENBURG, MARR;
      res Ellicott City, MD;
      dep MSA (G-236:65 with D-150), dep MHS/FCA (91).
M176 MUSGROVE Bible; eb 1870; eb 1842; em 1875; on CROOKS, CHENEY, CRIST;
      res How. Co., MD; dep CCGS (#40).
M177 John MYERS Bible; eb 1760; em 1782; on HIBBS, CORBLEY, BAILEY, GREGG,
      KIRBY, STEPHENSON, WATSON, REAMER; res NJ; Greene Co., PA;
      pub MBR 2:10.
M178 MYERS Bible; eb 1788; em 1873; on BABYLON, WAREHIME, MOTTER;
      dep BCGS (from Yingling).
M179 MYERS Bible; pd 1851; eb 1832; em 1853; on COOKERLY, REMSBURG;
      dep MHS/FCA.
M180 MYERS Bible; eb 1848; em 1873; on BABYLON, HARE, WAREHEME, MOTTER,
      HOFFMAN, COOPER, RAYER; dep CCGS (#54).
M181 Samuel MYERS Bible; eb 1841; em 1868; on MILLER, GARNER, NISWANDER,
      KERLEN, ALBAUGH; res Carr. Co., MD; PA; dep BCGS (from Yingling).
M182 MYERS Bible; eb 1938; em 1941; on GREEN, MEIER, ROBINSON, DAHLGREEN;
      dep CCGS (#21).

N001 NAGLE Bible; eb 1809; on ARNETT, AKEHURST, CALLAHAN; res Balto., Cecil
      Co.,MD; dep BCGS (under Cloman).
N002 NAGLE Bible; eb 1827; em 1853; on SHAW, COLEMAN, STOLTZ; res TN; dep BCGS.
N003 NAGLE Bible; pd 1835; eb 1895; em 1890; on HOUCK, BELL, PRICE, LUCY,
      FRANKLIN; res Carr. Co., MD; dep BCGS.
N004 NASH Bible; ins 1875; eb 1828; em 1849; on ADKINS, ROBINSON, BRIDGES;
      res TN; TX; ARK; dep MHS/FCA.
N005 NAYLOR Bible; eb 1868; em 1870; on BRADY; res Balto. and PG Cos., MD;
      pub PGCGS Bulletin 15/5:75; dep BCGS.
N006 NEAL Bible; eb 1832; em 1860; on HOPKINS, MORRIS, CHILDS, CAMERON,
      STAFFORD, HALLETT,HAIGHT; res QA & Talb. Cos., MD; DE; dep MHS/FCA.
N007 NEAL Bible; eb 1799; em 1846; on POWELL, WRIGHT, ENOCH, HOPKINS BAUM,
      GEORGE; res QA and Talb. Cos., MD; DE; dep MHS/FCA.
N008 NEAL Bible; eb 1868; em 1840; on BRADLEY, WALKER, BROHAUN, HARRINGTON;
      res Dor. Co., MD; pub DCGM 1-4:8.
N009 NEARING Bible; pd 1852; eb 1787; em 1818; on STARR, ROBSON; dep MHS/FCA.
N010 NELSON Bible; rs 1720-1918; res Balto. and Harf. Cos., MD;
      dep MSA (G-205:19 with D-150).
N011 NELSON Bible; eb 1798; on STURGIN; dep MHS/FCA.
N012 NETTLETON Bible; eb 1834; em 1868; on POWELL, RITTENHOUSE, RICHARDS;
      res Balto., MD; PA; dep MHS/FCA; dep MSA (G-560:110 with D-150).
N013 NEUBERT Bible; pd 1857; res Balto., MD; dep AAGS; (No family information).

BIBLES

N014 NEWCOMER Bible; pd 1816; eb 1796; em 1818; on TULLEY, TICE, KELLER,
    SEIBERT, EMMERT, KING, KROTZER; dep MHS/FCA.
N015 NEWCOMER-SHERRICK Bible; pd 1831; eb 1828; em 1828; on HAM, NICODEMUS,
    SHERRICK; res Wash. Co., MD; pub DAR (MdGRC 33:98).
N016 NEWHALL Bible; pd 1836; eb 1798; em 1830; on BATES, HEMPSTEAD, BENNETT,
    ABBOT; res Lynn, MA; KY; IL; DC; dep MHS/FCA.
N017 NEWNAM Bible; eb 1814; em 1850; on STOOPTS, SPARKS, WALRAVEN, AYRES,
    SMITH; res QA Co., MD; pub DAR (MdGRC 11:70).
N018 Levin B. NEWTON Bible; pd 1865; eb 1856; on DASHIELL, GILLIS, CATLIN,
    MURRELL; res Wetipiquin, Som. Co., MD (now Wico. Co.); dep WCFL
N019 NICHOLAS Bible; pd 1842; eb 1772; on FOSTER, OVERTHUM; res Bucks Co., PA;
    dep MdSAR 2743.
N020 NICHOLAS Bible; pd 1871; eb 1808; em 1840; on BIGELOW; res Buckingham
    Co., VA; Bennington Co., VT; pub BMGS 24-4:362.
N021 NICHOLS, Amos Bible; rs 1799-1883; res Dor. Co., MD; pub DOBR,39.
N022 NICHOLS Bible; pd 1815; em 1838; on STAVEN, PRATHER, NOEL; dep BCHS.
N023 NICHOLSON Bible; rs 1703-1947; dep MSA (G-252:22).
N024 NICHOLSON Bible; pd 1883; eb 1849; em 1973; on HALTON, HICKS, GRIGSBY,
    CARR, MERRIFIELD, KRUZE; dep BCGS.
N024 NICHOLSON Bible; pd 1883; eb 1849; em 1973; on NELSON, MULLIGAN, BROWN,
    BROYES, HUGGINS, ANDERSON, SMALL; dep BCGS.
N025 Aylett NICOL Bible; eb 1822; em 1847; on WILLIAMS, BARBOUR, BANDER,
    LEACHMAN, MAPHIS, APRINTIEL; res Prince Wm. Co., VA; DC;
    pub MBR 2:117.
N026 NICOLS Bible; pd 1795; eb 1770; on HAYWARD, WROTH, SMYTH; dep MHS/FCA.
N027 NIKIRK-PAGNE Bible; pd 1869; eb 1811; em 1839; on FAGUE, BOONE, MYERS:
    res DC; pub DAR (MdGRC 33:104).
N028 NOBLE Bible; eb 1792; em 1837; on GILBERT: res Harf. Co., MD;
    dep MHS (HBFR,53).
N029 Jonathann L. NOEY Bible; pd 1805; em 1826; on PERKIPELE, FAIN;
    pub MBR 2:20.
N030 NORMAN Bible; pd 1839; eb 1811; em 1809; on COWMAN, WEEMS, FRANKLIN;
    res A.A.Co., MD; dep MHS/FCA; dep AAGS.
N031 NORRIS Bible; rs 1778-1920; res QA and Caro. Cos., MD;
    dep MSA (G-223:40 with D-150).
N032 NORRIS Bible; eb 1785; em 1778; on CLEMENTS, BAGGS, PARNS, TUPPER,
    STRAUGHN; dep MHS/FCA (6).
N033 NORRIS; rs 1790-1895 Bible; dep MSA (G-640).
N034 NORRIS Bible; pd 1846; eb 1815; em 1838; pub NGSQ 60:131.
N035 NORWOOD Bible; eb 1813; em 1834; on WAGNER, MORRIS, MILLS;
    dep FCHS (original Bible).
N036 Leonard B. NOTTINGHAM Bible; pd 1828; rs 1805-1918; on BYRD, FLOYD,
    KENNARD, SAUNDERS, WISE, WADDY; res Balto., MD; VA;
    dep VSL (#2323, acc. #30453).
N037 NOTTINGHAM Bible; eb 1805; em 1827; on WADDY, KENNARD, FLOYD, BYRD,
    SAUNDERS, WISE; res VA; Balto., MD; dep BCHS (typed copy).
N038 NUNNALLY Bible; rs 1829-1942; dep MSA (G-214:29 with D-150).

O001 ODELL Bible; pd 1789; eb 1776; em 1760; on PHILLIPS, McCOLLISTER,
    CHAPMAN, ECKER, DICKSON; dep MHS/FCA.
O002 OFFUTT Bible; em 1785; on MAGRUDER, CRAWFORD, FORREST, CONTEE;
    res P.G.Co., MD; pub MGB 9:8.
O003 OFFUTT-LACY Bible; eb 1844; em 1869; on WILEY, WHITE, TRIMBLE, ALKER,
    BRETT, LACY, res NY; AL; KY; LA; pub DAR Mag. Nov.1980.
O004 OGIER Bible; eb 1830; em 1829; dep BCGS.
O004A OGIER Bible; res Montana, Calif.; dep BCGS

63

O005 OGLE Bible; rs 1746-1910; MSA (G-835).
O006 OLIVER-GUYTHER Bible; pd 1817; eb 1816; em 1890; on ROBINSON, GUYTHER;
          res Balto. City, St.Mary's Co., MD; dep SMGS.
O007 OLWINE Bible; eb 1819; em 1839; on JACKSON, ROBINSON, DUFFY, ASHMAN;
          res Balto., MD; KS, PA; dep BCHS.
O008 OREM Bible; rs 1713-1943; dep MSA (G-289, 289a).
O009 Robert ORME Bible; eb 1744; em 1769; on EDMONDSTON; res PG Co., MD;
          dep MGR 2:22.
O010 ORRICK Bible; rs 1756-1881; on SMITH, WEBB, DICKSON;
          dep MSA (G-205:20 with D-150).
O011 OSBORNE Bible; eb 1850; em 1909; on MINK, GRAYBEEL; res Harf.Co.,MD;
          Lancaster Co., PA; dep BCGS.
O012 OURSLER Bible; em 1778; pub NGSQ 6:32.
O013 OVERTON Bible; pd 1857; eb 1826; em 1852; on PIMM, KOONTZ, COATES,
          THOMAS, KNIPPLE, HEARDY; dep BMGS 14:21.
O014 OWENS Bible; eb 1729; em 1805; on ZIMMERMAN, COUNCILMAN, RUTTER, BIRCH,
          MULLER, BENT; pub MG 2:266.
O015 Thomas OWENS Bible; pd 1857; eb 1777; em 1813; pub MGB 6:1.
O016 OWENS Bible; pd 1807; eb 1777; em 1808; res A.A.Co., MD; pub NSGQ 19:109.
O017 OWENS-TRUETT Bible; rs 1813-1971; on BURTON, TRUETT; dep MSA (G-853).
O018 Samuel OWINGS Bible; eb 1702; em 1730; pub MG 2:272.
O019 Urath Randall OWINGS Bible; eb 1702; em 1729; pub MG 2:270.
O020 James Winchester OWINGS Bible; pd 1859; eb 1702; em 1729; pub MG 2:275.
O021 OWINGS Bible; eb 1740; em 1811; on REISTER, LAWRENCE; pub MGB 3:18.
O022 OWINGS Bible; pd 1813; eb 1762; em 1788; on DORSEY, LAWRENCE, SOLLERS,
          WARFIELD; res How. Co., MD; pub MGB 14:37.
O023 Caleb OWINGS Bible; pd 1767; eb 1769; em 1768; pub NGSQ 5-4:63.
O024 Edwin OWINGS Bible; eb 1813; em 1845; on BUTLER, BAXTER, KIDSON;
          pub MGB 16:1.
O025 James Winchester OWINGS Bible; eb 1851; em 1832; pub MG 2:274.
O026 Beal OWINGS Bible; pd 1851; on JESSOP, FOUDRAY; res Balto. Co., MD;
          dep BCHS (typed copy).

P001 PACKETT Bible; eb 1736; em 1778; on HARFORD, COOPER, SUTTON, WALKER,
          SCRIMGER, HAMMOND; dep BCGS (MBR 2:31).
P002 PACKETT Bible; eb 1808; res Richmond Co., VA.; dep BCGS (MGB 2:33).
P003 PAGE Bible; pd 1790; eb 1766; em 1764; on GROVINE, WICKES, WROTH, COULTER;
          res Kent Co., MD; pub DAR (MdGRC 8:223).
P004 PALMER Bible; eb 1798; em 1825; on TILLOW, KELLEY, JESSUP, PERRIGOR,
          ELLISON, HAWTHORNE,SPERRY; res Greenwich, CT; NY; TN;
          dep MHS.
P005 PALMER Bible; eb 1873; em 1872; on GUNNELL; res Phila., PA; dep BCGS.
P006 PARISH Bible; rs 1859-1925; pd 1856; on ANDERSON, DUN, EPES, GATTIS,
          PALMER, TAYLOR, WILLIAMS, WOOLTON; res MD, AL, NC, VA;
          dep VSL (#2388, acc. #19741).
P007 PARKER Bible; pd 1802; eb 1756; em 1777; on SAVAGE, BRITTINGHAM;
          res Wico. Co., MD; pub DAR (MGRC 11:158).
P008 PARKER Bible; eb 1777; em 1822; on WILLIAMS, FOOKS, PITTS, ATKINSON,
          MARRINER, WHITE; res Wico. Co., MD; pub DAR (MGRC 11:161).
P009 PARKER Bible: rs 1886-1961; dep MSA (G-597).
P010 PARLETT Bible; eb 1839; on KNIGHT; res Harf. Co. & Annapolis, MD.;
          pub BMGS 21-4:309-310.
P011 PARSLY Bible; eb 1759; res Mont.Co., MD;
          pub BMGS 16:1:38.
P012 PARSONS Bible; rs 1734-1859; dep (G-442).
P013 PATTERSON Bible; eb 1730; on NEIL; dep BCGS (from DAR).

P014 PATTERSON Bible; eb 1776; em 1801; on SUTER, BARNES; res Bucks Co., PA; Georgetown, DC; pub MGB 11:39; pub DAR (MdGRC 9:20).

P015 PATTERSON Bible; eb 1784; em 1805; on HARVEY, PHILLIPS, NORTHERN, FOSTER, HUMPHREY; dep BCGS (MBR 2:26).

P016 PATTERSON Bible; rs 1816-1943; dep MSA (G-189, G-205:16).

P017 PATTERSON Bible; eb 1837; em 1862; on de la ROCHE, JOHNS, BATES, GREENLEAF, COOKE, McGREEVY; res Georgetown, DC; Balto. & Harf. Co., MD; pub BMGS 19-3:177.

P018 PATTERSON Bible; eb 1868; em 1889; on HASSON, JACKSON, MILLER, BEAVEN, GARDNER, JONES; res Cecil Co., MD; dep MHS/FCA.

P019 PATTERSON Bible; rs 1872-1916; pd 1872; on McGREW, EDMUNDSON, PHILLIPS; res MD, VA, PA, FL; dep VSL (#2408, acc. #29745).

P020 PATTERSON Bible; pd 1849; eb 1819; em 1843; on LeCOMPTE, BELL, SMITH, SUARDE; res Dor. Co., MD; pub DOBR,41.

P021 PATTERSON Bible; pd 1817; eb 1789; em 1788; on McKEEL;, res Dor. Co., MD; dep MHS/FCA.

P022 PATTERSON Bible; pd 1817; eb 1789; em 1817; res Dor. Co., MD; pub MGB 4:13.

P023 PATTERSON Bible; pd 1828; eb 1759; em 1788; res Dor. Co., MD; pub MGB 4:13.

P024 PATTERSON Bible; eb 1819; em 1817; res Dor. Co., MD; pub MGB 4:14.

P025 PATTON Bible; pd 1829; eb 1803; em 1825; res Orange Co., NC; Haywood Co., TN; dep MdSAR #2559.

P026 PAYNE Bible; pd 1833; eb 1833; em 1833; pub MGB 2:13.

P027 PEARCE Bible; eb 1735; em 1732; pub MG 2:279.

P028 David PEARCE Bible; eb 1756; em 1798; on BELL; dep BCGS (MBR 2:30).

P029 PEARCE Bible; eb 1837; em 1866; res Balto. Co., MD; dep BCGS (photostat of original pages).

P030 PEARCE Bible; rs 1835-1915; on CLEMSON, DUDDERAR, LINDSAY; dep NGS (Bible Records Collection).

P031 PARRE Bible; pd 1860; em 1857; on LINDSAY, BUCKINGHAM; res Carr. Co., MD; pub MDG 25:13; dep NGS (Bible Record Coll).

P032 PEASE Bible; rs 1838-1948; on BALDWIN, BOWIE; res MD, NY, VA, Washington DC; dep VSL (#2428, acc.#30270).

P033 PEMBERTON Bible; pd 1730; eb 1769; em 1767; pub GPF/PGM 3:747.

P034 PENDLETON Bible; eb 1749; em 1788; pub NGSQ 19-1:16.

P035 PENNINGTON Bible; pd 1834; eb 1810; em 1828; on HOLDING, MILLER, LYSINGER, PRYOR, CARTER, REED, KRIEL; dep MHS/FCA.

P036 PENNINGTON Bible; pd 1834; eb 1842; em 1822; res Kent Co., MD; dep MdSAR 2553 (photocopy).

P037 PETTEBONE Bible; eb 1852; em 1856; on HANS, MARSHALL, COLE, DURSILL; dep MHS/FCA (Hancock-Leonard-Pettebone).

P038 James PETTIT Bible; eb 1762; em 1783; on BAKER, HARRISON, BURKE, HENNYS, CAMPBELL, NORTON, CLAY; dep BCGS (MBR 2:44).

P039 PFONTY Bible; pd 1889; eb 1770; em 1831; on SLOTHOVER, SMITH, ROOP, GABY, OSCER, SCHILDT, BALDNER, SUNBRUIN, REPP, ORVALE, ALVIN; dep BCGS.

P040 Jacob PHILLIPS Bible; eb 1786; em 1785; on ISAACS; dep BCGS (MBR 2:29).

P041 Samuel PHILLIPS Bible; eb 1857; em 1830; res Princess Anne, MD; pub MDG 22-4:108.

P042 PHILLIPS Bible; pd 1807; eb 1807; em 1853; on PEARSON, WILLIAMS; res Dor. Co., MD; pub DOBR,43.

P043 William S. PICKETT Bible; eb 1735; em 1759; METCALFE, YOUNG, FISHBACK, JACKSON, BRADY, CHAMPERLAIN, SMITH, CHANNELL, RICHARD; dep BCGS (MBR 2:34).

P044 James S. PICKETT Bible; eb 1768; em 1800; on SMITH, HAMPTON, DAVE, HARRIS, WALKER, THOMAS, KERFORT, HAUGHTON, WORMLEY; dep BCGS (MBR 2:35).

INVENTORY OF MARYLAND BIBLE RECORDS

P045 William PICKETT Bible; eb 1782; em 1827; on THOMPSON, MAFEN, BENSON,
        MORROW, FAUCETT, MURDLE; res Orange Co., NC; dep BCGS (MBR 2:38).
P046 William S. PICKETT Bible; eb 1810; em 1842; on WALKER, SAFFARENS,
        ROBINSON, SMILEY, CHALMERS, GOULD, SCOTT, HOUSER, PHILLIPS;
        res Columbia, TN; TX, NY, LA, Fauquir Co., VA; pub MBR 2:39.
P047 PICKETT Bible; pd 1874; eb 1849; em 1872; on WEBB, HIGGENBOTTOM; res IO;
        dep CCGS #11.
P048 PIERCE Bible; pd 1873; eb 1838; em 1835; on GIMPER, SPILLMAN, GILBERT,
        SOFSR, BRITE; res Talb. Co., MD; dep AAGS.
P049 George Washington PILCHARD Bible; eb 1804; em 1890; on MARSHALL, PAYNE,
        SMITH; res Worc. Co., MD; pub MDG 4-3:55.
P049A PINDELL Bible; rs 1780-1870; dep MSA (G-570:1).
P049B PIPER Bible; rb 1852; on LEWIS; res NH; dep HCGS.
P049C PLACE-HALL-GRAHAM Bible; pd 1831; em 1836; on HALL, GRAHAM; res NY;
        dep BCGS.
P050 PLACK Bible; eb 1871; res Balto.City, MD; dep BCGS.
P051 PLUMMER Bible; pd 1791; eb 1745; dep MHS/FCA (E.W. Jackson, Chart).
P052 PLUMMER Bible; eb 1832; em 1859; on STRIDER, ANDERSON, ZIMMERSON, BLUE,
        WARD, TORSCH, HERSPERGER, ROELKE,WHEATON, RODGERS;
        pub DAR (MdGRC 25:4).
P053 PLUMMER Bible; eb 1856; em 1881; on GUE, CLAGETT, BOSWELL, SHELLY;
        pub DAR (MdGRC 33:60).
P054 PLUNKERT Bible; pd 1890; eb 1874; em 1894; on MEHRING; res Littlestown, PA;
        dep CCGS 23.
P055 POCOCK Bible; rs 1720-1918; res Balto. & Harf. Co., MD;
        dep MSA (G-205:19 with D-150).
P056 POE Bible; pd 1819; eb 1783; em 1818; on ZIEGLER; pub DAR (MdGRC 9:63).
P057 POFFENBERGER Bible; pd 1834; eb 1812; em 1838; on KAUFFMAN, WHALEY,
        COOPER, KIGHT, FRYE, NICKLES; res Ohio; Frostburg, MD;
        pub MDG 7-3:58; pub DAR (MdGRC 33:80).
P058 POOLE Bible; pd 1815; eb 1769; em 1794; on MAYNARD, GAITHER; dep CCGS.
P059 POOL Bible; eb 1781; em 1807; on BARNES, COOK; CCGS 38.
P060 POOL Bible; eb 1847; em 1846; res Carr. Co., MD; dep CCGS 39.
P061 POOLE Bible; rs 1778-1914; res Montgomery Co., MD;
        dep MSA (G-560:83 in D-150).
P062 POPE-THOMPSON-STEWART Bible; eb 1812; em 1836; on THOMPSON, STEWART;
        pub DAR (MdGRC 33:57).
P063 PORTER Bible; eb 1765; em 1787; pub MGB 2:18.
P064 PORTER Bible; eb 1788; em 1840; on ABEL, HEART, PETTIGREW, KARNES,
        GOODMAN, LANDON; res CT, MA, Balto., MD; dep MHS.
P065 PORTS Bible; eb 1880; em 1912; on MEYERS, PRICE, TOWNSEND, FREELMYER;
        res Carr. Co., MD; BCGS (Miller Coll.).
P066 Benjamin POSEY Bible; eb 1778; em 1802; on WILLIAMSON; dep BCGS (MBR 2:46).
P067 POSEY Bible; rs 1737-1927; MSA (G-323:1).
P068 POSEY Bible; eb 1750; em 1772; on MATHEWS, THORNTON, RANDOLPH, DAVIS,
        STREET, WASHINGTON, CAMPBELL, CHURCHILL; pub MBR 2:24.
P069 POSEY Bible; rs 1792-1884; res St.M. Co., MD; dep MSA (G-560 with D-150).
P070 POWELL Bible; rs 1834-1939; res PA; dep MSA (G-560:110 with D-150).
P071 POWELL Bible; rs 1812-1927; res Som. Co., MD;
        dep MSA (G-560:95 with D-150).
P072 Warren PRETTYMAN Bible; pd 1848; eb 1765; em 1793; on WHARTON, McCUBBIN,
        BRIEN, POWELL; res Balto. & How. Cos., MD; DE; dep DBR 12:1.
P073 PRICE Bible; pd 1791; eb 1777; em 1799; on MONTGOMERY, PENN-INGTON, SEWELL;
        res Cecil Co., MD; dep AAGS.
P074 Warwick PRICE Bible; eb 1808; em 1840; on MATTHEWS, JONES, UNDERWOOD, BELL;
        dep BCGS.

P075 PRICE Bible; eb 1809; em 1838; on HOPKINS, HYSON, WALTON, BETTERTON,
     HERUE, BEYER; res Balto., MD; pub BMGS 25-1:117.
P076 Mordecai PRICE Bible; pd 1850; eb 1833; em 1857; on ARMACOST; dep BCGS.
P077 PRICKETT Bible; eb 1758; em 1780; on KINDLE; pub MBR 2:45.
P078 Benjamin PRIGMORE Bible; pd 1829; eb 1761; em 1802; on DOWNING, KRAUS,
     SCOTT, TUCK, HALL, BEATY, WINGFIELD; res MD; MO.; pub BMGS 23-4:349.
P079 Duke Young PRIGMORE Bible; eb 1826; em 1856; on HILL, CLAY, RHODES,
     JACKSON, BLENK, THOMPSON, VANMETER; res MO; pub BMGS 23-4:351.
P080 PRITCHARD Bible; pd 1858; eb 1857; em 1857; on RAWHOUSER, CONN;
     res Harf. Co., MD; York Co., PA; dep MHS (HBFR,42).
P081 John Wingate PRITCHETT Bible; eb 1824; em 1873; on BRAMBLE, CANNON, JONES,
     LEWIS; res Dor. Co., MD; pub DOBR,44.
P082 Moses Edward PRITCHETT Bible; eb 1849; em 1873; on CANNON, res Dor. Co.,
     MD; pub DOBR,44.
P083 Zebulon PRITCHETT Bible; eb 1776; em 1865; on BLOODSWORTH, INSLEY, MURPHY,
     LEWIS; res Dor. Co., MD; pub DOBR,44.
P084 PRITCHETT Bible; eb 1865; em 1857; on MOORE; res Dor. Co., MD;
     pub DORB p.44.
P085 PUGH-BALLOU Bible; rb 1801; on MARTIN, DAVIS, SPENCER, CORNETT, WOOD;
     res Grayson Co., VA; dep BCGS.
P086 PURDY Bible; eb 1829; on COPPERS; dep MHS/FCA ("Hancock").
P087 PURNELL Bible; pub PGM 3:527.
P088 PURNELL Prayer Book; eb 1748; em 1744; pub NGSQ 21:107.
P089 Chessed PURNELL Prayer Book; eb 1788; em 1788; pub NGSQ 21:108.
P090 John Selly PURNELL Bible: res Eastern Shore, MD; pub NGSQ 21:108.
P091 Lanta PURNELL Bible; pd 1813; eb 1730; em 1759; pub NGSQ 21:107.
P092 PURSER Bible; eb 1852; em 1880; on CATON, CAYTON; res Beaufort Co., NC;
     dep BCGS.
P093 PYE Bible; pd 1708; eb 1730; on BOOTH; dep MHS/FCA.

R001 RADCLIFFE Bible; eb 1797; em 1865; on HARRISON, GARDE, KING, KEMP, BRIDGES,
     WINFRED; pub CC 9-2:20.
R002 Laurence RAMEY Bible; eb 1759; em 1784; on NIMON, GILBERT, SHIELDS,
     LAYCOCK, McLAUGHLIN, WATERFIELD; res Berkeley Co., VA;
     pub MBR 2:53.
R003 RAMSBURG-REMSBURGH Bible; eb 1750; on WHIPP, HEFFNER, REMSBURGH;
     dep FCHS (original).
R004 RANSDELL Bible; eb 1763; em 1832; on SANFORD; dep MHS/FCA.
R005 RATCK Bible; pd 1874; eb 1840; em 1864; res Kent Co., & Balto., MD;
     dep BCHS (original).
R006 RATHEL Bible; rs 1746-1837 Bible; dep MSA (G-132).
R007 RATLIFF Bible; eb 1755; em 1785; on BRIDGES, ORR; pub MGB 9:25.
R008 Not assigned
R009 RAWLEIGH Bible; eb 1806; em 1806; on THOMPSON, HANDLEY; res Dor. Co., MD;
     pub DOBR,45.
R010 Ashael RAWLINGS Bible; eb 1742; em 1763; on CHILTON, ENGLISH, KENNEDY,
     THURMAN; pub MBR 2:73.
R011 Charles RAWLINGS Bible; eb 1828; em 1860; on HICKMAN, COLE, CARREN,
     SWACKER, SHIELDS, DAVIS; DAR Mag., Jan. 1981 pg.111.
R012 Hosea RAY Bible; eb 1776; em 1796; on LAMB, GIBBS, GARRETT, NORMAN,
     BROWNING, HILL; pub MBR 2:47.
R013 RAYMOND Bible; rb 1764; res Harf. Co., MD; dep HCGS.
R014 RAYMOND Bible; eb 1769; em 1842; on FELL, ALLEN, BOND, LENOX, CABURN,
     PENTZ; res Harf. Co., Balto., MD; VA; DC; Ireland;
     pub BMGS 19-1:21-23.

R015 READ Bible; pd 1834; eb 1789; em 1816; on ALEXANDER;
dep MHS.
R016 W. H. REASEN Bible; pd 1891; eb 1809; em 1820; on NELSON, COLE, GORRELL,
ARTHUR, ALEINE, HAYMAN; dep BCGS.
R017 REDDEN Bible; eb 1817; em 1891; pub MDG 4-3:55.
R018 READ-ABRAHAMS Bible; eb 1794; em 1836; on ABRAHAMS; res Cecil Co., MD;
pub NGSQ 41-1:29.
R019 Rev. Daniel Meredith REESE, Bible; eb 1809; em 1829; pub NGSQ 33-1:42.
R020 REESE Bible; pd 1848; eb 1823; em 1850; on ROOP, MORROW, PFOUTZ, BANKERT;
res Balto. Co., MD; Reno, NV; dep BCGS.
R021 Robert A. REGERSTER, Bible; pd 1872; eb 1816; em 1840; on JONES, CARTER,
TREADWELL; res Balto. City & Co., MD; pub BMGS 15-4:238.
R022 REGESTER Bible; pd 1890; eb 1851; em 1925; on SHARGREEN, THOMAS, SAUNER;
res Balto., MD; pub BMGS 15-4:236..
R023 REID Bible; eb 1835; on REED, REIDE; pub DOBR,45.
R024 REILLY Bible; rb 1753; res Balto., MD.; dep HCGS.
R025 REMSBURG Bible; pd 1762; eb 1736; em 1756; on BRUNNER, WHIPP, HEFFNER;
res Fred. Co., MD; dep FCHS.
R026 John RENFRO Bible; eb 1760; em 1781; pub MBR 2:55.
R027 RENSHAW Bible: rs 1797-1946; res Som. Co., MD; dep MSA (G-560 with D-150).
R028 James RENTFRO Bible; eb 1763; em 1783; HUFF; pub MBR 2:55.
R029 REYNOLDS Bible; ins 1875; eb 1793; em 1836; on KIRK, MENDENHALL, MEARNS,
MICHURN, DICKEY; res Cecil Co., MD.; dep BCGS (from DAR).
R030 REYNOLDS Bible; rb 1793; on CLAYTON, HOBSON; dep HCGS.
R030A REYNOLDS Family Record; rb 1814; dep BCGS.
R031 REYNOLDS Bible; eb 1829; em 1854; on BATCHER, KERSTATER; res Clearspring,
MD; pub PGCGS Bulletin 15-7:114 (Mar.1984).
R032 RHODES Bible; pd 1818; eb 1822; em 1815; on HALL, GOTT, CATTERTON;
res Calv. Co., MD; dep AAGS.
R033 RICE Bible; ins 1842; eb 1824; em 1824; on PRITCHARD, MOORE, RANDALL,
HOOK; pub BMGS 10:88.
R034 RICHARDS Bible; eb 1809; em 1807; on VERNON, WEBSTER, HELFRICH, SPEAR,
McCUBBIN, JOHNY; res Balto., MD; Del. Co., PA; pub BMGS 24-2:151.
R035 RICHARDS Bible; res Carr. Co., MD; dep BCGS (photocopy).
R036 RICHARDSON Bible; eb 1707; em 1768; COALE, PIERPONT, DAWSON; res AA Co. MD;
Fauquier Co. VA; DC; pub MGB 11-6:16.
R037 RICHARDSON Bible; eb 1794; em 1841; on WILSON, PARROTT, WILKINS, SKINNER,
HACKETT, DEAKYNS; COWGILL, BOWERS, COVINGTON, KIDD:
res QA, Talb. Cos. MD; dep MSA (G-560:97).
R038 RICKETTS Bible; ins 1841; pd 1825; em 182(?); on STRONG, BOWEN, DAVIS,
MILLER, FOARD, BRANNAN, BALDWIN; dep MHS (HBFR,12).
R039 Thomas RICKETTS Bible; eb 1883; em 1883; on DAVIS, MYERS, LOWRY, LURTZ,
NORMAN, FRANZON; res Havre de Grace, MD.;
dep MHS (HBFR,12).
R040 Jacob RIDENOUR Bible; pd 1848; eb 1824; res Wash.Co. MD; pub MDG 7:2:31;
pub DAR (MdGRC 33:86).
R041 RIDENOUR Bible; pd 1870; eb 1831; em 1917; on SMITH;
pub DAR (MdGRC 33:106).
R042 Col. John RIDER Bible; eb 1684; em 1705; on HICKS, BILLINGS, STEELE;
res Dor. Co. MD; pub DOBR,45.
R043 RIDER-BRANDAU Bible; pd 1861; eb 1809; em 1838; on BRANDAU, SHOPE, KORB,
KLAUENBERG, KOLB, PRESCOTT, PACE; res Balto.,Wheaton, MD; PA;
pub BMGS 25-2:191; dep BCGS.
R044 RIDGELY Bible; pd 1792; eb 1764; em 1791; pub MG 2:301.
R045 RIGDON Bible; eb 1742; em 1781; on JOHNSON, AMOSS, WATERS, RISTEAU,
LUCKEY, NELSON; res Balto. & Harf. Cos. MD; pub CMF 1:87.

R045A RIGGIN Bible; eb 1770; em 1784; res Princess Anne, MD; pub MDG 22-4:107.
R046 RILEY Bible; eb 1740; em 1767; on TAYLOR; res Ireland; SC;
    pub MBR 2:49.
R047 Abraham RILEY Bible; eb 1782; em 1808; on GARDNER, BONNER, PRUETT;
    pub MBR 2:51.
R048 James RILEY Bible; eb 1834; on WILLINGHAM, BARNETT, WILEY, MASON, MULLINS,
    BONNER, ELLISON, SELMON, SMITH; pub MBR 2:53.
R049 RINEHART Bible; pd 1859; eb 1834; em 1860; on GRABILL, BAUGHER, RUDISELL,
    ARTHUR, WANTZ, MYERS; res Emmittsburg, MD; NY; Switzerland; dep BCGS.
R050 RINGGOLD Bible; eb 1773; em 1772; on CARROLL; dep MHS/FCA.
R051 RINGGOLD Bible; pd 1832; eb 1844; em 1832; on BROWNE; dep MHS/FCA..
R052 ROACH Bible; eb 1765; on GREENWELL, THOMPSON, WILLIAMS,
    pub DAR (MdGRC 4:43, possibly incomplete).
R053 ROBERTS Bible; pd 1802; eb 1753; em 1776; on FRY, PATTERSON, TIMMIUS,
    WILFORD, GILLIS; res Wake Co., SC; dep AAGS.
R054 Benjamin ROBERTS Bible; pd 1827; eb 1775; em 1776; on McKAIN, MONEY,
    DAWSON, BALL, HARTUP, PURVIANCE; res MD.; Jefferson Co.,OH;
    pub MGB 12:35; correction in MGB 13-31,63.
R055 James ROBERTS Bible; eb 1805; em 1840; on DAWSON, PRUVIANCE, WOOD, FORNER;
    pub MGB 12:36.
R056 ROBINS Bible; rs 1794-1957; pd 1895; res MD and AL;
    dep VSL (#2669 acc. #30268).
R057 ROBINSON Bible; eb 1746; em 1792; on TERRY, CALDWELL, WYATT, OWEN,
    de JARNETTE, DUDLEY, CAIN, McKENZIE, FAIR, McCAIN, McGOWEN,
    REESE, GODDALL, BROWN; pub MBR 2:61.
R058 ROBINSON Bible; rb 1801; on CORNER, RICHARDSON, BEEMAN; res Balto. City
    & Harf. Co., MD; RI; dep HCGS.
R059 Cornelius RIBINSON Bible; eb 1805; em 1828; on de JARNETTE, MAY;
    pub MBR 2:54.
R060 ROBINSON Bible; rs 1818-1861; dep MSA (G-550:1).
R061 William H. ROBINSON Bible; eb 1818; em 1854; on JONES, PRITCHETT;
    res Dor. Co., MD; pub DOBR,47.
R062 ROBINSON Bible; eb 1827; pub DCGM 1-3:7.
R063 ROBINSON Bible; eb 1828; em 1854; on LONG, TURNER, WENTZ, VIVIAN, DOD,
    PUTNAM, CHICHESTER; res PG Co., MD; dep AAGS.
R064 ROCKWELL-ROBERTS-BLANCHARD Bible; pd 1868; eb 1781; em 1856; on ROBERTS,
    McKEE, BLANCHARD, WETZLER, KING; res VT; MA; IL; BCGS (in Yingling).
R065 RODGERS Bible; eb 1807; em 1806; on DENISON; dep MHS/FCA (105).
R066 RODOCK Bible; pd 1826; eb 1854; em 1912; on HOUCK, BUSHWALLER, NIEUABER,
    DOVAY; res Fred. Co., MD; NY; dep FCHS (original bible).
R067 ROE Bible; rs 1767-1886; res Caro. and QA Cos., MD;
    dep MSA (G-223:42 with D-150).
R068 ROGERS Bible; eb 1748; on MORGAN, CRAWFORD, ELY, JONES;
    res Harf. Co., MD; pub DAR (MdGRC 4:69).
R069 John H. ROGERS Bible;ins 1811; eb 1775; em 1807; on HAGLE, SPEDDEN, WARNER,
    BROWNE, HOLDEN, PETERSON; res Balto., MD;
    dep MHS/FCA (105) photocopy not fully legible.
R070 ROGERS Bible; em 1825; on COTTRELL, St. GERMAIN, HARVEY, PENN, HOOPER,
    NICKERSON; res NY; MA; England; dep MHS/FCA (105).
R071 ROLPH Bible: rs 1824-1929; res Kent Co., MD; dep MSA (G-189:5 with D-150).
R072 ROOP Bible; pd 1846; eb 1823; em 1850; on ENGLER; res Carr. Co., MD;
    dep BCGS (in Yingling).
R073 ROOP Bible; pd 1884; eb 1864; em 1890; on BUCHER, PFOUTY, KNIGHT, DITMARS,
    CROUT; dep BCGS (in Yingling).
R074 ROSENBERGER Bible; pd 1892; eb 1860; on BEARD, WALKING;
    dep BCGS (in Yingling).

R075 ROSENCRANSE Bible; eb 1804; em 1830; on SLAGLE, TRANSUE, JONES, SERFOS, WASSER, DIETRICH; dep MHS/FCA; dep MSA (G-560:111 with D-150).
R076 ROSS Bible; eb 1856; em 1851; on DOLLY, WINDSOR, WHEATLEY; res Dor. Co., MD; pub DCGM 4-2:7.
R077 ROSSE Bible; rs 1775-1838; dep MSA (G-645).
R078 ROULHAC Bible; pd 1818; eb 1753; em 1818; on RASCOE, ROBINSON, ANDERSON, DIXON, HOLDEN, GRAY; res N.E. NC; dep AAGS; dep MHS/FCA.
R079 ROULHAC Bible; pd 1851; eb 1824; em 1850; on DIXON, HINES, BAKER, HARRISON, HOLLAWAY, GAPPAN; res N.E. NC; dep AAGS; dep MHS/FCA.
R080 ROYER-RYER Bible; eb 1900; on RYER; res Westminster and Lancaster, PA; dep BCGS (in Yingling).
R081 Scott ROYER Bible; pd 1879; eb 1883; em 1881; on MUMMA; res Hagerstown, MD; Columbus, OH; dep BCGS (in Yingling).
R082 Reuben RUCKER Bible; eb 1755; em 1776; on McDANIELS, BURFORD, PARKER, WARE; pub MBR 2:69-70.
R083 Isaac RUCKER Bible; eb 1797; em 1793; on HIGGIN, BOTHAM, CHRISTIAN, WINGFIELD; pub MBR 2:68.
R084 Theodosia RUDDELL Bible; eb 1757; em 1779; on LYNN; res Ruddell Sta., VA; pub MBR 2:43.
R085 RUNKLES Bible; pd 1840; eb 1828; em 1827; on GRIMES; res Fred. Co., MD; pub WMG 1-4:180.
R086 RUNKLES Bible; eb 1926; em 1977; on AVERLY; res Kemptown, MD; dep BCGS.
R087 Willliam RUSH Bible; eb 1755; em 1775; on TERRILL; pub MBR 2:76-77.
R088 Grisby RUSH Bible; eb 1784; em 1803; on HARRIS; pub MBR 2:77.
R089 RUSSELL Bible; pd 1767; eb 1769; em 1766; res Balto., MD; pub NGSQ 65-4:310.
R090 RUSSELL Bible; eb 1781; em 1804; on TITTLE, BYRON, GEORGE, GREENWOOD; pub DAR (MdGRC 13:118).
R091 RUSSELL Bible; eb 1861; em 1889; on HORSEY; res Wilmington, DE; dep MHS/FCA.
R092 RUTHERFORD Bible; rs 1766-1933; dep VSL (#2728-2730, acc. #20644).
R093 RUTHERFORD Bible; pd 1848; eb 1849; em 1848; on CLAYLAND, BURCKARET, IGLEHART, GRASON, HARRYMAN, STEWART; res Towson, MD; Louisville, KY; dep BCGS #503.
R094 Col. Joshua RUTLEDGE Bible; eb 1759; em 1838; on NELSON, McCOMES, RICHARDSON, WARD, AMOS, WELSCH, STERTT, JOHNSON, WILSON; pub Turner Genealogy Newsletter #2 (1972) p.2 in MHS/FCA.

S001 SACKETT Bible; pd 1819; eb 1763; on BEACH, BECKER, WATERMAN, BUEL, MORGAN, SLUYTER, TAYLOR; pub DAR (MdGRC 8:132-2).
S002 SANDERS Bible; rb 1806; res Kuhlstatt, Germany: dep HCGS.
S003 SANGER Bible; pd 1907; eb 1842; em 1892; on GRAYBILL; dep BCGS (in Yingling).
S004 SANGSTON Bible 1832-1892; res Balto., MD; VA; dep MSA (G-560:106 with D-150).
S005 James W. SARGENT Bible; eb 1770; em 1791; on McNEAL, WELLS; res Fred. Co., MD; OH; Lester,280.
S006 SAUMENIG Bible; rs 1833-1962; dep MSA (G-918).
S007 SAUTER Bible; eb 1868; em 1849; on THOMAS, BROWN, REINHOLD; res Balto. City and Co., MD; dep CCGS.
S008 Hezekiah S. SCARBOROUGH Bible; rb 1785, on RUCKMAN, RUTMAN, ALBERT, STOKES, MOULTON, SCHLOER, MOORE, REYNOLDS, CLEMENTS, HUFF, FOARD, PYLE, BAILEY, COX, GARDNER, HOLLOWAY, SNODGRASS, WEBB, PRICE; res Harf. Co., MD; dep HCGS.
S009 Andrew Howlett SCARBOROUGH Bible; rb 1873; on RITCHIE, WILLIAMS, TALLMAN, BOYLE; res Harf. Co., MD; dep HCGS.

S010 SCARBOROUGH Bible; rb 1875; on SMITH, DELWORTH, WILSON, DAVIS, ENGLAND,
    RUTLEDGE; REYNOLDS, STREET, PIERCE, TYSON, CRUNLISH, WILHEIM;
    res Harf. Co., MD; dep HCGS.
S011 SCARBOROUGH Bible; eb 1903; on BALDWIN; dep BCGS (539); pub BMGS 22-3:232.
S012 SCHELL Bible; eb 1820; em 1845; on FRIFEGLE, KNOLL, SHAFFER, OYSTER, RUHL,
    LIEBLING; res Balto. Co., MD; PA; OH; pub OSR,446.
S013 SCHEMINANT Bible; pd 1874; eb 1828; em 1852; on CORRIGAN, MANGUM;
    res AA Co., MD; dep BCGS (504).
S014 SCHERER Bible; eb 1716; em 1765; on MACK, TEACKLE, PARKER, TANKARD, BELL,
    KILLAM; dep MHS.
S015 SCHLEIGH Bible; pd 1812; eb 1790; em 1831; on BECK, GONDER, HARDING,
    HALLER, KANTNER, HEARD, STOCKMAN, KESSLER, MEALY, MORGAN, COOMS;
    pub DAR (MdGRC 33:119-120).
S016 SCHOOLFIELD Bible; pd 1815; eb 1763; em 1787; on WHEELER, GUNBY, HENDERSON,
    BEAUCHAMP, MERRILL; res Worc. Co., MD; dep MSA (G-560:98 with D-150);
    dep MHS/FCA.
S017 SCHUFF Bible 1877-1934; on MILLER, STITELY; res Thurmont, MD; dep NGS.
S018 SCHULTZ Bible; eb 1848; em 1873; on HENDRIX;
    dep MHS/FCA (Bible Records Coll. DAC).
S019 SCHWERER-ROGERS Bible; eb 1835; em 1865; on SAPPINGTON, WILMER, STALLINGS,
    DAWSON, RALEIGH, WAGNER, MAGRUDER; res Kent Co., Balto., Annapolis,
    MD; DC; NY; dep BCGS.
S020 Thomas SCOTT Bible; pd 1715; eb 1718; em 1742; on WILLIAMS, GATEWOOD;
    res Caro. Co., VA; pub MBR 2:83.
S021 Samuel SCOTT Bible; eb 1754; em 1784; on ROY, PAYNE, HOLCOMB, KENDALL;
    pub MBR 2:82.
S022 SCOTT Bible; eb 1868; em 1867; on BELL, McILVAIN; res Balto., MD;
    dep MHS.
S023 SCOTTEN Bible; on PERRY; res Harf. Co., MD; York Co., PA; dep HCGS.
S024 J.I. & J.B. SCRIVENER, Bible; eb 1830; em 1902; on MONETT, RAWLINGS;
    pub O'Brien, p.310.
S025 FLETCHER-NASON Bible; on SEAWARD, MASON; res Balto., MD; ME;
    pub NEHGR 88:331.
S026 SEIBERT Bible; eb 1825; on RONEY; res Wash., Co., MD;
    pub DAR (MdGRC 33:89).
S027 Louis B. SEIBOLD Bible; pub HCMR vol.75.
S028 SEIFERT Bible; eb 1857; em 1876; on ROHDE; dep MHS/FCA.
S029 SELLMAN Bible; pd 1791; eb 1755; em 1754; on WAYMEN, RANKIN, WALLACE,
    MAYNARD, HOMEWOOD; res AA Co., MD; pub DAR (MdGRC 35:9).
S030 SELLY Bible; eb 1809; em 1860; pub MGB 3:26.
S031 SELBY Bible; eb 1852; em 1877; pub MG 2:277.
S032 SELLMAN Bible; rs 1689-1875; dep MSA (G-258:17).
S033 SELLMAN Bible; rs 1689-1957; MSA (G-569).
S034 SELLMAN Bible; rs 1770-1937; MSA (G-570:3).
S035 Thomas Pennington Bennet SETH Bible; pd 1846; eb 1803; em 1802;
    res Talb. Co., MD; pub MDG 24-1:25.
S036 SETH Bible; eb 1785; on O'BRYON, DOWNS; pub DAR (MdGRC 7:39).
S037 SETH Bible; rs 1789-1948; dep MSA (G-363).
S038 SEWARD Bible; rb 1677; res QA Co., MD; dep MSA (G-560:99).
S039 SEWELL Bible; pd 1867; eb 1802; em 1823; on HOLLINGSWORTH, HOPKINS,
    THOMAS, McCLOONEY, OAS, TYSON, WEITZEL, WARNER, LLOYD, WELCH,
    TREFFENBERG, HENDRIX, BULL, BANNER, WILSON, WATSON;
    res Cecil Co., MD; dep AAGS; dep MHS/FCA.
S040 SEWELL Bible; eb 1821; em 1819; on SKINNER, RAWLEIGH, HANDLEY;
    res Dor. Co., MD; pub DOBR,47.

S041 SEYMER Bible; pd 1882; on SEYMER, DEWEY, SCHEIHING; res Balto., MD;
dep AAGS; dep MHS/FCA.
S042 Joseph Carter SHACKELFORD Bible; eb 1818; em 1843; on JONES;
res Edmonson Co., KY; pub MBR 2:93.
S043 SHAMBERGER Bible; pd 1884; eb 1787; em 1790; on ETER, SOUDER, BECKLEY,
KLARE, WEAVER, ABBOTT, FITZELL; res MD; PA; dep AAHS (original).
S044 SHANNON Bible; pd 1877; eb 1855; em 1871; dep BCGS.
S045 SHARP Bible; eb 1781; em 1834; res PA; OH; dep MdSAR (2514).
S046 SHAW Bible; rs 1745-1830; dep MSA (G-465).
S047 Hugh SHAW Bible; eb 1766; em 1791; on McHENRY, GALT, KRISE, BARRICK,
SHEPHERD, HOGUE, JOHNSON, KLING, WAESCHE, BAUGH; res MD; OH;
pub DAR (MdGRC 7:64).
S048 SHAW Bible; pd 1845; eb 1773; em 1826; on FOSKET, SAGE; res Berkshire
Co., MA; dep MHS/FCA.
S049 SHAW Bible; pd 1849; eb 1816; em 1849; on JOHNSON; res Balto. Co., MD;
dep MdSAR (2568); dep MHS/FCA.
S050 George E. SHELLEY Bible; pd 1875; eb 1864; em 1864; on PRICE, NELSON,
MATTHEWS, GONTEE; res Balto. Co., MD; dep BCGS.
S051 SHENTON Bible; eb 1841; on DUNNOCK; pub DOBR,47.
S052 SHERMAN Bible; pd 1778; eb 1778; em 1835; on RAWLEIGH, HARRISON, HOLLAND,
COLESCOTT, HAYS, PECK; res Dor. Co., MD; pub DOBR,48.
S053 SHERMAN Bible; pd 1829; eb 1831; em 1820; on WEBB, RAWLEIGH, GAMBRIEL,
WELSTER, CLIFTON, LARRIMORE, SHARP, BRADLEY; DOBR,51.
S054 SHERMAN Bible; pd 1870; eb 1849; em 1842; on HARE, CRAMER, ZEPP,
ZIMMERMAN; res MD; CCGS (55).
S055 SHERTZER Bible; pd 1846; eb 1820; em 1840; on TREGE, MERRITT, HOOVER;
res Balto.,Churchville, MD; Phila., PA; San Francisco, CA;
pub BMGS 23-2:172.
S056 SHERWOOD Family Record; eb 1632; em 1689; res Talb. Co., MD;
pub NGSQ 12-2:27.
S057 SHERWOOD Bible 1668-1878 Bible; dep MSA (G-142 with G-125 Hall Collection).
S058 SHERWOOD Bible; pd 1836; eb 1770; em 1878; on PANTIER, JEWELL, HYATT,
MOFFETT; pub MGB 21:1.
S059 SHIPLEY Bible; eb 1840; em 1838; on GILLIS, TURNER, FARVER, HAINES,
GOSNELL, BRANDENBURG, LAMBERT, LEURS, WILSON, BARNES, SMITH;
dep CCGS (#6); dep BCGS.
S060 Thomas J. SHIPLEY, Bible; eb 1862; pub DAR (MdGRC vol.33).
S061 SHIPLEY Bible; pd 1844; eb 1734; em 1863; on CRONISE, GATES, COST;
pub MGB 17:35.
S062 SHIPLEY Bible; eb 1767; pub DAR Mag. May 1967, p.546.
S063 SHIPLEY-BARNETT Bible; eb 1804; em 1832; on EGGLESTON, SHOCKEY, CLAYTON,
HOOPER, MAHAN, WOOD, McMILLIN, HUFFORD, BARNETT, COLT, AVERY, BURKE;
res Balto. Co., MD; IO; MO; pub BMGS 15-1:22.
S064 SHIPLEY-PORTER Bible; pd 1873; on PORTER dep BCGS (typed copy).
S065 SHORES Bible, rs 1811-1947; dep MSA (G-305:2).
S066 SHUMAN Bible; pd 1829; eb 1815; em 1837; on LINGMAN, SCHAFFER;
res Carr. Co., MD; dep CCGS (#34).
S067 SHIPLEY Bible; pd 1847; on BARNETT; res Balto., Carr. Co., MD; IO, MO;
pub BMGS 15-1:26.
S068 SHORT Bible; pd 1853; eb 1832; em 1853; on PARKER, BERSCH, ADAMS;
pub BMGS 28-2:234-235.
S069 Oliver F. SIMMONS Bible; eb 1868; em 1860; on WOOD, HOOPER;
pub O'Brien p.311.
S070 Jesse H. SIMPERS Bible; eb 1797; em 1821; pub NGSQ 33-1:40.
S071 Willain SIMPERS Bible; pd 1803; eb 1795; em 1794;
res Cecil Co., MD; pub NGSQ 32:2:71.

72

S072 SIMPSON Bible; pd 1862; eb 1784; em 1809; on SUDLOW, FULLER;
  pub BMGS 19-2:125.
S073 SIMPSON Bible; pd 1853; eb 1775; on BAKER, FADE; pub MGS 16:42.
S074 SINCLAIR Bible; eb 1895; em 1905; on TODD, MILLER; res Dor. Co., MD;
  pub DCGM 1-2:6-7.
S075 Samuel SIX Bible; pd 1850; eb 1830; em 1858; on STALEY, FRALEY;
  res Thurmont, MD; pub DAR (MdGRC 7:219).
S076 SIX Bible; pd 1816; eb 1820; em 1835; on HAINES, WASE, MURDOCH; res Ohio;
  dep AAHS (typed copy).
S077 David SKELTON Bible; pd 1770; eb 1827; em 1853; on BLAKESLEE, KING,
  GOLDWITH, SWANSON, HOUSEHOLDER; res PA; pub DAR (MdGRC 33:66).
S078 Jesse SKILTON Bible; pd 1813; eb 1764; on HARVEY; pub DAR (MdGRC 33:65).
S079 SKIDMORE Bible; rs 1789-1914; on ALLEN, BOYD, MORGAN, WIMSATT; res MD; VA;
  dep VSL (#2849, acc. #29741).
S080 SKINNER Bible; pd 1809; eb 1811; em 1810; pub MG 2:324.
S081 SKINNER Bible; eb 1885; em 1852; on KLINE; res New Haven, OH;
  pub CMF 2:25.
S082 SKIRVEN Bible; pd 1866; eb 1866; em 1866; on BARD; res Kent Co., MD;
  Norwich, CT; pub DAR (MdGRC 11:125).
S083 SLEMAKER Bible; eb 1716; em 1745; on GILES, HART, GREATHOUSE, ELLIOTT,
  HYDE, SMITH, DUVALL; res Balto., Annapolis, Allegany Co., Kent Is.,
  MD; Reichenberg, Germany; pub BMGS 19-3:145-147.
S084 SLICER Bible; pd 1775; eb 1797; res Balto. Co., MD; PA; DC; dep MHS/FCA.
S085 SMALL Bible; pd 1859; eb 1863; on SMITH, FULKERSON, DUBBER, PURDUE,
  ELZER, BRACKER; MILLER, STEWART, MARCOW; res Warrick Co., IN;
  dep AAGS.
S086 Archibald SMITH Bible; pd 1808; eb 1717; res Som. Co., MD; NH;
  pub NEHG Reg 96:206-207.
S087 SMITH Bible; rs 1720-1918; res Balto., Harf. Co., MD;
  dep MSA (G-205, G-214:19 with D-150).
S088 Isaac SMITH Bible; rb 1734; pd 1891; on HOPKINSON, PARKER, TEACKLE;
  res MD; VA; IN; dep VSL (#2868, acc.#30453).
S089 SMITH Bible; rs 1740-1957; res AA Co., MD; dep MSA (G-711).
S090 Samuel SMITH Bible; eb 1745; em 1808; res Berkely Co., VA;
  dep BCGS (photocopy).
S091 James SMITH Bible; eb 1767; em 1794; on CLARK, BROWN, DICKSON, LEONARD,
  BAUERMAN, DAILEY; res Jones Co., NC; pub MBR 2:78.
S092 SMITH Bible; pd 1822; eb 1798; res Balto. Co., MD; dep CCGS.
S093 SMITH-YOUNG Bible; pd 1827; eb 1797; em 1819; on YOUNG;
  dep BCGS (photocopy).
S094 SMITH-SPEAR Bible; pd 1869; eb 1808; em 1831; on SPEAR, COLL, FUNK,
  DURANT, BRILL; dep BCGS (#496).
S095 SMITH Bible; pd 1852; eb 1809; em 1845; on HOPKINS, HOLLAWAY, STEPHESON,
  WILSON, PATTERSON, HANNA, ELLIOTT; res VA; dep MHS (HBFR,37).
S096 SMITH Bible; eb 1809; res Kent Co., MD; pub DAR (MdGRC 7:316); KBG1,55.
S097 SMITH-BALLARD Bible; eb 1811; em 1832; res Balto., Som. Co., MD;
  dep BCGS (photocopy).
S098 SMITH Bible; rs 1812-1889; on BRYAN, HARRINGTON, SHEPPARD, TOLL; res MD;
  DE; VA; PA; VSL (#2883, acc.#30433).
S099 SMITH Bible; rb 1806; on MARTIN; res York and Lancaster Cos., PA;
  dep HCGS.
S100 SMITH Bible; eb 1816; em 1841; on HUNGERFORD, DARLY, HALL, McINTYRE,
  THOMAS; dep BCGS (499).
S101 SMITH Bible; rs 1819-1837; dep HCGS.
S102 SMITH Bible; rs 1822-1877; res Caro. Co., MD;
  dep MSA (G-560:100 with D-150).

INVENTORY OF MARYLAND BIBLE RECORDS

S103 SMITH Bible; rs 1822-1866; dep MSA (G-518:3).
S104 SMITH Bible; eb 1829; on BARGER, CRUTCHER; pub MGB 21:31.
S105 SMITH Bible; eb 1838; em 1832; on JENKINS, ADAMS, CREIGHTON;
     res Dor. Co., MD; pub DCGM 3-3:3.
S106 SMITH-MARTIN Bible; rb 1838, on FREDEKING, LEINBACH, JORDAN, FLANAGAN,
     HERSHEY, BEAR, TRENT, TERRY; res York Co., PA; dep HCGS.
S107 SMITH Bible; eb 1852; em 1875; on PENNINGTON;
     dep MHS/FCA (with Pennington Bible 1834).
S108 SMITH Bible; pd 1859; eb 1877; res Tyrone, PA; dep AAGS.
S109 SMITH-MITCHELL Bible; eb 1865; em 1864; res Lawrenceburg, TN;
     dep MdSAR (#2559).
S110 SMITH Bible; pd 1874; eb 1876; em 1878; on DODD, YOUNG, res Smithville, NJ;
     dep AAGS.
S111 SNADER Bible; pd 1888; eb 1862; em 1887; on ROGER, SCHWERGART, SAPPINGTON;
     res Carr, Co., MD; dep BCGS (in Yingling).
S112 SNOWDON Bible; pd 1846; eb 1824; em 1848; on DAY, LEE, DUNN, KAPTAIN,
     BECKMAN, MADDOCKS; OLSON, HILL, DEAN; res Medford, MA; dep AAGS;
     dep MHS/FCA.
S113 Philip SNYDER Bible; pd 1872; eb 1849; on HALLER, BRITT; res Balto., MD;
     dep AAGS.
S114 Alexander SOMERVELL Sr. Bible; em 1795; on IRELAND, PARRAN, SEWELL,
     HELLEN, McDANIEL, WEEMS, SEDURCH; pub O'BRIEN p.311.
S115 Adam SPACH Bible; eb 1720; em 1752; on HUNTER, TEACH, KOSTNER, EBERT, LONG,
     HEGE, ABREHLER; res Fred., MD; NC; Germany; pub MBR 2:74.
S116 SPENCE Bible; eb 1767; em 1807; on DAVIDSON, SCOTT, SCARBOROUGH, BOYD;
     pub DAR (MdGRC 11:52).
S117 SPENCER-HOLCOMBE-KEENER Bible; eb 1796; em 1782; on HOLCOMBE, KEENER;
     res Talb. Co., MD; AL; pub MDG 12-3:64.
S118 Silas L. SPENCER Bible; rb 1830; on MITCHELL, COOPER, AMOSS, KING, GROSS,
     FRIZZELL; res Harf. Co., MD; dep HCGS.
S119 Richard Littleton SPENCER Bible; rb 1858; on COOPER, HOPKINS, BANGS,
     STRAUFF, CURRY, POTEET, HENDERSON, GROSS, THOMPSON, GOLANDER,
     BISHOP, PULLEN; res Harf. Co., MD; dep HCGS.
S120 SPICKLER Bible; pd 1851; eb 1827; em 1847; on FRISBY, TILGHMAN, SHELLER,
     WOLFENSBARGER, STAUFER; pub DAR (MdGRC 33:118).
S121 Samuel SPICKLER Bible; eb 1795; on MILLER; pub DAR (MdGRC 33:114).
S122 SPICKNALL Bible; rs 1882-1920; dep MSA (G-550:4).
S123 SPRIGGS Bible; rs 1881-1939; dep MSA (G-644).
S124 SPURRIER Bible; rs 1779-1898; res Fred. & Carr. Cos., MD;
     dep MSA (G-863:1).
S125 Mary A.M. Albaugh SPURRIER Bible; pd 1848; eb 1779; em 1818; on MILLER,
     ALBAUGH; res Fred. & Carr. Cos., MD; dep CCGS.
S126 SPURRIER-BURGESS Prayer Book; rs 1790-1804; dep MSA (G-159 with D-150).
S127 Thomas B. SPURRIER Bible; pd 1860; eb 1828; em 1850; on ALBAUGH, UHLER,
     KING, FOUNTAIN; res Fred. & Carr. Cos., MD; dep CCGS.
S128 SPURRIER Bible; pd 1860; eb 1828; em 1850; on ALBAUGH, UHLER, KING,
     FOUNTAIN; res Fred. Co., MD; PA; pub BRP 1:107.
     Note: S127 and S128 may be different reports on the same Bible.
S129 STACKETT Bible; rs 1689-1857; dep MSA (G-569).
S130 STAMETS-GIST Bible; eb 1803; em 1869; on BROWN, BLUNT, GIST; pub MGB 16:4.
S131 STAMFORD Bible; eb 1740; em 1765; on STANDIFORD; res Balto. Co., MD: KY;
     pub Ardery 2:217.
S132 Thomas STANLEY Bible; eb 1757; em 1796; on VOTAW; dep BCGS (MBR 2:76).
S133 John STANLEY Bible; eb 1795; em 1821; on CREW, HALL, MACY, LANN, VOTAW,
     JOHNSON; pub MBR 2:77.

BIBLES

S134 STANLEY-SWEENEY Bible; eb 1854; em 1902; on AURT, SWEENEY; res Balto.,
     Marlboro, MD; pub NEHG Reg 107:235.
S135 STANSBURY Bible; rs 1803-1877; dep MSA (G-584).
S136 Albert G. STANSBURY, Bible; pd 1837; eb 1837; em 1876; res KY; GA; IN; MO;
     pub MGB 5:5.
S137 Eli STANTON Bible; pd 1863; rs 1844-1903, on BROADWATER; res Garrett Co.,
     MD; VSL (#2942, acc. # 30391).
S138 STAPLEFORD Bible; rs 1746-1837; dep MSA (G-132).
S139 STARKEY Bible; rs 1834-1927; res Som. Co., MD;
     dep MSA (G-560:101 with D-150).
S140 START Bible; rs 1802-1941; res Kent Co., MD;
     dep MSA (G-560:102 with D-150).
S141 STARTZMAN Bible; pd 1884; eb 1853; em 1877; on MIDDLEKAUF, MARTIN, HENDRY,
     ENSMINGER, SUMMER; res MD; dep MdSAR 2606; dep MHS/FCA; dep BCGS.
S142 STEBBING Bible; rs 1821-1842; res Cecil Co., MD;
     dep MSA (G-214:29 with D-150).
S143 Thomas STEEL Bible; eb 1768; res Chester Co., PA; pub DAR (MdGRC 9:109).
S144 STEELE Bible; eb 1768; on HILL; res Delaware Co., PA;
     pub DAR (MdGRC 4:50), typed copy.
S145 Hugh STEERS Bible; eb 1758; em 1790; on DAVIS, THOMPSON, DARNELL, THARP,
     FITZGERALD; pub MBR 2:92.
S146 STEIGELMAN Bible; pd 1854; eb 1797; em 1852; on LAMB, RICE; res Balto.,
     Annapolis, & Talb. Co., MD; pub PGCGS Bulletin 19-3:39, Nov. 1987.
S147 Leonard STEPHENS Bible; eb 1816; em 1813; on SANFORD; pub MBR 2:181.
S148 STEPHENS Bible; on COCHRAN; res Md; PA; dep HCGS.
S149 Thomas STEVENS Bible; pd 1735; eb 1735; em 1734; dep MHS/FCA.
S150 Richard STEVENS Bible; eb 1783; em 1782; on CARTER; pub MBR 2:96.
S151 STEVENS Bible; eb 1809; on VOSS, LIDEN; res Denton, MD; pub DBR 12:8.
S152 STEVENS Bible; eb 1825; em 1849; on ROGERS, LINN, WITT, SMITH, OATIS,
     WYATT, FINLEY; pub BMGS 19-2:122-123.
S153 STEVENSON-BOONE Bible; pd 1696; eb 1763; em 1784; on McKELVEY, TAYLOR,
     BOWEN, BOONE, GLANVILL, HOPKINS; res Balto. Co., MD;
     pub OSR,490-491; dep BCHS (typed copy).
S154 Isaac STEWART Bible; eb 1743; res VA; pub MGB 4:29.
S155 STEWART Bible; eb 1785; em 1804; on FRAZIER, LAWS, RICARDS, FRAME;
     res Dor. Co., MD; pub DCGM 2-1:1, 18 and 2-3:5.
S156 STEWART Bible; rs 1814-1839; dep MSA (G-823, G-834).
S157 STEWART Bible; eb 1848; em 1871; on OSBORN; res Van Wert, OH; dep CCGS #9.
S158 STEWART Bible; em 1862; on POPE, MARLOW, MARTIN, MAGRUDER;
     pub DAR (MdGRC 33:58).
S159 STEWART Bible; pd 1868; eb 1869; em 1868; on BEATLEY, BLASS, MAC,
     QUARRIE; res Balto. MD; dep CCGS.
S160 STINCHCOMB Bible; rs 1825-1945; dep MSA (G-238).
S161 STODDARD Bible; eb 1765; em 1791; on TAVENER, JONES, MILLARD; res MA; CT;
     dep MHS.
S162 John H. STOKES Bible; rb 1785; on SCARBOROUGH, STACKS, REYNOLDS, CLEMENT,
     MOORE, MOULTON, RUCKMAN, ALBERT, HUFF, BAILEY, GRIFFITH;
     res Harf. Co., MD; dep HCGS.
S163 STOLL Bible; em 1865; on SCHREINER, RADECKE; res Balto. MD;
     dep AAGS; dep MHS/FCA.
S164 STONE Bible; eb 1766; em 1789; on BEDELL, KESTER, NICHOLSON, SHERRILL,
     MERRIWETHER, RUSSELL; res AL; dep MHS/FCA.
S165 STONER Bible; eb 1755; on OVERHOLSSERN, DIEHL; res Fred. Co., MD;
     pub BMGS 14:39.
S166 STOUT Record; rs 1761-1778; dep MHS (HBFR,35) deaths only.
S167 STOVER Bible; eb 1809; em 1833; on FOSTER; pub DAR (MdGRC 33:91).

S168 STRAUGHN Bible; eb 1770; em 1797; on CUTLAR, HARPER; dep MSA (G-233:50); dep MHS/FCA (6).
S169 STREETT Bible; RB 1879; on MITCHELL; res MD; dep HCGS.
S170 STRONG Bible; pd 1812; eb 1816; em 1846; on HUFFMAN, PRICE, DWYER, WALTERS, AMBERG, RINGGOLD; res Kent Co., MD; VA; Mass.; pub KBR p.33; dep MHS typescript.
S171 John STRODE Bible; eb 1724; em 1758; on BOYLES, CONSTANT, ECTON, LANE, FORMAN, DUNCAN, McMILLAN, WILSON, McCOWAN, LANDER, STORM; pub MBR 2:94-95.
S172 John STRODE Jr. Bible; eb 1768; em 1791; on McMILLAN; pub MBR 2:95.
S173 STRUTHERS Bible; eb 1872; em 1871; on COX, RICE, WESSELL, VOLKERS, ELLCOTT, COCK, LANTZ, WELSH, BARBER, MALTUS, NALL, SCHERT; res NJ; dep BCGS (#497).
S174 STUDYBAKER Bible; rb 1838; res IN; dep HCGS.
S175 Foxhall STURMAN Bible; eb 1720; em 1745; on CHILTON, MUSE, PARKER; pub MBR 2:75.
S176 SUDLER-EMORY Bible; pd 1806; eb 1740; em 1765; on WELLS, JACKSON, RALSTON; res Kent Co., MD; pub DAR (MdGRC 8:236).
S177 John SUGGETT Bible; eb 1751; em 1772; on DAVIS; pub MBR 2:91.
S178 SULLIVAN Family Records; eb 1793; em 1812; on COLLINS, HITCH, KINNEY, ELLIS, KINDRED, FOOKS, BACON, WOOTEN; res Sussex Co., DE; pub MDG 1-2:44,64,86; 2-3:69.
S179 SULLIVAN Bible; eb 1801; em 1867; on BARWICK, CASTATOR, SLOVIS, VAN METER, KINNEMON; dep MHS/FCA.
S180 SULLIVANE-ENNALLS-HAGGAMAN Bible; on ENNALLS, WAGGAMAN; pub CC 9-1:11, (1982-83).
S181 SUPPLEE Bible; eb 1748; em 1806; on WHETHERILL, McGLATHERY, CREELY, SMITH, LEE, LEWIS, TEANY, MYERS; pub DAR (MdGRC 13:12).
S182 Jay SUTTON Bible; eb 1790; em 1811; on GILLESPIE, JACKSON, SUTHERLAND, WASHBURN, REYNOLDS, CATLIN; res Huron Co., OH; dep AAHS (typed copy).
S183 Randolph SWANN Bible; pd 1892; eb 1874; em 1907; on SIMPSON, MILES, WILLIAMS; res Wico. & Chas, Cos., MD; dep SMGS.
S184 SWEARINGEN Bible; eb 1760; em 1785; on BENNETT, WERNENGER, BARNES, KIGER; pub DAR Mag. 80:582.
S185 Stephen Booker SWENNY, Bible; eb 1821; em 1821; on HUGHES, ENROUGHTY, WHITLOCK, WOODWARD, WYATT, BARNES, WILLIS; res New Kent & Hanover Cos., VA; pub MBR 2:86.
S186 Martin SWEENY Bible; eb 1832; em 1850; on BARNES, HUTCHESON, PEATROSS; pub MBR 2:89-90.
S187 SYLVESTER Bible; eb 1790; on RYCHER, CASE, SHERER, TISCHER; pub BMGS 17-3:132.

T001 TABB Bible; rs 1824-1930; on ALLMAND, BROWN, CLAYBROOK, CRUMP, LEMMON, LIGHTFOOT, TUCHER, WELLFORD; res MD; VA; dep VSL (#3017, acc #20651).
T002 TAIT Bible; rs 1768-1836; dep VSL (#3019, acc #30322).
T003 TALBOTT Bible; rs 1796-1855; res Balto. Co., MD; dep MSA (G-236:57 with D-150).
T004 TANNER Bible; eb 1820; em 1848; res Campbell Co., VA; dep MdSAR (2576).
T005 TARBUTTON Bible; eb 1841; res Kent Co., MD; pub DAR (MdGRC 13:144).
T006 TARLTON Bible; pd 1840; eb 1829; em 1828; on MOORE; res St.M. Co., MD; dep MHS/FCA (21 with Cardeau).
T007 TARR Bible; eb 1761; res Snow Hill, MD; KY; pub Audery 2:219.
T008 John TAYLOR Bible; eb 1696; em 1716; on PENDLETON, PENN, LEWIS, WALKER, LYNN, POLLARD, ANDERSON, BULLOCK; pub MBR 2:122-125.
T009 TAYLOR Bible; eb 1731; em 1771; on BYNE, TURNER, BALDWIN, OLIVER; pub MBR 2:106-108.

BIBLES

T010 Edmund TAYLOR Bible; eb 1741; em 1771; on DAY, WINSTON, REDD, TOMPKINS,
     BURNLEY, MARSHALL, RICHARDSON, SHEPHERD, MORRIS, SHEPARD;
     pub MBR 2:97.
T011 Joseph TAYLOR Bible; rb 1720; pd 1827; dep VSL (#3041,acc. #30433).
T012 TAYLOR Prayer Book; eb 1742; res AA Co., MD; pub MDG 23-1:20.
T013 TAYLOR Bible; rs 1766-1944; res Cecil Co., MD;
     dep MSA (G-236:69 with D-150).
T014 TAYLOR Bible; rs 1792-1948; res Som. Co., MD; VA;
     dep MSA (G-560:112) with D-150).
T015 TAYLOR Bible; pd 1844; eb 1813; em 1839; on PHILLIPS, HUGHES, TRUITT,
     MUMFORD, MORSBERGER, LYNCH, TOADVINE, BAYSINGER; dep BMGS 19:26-28.
T016 TAYMAN-GARNER-PARKER Bible; rs 1886-1961; on PARKER,
     .GARNER; dep MSA (G597).
T017 John TENNEN Bible; rb 1749; pd 1973; on BANNING, ELLIOTT, FORD, GREIMAN,
     NOEY, HOPPER, KLING, TEVIS; res MD; DE; MO; NY; VA;
     dep VSL (#3069, acc. #30391).
T018 TERRILL Bible; eb 1740; em 1760; on WILLIS; pub MBR 2:111.
T019 Jacob L. TERRY Bible; eb 1894; em 1884; on STINCHCOMB, HANNA, EVERETT,
     LYNCH; res Harf. Co., MD; dep BCGS.
T020 THOMAS Bible; eb 1683; pub MDG 18-2:43.
T021 Samuel THOMAS Bible; inss 1799; eb 1742; on BAGGS, GRAHAM, STEPHENS,
     WALES; res QA & Caro. Cos., MD; pub BMGS 24-1:78-80.
T022 William and Hannah THOMAS Bible; eb 1756; em 1801; res Cecil Co., MD;
     pub NGSQ 40:140.
T023 Giles THOMAS Bible; pd 1784; eb 1763; em 1786; pub NGSQ 66-1:64.
T024 THOMAS Bible; eb 1764; em 1893; on THRELKELD, ROYALTY, RANSDELL, DEVINE,
     CURRY; dep MHS/FCA (Bible Rec. Coll. DAC).
T025 Tristram THOMAS Bible; eb 1770; em 1780; on HOLLINGSWORTH, CLOTHEIR;
     pub Mid South Bible Records p.329-330.
T026 Theodore and Mary THOMAS Bible; eb 1772; res Cecil Co., MD;
     pub NGSQ 40:140.
T027 THOMAS Bible; eb 1791; em 1842; on BOWMAN, WEBB, COVERDALE, RICHARDS,
     CUBBAGE; res DE; dep MHS/FCA.
T028 THOMAS Bible; pd 1850; eb 1793; em 1816; on TUBMAN, LEIPER;
     res St.M. & AA Cos., MD; PA; pub BMGS 21-2:176.
T029 THOMAS Bible; rs 1806-1923; on BEVYLEY, BROWN, CARTER, JONES, MOONEY,
     PAVARD; res Elkton, MD; dep NGS Bible Rec. Coll.
T030 David Ogle THOMAS Bible; pd 1839; eb 1838; em 1838; on STAUFFER, WARFIELD,
     MYER, CLARK, SMITH, SPRAGENS, WARNER, BALDWIN, HODGEN;
     res Fred. Co., MD; pub NGSQ 8-2:36.
T031 THOMAS-MOORE Bible; eb 1848; em 1871; on SMITH, REW, BROADWATER, MILES,
     MOORE; pub BMGS 13:216.
T032 THOMAS-MOORE-TULL Bible; eb 1848; em 1871; on MOORE, TULL;
     pub MDG 12-3:67.
T033 Roger THOMPSON Bible; eb 1750; em 1781; on WHITE; pub MBR 2:101.
T034 Thomas THOMPSON Bible; on TRACY, HAMILTON, WARD, KIVET; res Loudoun Co.,
     VA; pub MBR 2:121.
T035 THOMPSON Bible; eb 1782; on JARVIS, BAILEY, LEWIN, JONES, HUFF,
     SCARBOROUGH, CATHCART, BARBER, McFADDEN; res Harf. Co., MD; dep BCGS.
T036 THOMPSON Prayer Book; eb 1787; em 1786; on HARPER, WEBB; res Dor. Co., MD;
     pub DCGM 4-3:17.
T037 THOMPSON Bible; eb 1787; em 1827; on JOHNSON, WILLS, DAVIS, STONESTREET,
     GREEN; dep MHS/FCA.
T038 THOMPSON Bible; pd 1845; eb 1793; em 1824; on WOOD, CHESNEY;
     res Harf. Co., MD; dep MHS (HBFR,54).

T039 THOMPSON Bible; eb 1824; em 1872; on DEMPSEY, POWELL, RATLEDGE, BOYS;
     res DE; dep BCGS (from DAR).
T040 Robert Vinton THOMPSON Bible; pd 1884; eb 1852; em 1877; on CONNELL,
     TIBBETTS, BURGESS, FLETCHER, BARNES, BIDDLE, MULDOON, WHITNEY;
     res Howard Co., MD; pub DAR (MdGRC 35:87).
T041 THOMPSON Bible; eb 1874; em 1874; on BAKER, WHERRETT, TORREY, YOUNG;
     res Balto., MD; Boston, Mass; pub BMGS 22-3:234.
T042 THOMPSON Bible; eb 1879; on RATTEDGE; dep BCGS (from DAR).
T043 James THOMSON Bible; eb 1755; em 1774; on IVEY, GRICE, MOORE;
     pub MBR 2:113.
T044 Anthony THORNTON Bible; eb 1727; em 1746; on TALIAFERRO, FITZHUGH,
     BUCKNER, ROOTES, STANLEY, JONES, GRYMES, LAUGHLIN; pub MBR 2:99.
T045 George Washington THORNTON Bible; eb 1737; em 1773; on ALEXANDER, POSEY;
     res Stafford Co., VA; pub MBR 2:112.
T046 George THORNTON Bible; eb 1752; em 1774; on STANLEY; pub MBR 2:102.
T047 THORNTON Bible; pd 1887; eb 1891; em 1890; on WALTERS; res CA; dep BCGS.
T048 THRUSTON Bible; rs 1832-1892; res Balto., MD; VA;
     dep MSA (G-560:106 with D-150).
T049 William R. THURMAN Bible; eb 1813; em 1837; on STEPHENSON, ROGERS, PARHAM;
     res Bledsoe Co., TN; pub MBR 2:120.
T050 TILLARD Bible; rs 1788-1921 Bible; dep MSA (G-570:4).
T051 TIMMONS Bible; eb 1800; em 1827; on REIFSNIDER; pub DAR (MdGRC 33:110).
T052 TIMMONS Bible; pd 1877; eb 1841; em 1868; on GABLER; res Franklin Co., PA;
     pub DAR (MdGRC 33:11).
T053 TINDALL-DOWNS Bible; pd 1874; eb 1840; em 1840; on DRAY, WILLIAMS,
     RAWLINGS, RICE, STEUART; pub DAR (MdGRC 35:13).
T054 TOWLES-POOLE Bibles; rs 1801-1897; on BEARDSLEY, DeCAMP, DICKERSON, JONES,
     MACKEY; res MD; VA; dep VSL (#3122, acc. #28126).
T055 TOWNSEND Bible; pd 1830; eb 1800; em 1830; on LINDSAY, SELBY, ROBISON,
     FREEHAN, BEVANS, MUNK; res Worc. & Dor. Cos., Balto., MD; IL; DC;
     dep MHS/FCA.
T056 TOWNSEND Bible; rs 1824-1929; res Kent Co., MD;
     dep MSA (G-189:5 with D-150).
T057 TOWSON Bible; eb 1735; em 1788; on IRWIN, SMITH, BOYD, PORTERFIELD, HAMME,
     COAKLEY, BISHOP, KENLY, PRICE, BRADY, BRIDGES, PAULDING, LANDELL;
     res Balto. & Wash. Cos., MD; pub NEHG Reg 79:327-329.
T058 John TRABUE Bible; eb 1762; em 1793; on PENDLETON; pub MBR 2:115.
T059 Henry TRACY Bible; pd 1834; eb 1773; em 1795; pub DAR (MdGRC 33).
T060 Jonathan TRACEY Bible; pd 1822; eb 1812; em 1813; res Balto. & Carr. Cos.
     MD; dep BCGS (photocopy).
T061 TREFFENBERG Bible; eb 1802; em 1825; on BULL, BANNER, SEWELL, PRICE,
     HOPKINS, SAMPSON, COPENHAVER; res Cecil Co., MD; Sweden; dep AAGS;
     dep MHS/FCA.
T062 TREHEREN-ATKINSON Bible; eb 1806; em 1827; on ATKINSON; res Som. Co., MD;
     pub MDG 22-2:46.
T063 TRUITT Bible; eb 1802; em 1872; on POWELL, WARD, PERDUE, JONES, KELLY,
     SELBY; pub DAR (MdGRC 11:163).
T064 TRUITT Bible; eb 1757; em 1783; on GODFREY, RENDER; pub MBR 2:108.
T065 TRUITT Bible; rs 1813-1917; on OWENS, BURTON; dep MSA (G-853).
T066 TRIMMER Bible; pd 1872; eb 1838; res York Co., PA; dep MdSAR #2515.
T067 Robert TUCKER Bible; eb 1710; em 1739; on CORBIN; res King and Queen Co.,
     VA; pub MBR 2:116-119.
T068 TUCKER Bible; eb 1781; em 1809; on CHADSEY, REID; res Mont. Co., MD;
     Marion Co., KY; pub PGCGS Bulletin 18-7:117 (March 1987).
T069 TULL Bible; pd 1850; em 1771; on HALL, EVANS; res Som. Co., MD;
     pub DAR (MdGRC 13:162).

T070 TULL-FITZGERALD Bible; eb 1812; em 1834; res Som. & Worc. Cos., MD;
      pub DAR Mag. Nov. 1960 p.660.
T071 TULL Bible; rs 1816-1870; dep MSA (G-505).
T072 William TUNNELL Bible; eb 1760; em 1781; on McCLAUD; pub MBR 2:98.
T073 TURNBULL Bible; eb 1871; em 1871; on LITCHFIELD, JONES, TRUCHART, KIDDER,
      POPE; res Balto. MD; dep MHS/FCA (under Christie).
T074 TURNER Bible; eb 1752; res MD; Bourbon Co., KY; pub Ardery 2:220.
T075 John TURNER Bible; eb 1757; em 1832; on YOUNG, GILL, MICHENER;
      pub MBR 2:103.
T076 TURNER Bible; inss 1835; eb 1772; em 1798; on RANDOLPH, CARTER, POWELL,
      HALL, FAUNTLEROY, PALMER, HUNT, TAYLOR, BASCOM, LUFFBOROUGH;
      dep MSA (G-560:113 with D-150); dep MHS/FCA(125).
T077 Joseph TURNER Jr. Bible; eb 1790; em 1812; on SINCLAIR, CHANDLEE, PLATTE,
      HATTO; res Balto. MD; dep MHS/FCA (125).
T078 TURNER Bible; rs 1798-1855; res PG Co., MD; dep MSA (G-919:1).
T079 TURNER Bible; inss 1854; eb 1853; em 1852; on McDANIEL, JONES, TOWNSEND;
      res Kent Co., MD; Phila., PA; dep MHS/FCA.
T080 TURNER Bible; rs 1855-1915; dep MSA (G323:2).
T081 TURNER Bible; rb 1858; on WEBB, HOWELL, BLEDSOE, POINDEXTER, HUTTON,
      MEDLIN, REEVE; res Wilks Co., NC; dep HCGS.
T082 TURNER Bible; em 1879; on PITTEMGER, DEATRICH; pub DAR (MdGRC 33:93).
T083 TURNER Bible; pd 1850; eb 1842; em 1841; on PARK, ASHCRAFT;
      res Gloucester Co., NJ; dep CCGS (#49).
T084 Maj. Francis TURPIN Bible; eb 1723; on SMOOT, DOUGLAS, WRIGHT, WILLISON,
      DAVIS; res Dor. Co., MD; pub DAR Mag. 66:673.
T085 William TURPEN Bible; eb 1744; em 1781; on WRIGHT, OGLE, SMOOT;
      res Dor. Co., MD; pub DAR Mag 66:672.
T086 TUTTLE Bible; eb 1836; em 1833; on HOWELL, TERRY, PRESCOTT, PURDY;
      res MD; DC; NY; pub DAR (MdGRC 33:126).

U001 UHLER-NACE Bible; eb 1751; em 1778; on NACE, ANDERSON, DEADY, BURGESS,
      GALLOWAY, WATTS; res Talb. & AA Cos., MD; pub DAR (MdGRC 3:64).
U002 UNDER Bible; em 1889; on EDDINGTON; res IL; CO; OR; dep BCGS (#501).
U003 UPPERCO Bible; eb 1788; em 1852; on VAN BIBBER, WHEAT, STOCKSDALE, MITTEN,
      REIGHLER, SAMPSON, TURNER, BREYMAIER, STANLEY; res Balto. and Balto.
      Co., MD; pub BMGS 23-2:174.
U004 UPPERCO Bible; pd 1853; eb 1821; em 1852; res Balto., Carr. Co., MD;
      dep BCGS (photocopy of original).
U005 UPPERCO Bible; eb 1859; em 1886; dep BCGS (photocopy of original).
U006 UPSHUR Bible; rs 1844-1908; pd 1850; on BLANDING, MARTIN, ROBINSON;
      res MD; VA; SC; dep VSL 3187, 3188 (acc #30453).
U007 USILTON Bible; eb 1791; res Kent Co., MD; pub DAR (MdGRC 11:80).

V001 VALIANT Bible; eb 1872; em 1871; on OLIVER, FAY, WEST, CARNAN, CAUTHORNE;
      res Balto., MD; dep BCGS.
V002 John VANCE Bible; eb 1753; em 1778; on SLACK; pub MBR 2:127.
V003 Samuel VANCE Bible; eb 1762; em 1798; on WATERS; pub MBR 2:127.
V004 VANCE Bible; eb 1801; em 1820; on HARPER, WATERS; pub MBR 2:126.
V005 VANNORT Bible; pd 1837; eb 1806; em 1831; on ADAMS, ALLEN, USILTON,
      BARTHOLOW, SIMPERS; res Kent Co., MD; pub KBR p.22.
V006 VAULX Bible; eb 1914; em 1772; on HOBSON, ARMSTRONG, COWAN, CROCKETT;
      res TN; NC; dep MHS/FCA.
V007 VEAZEY Bible; inss 1802; eb 1774; em 1794; pub NGSQ 55-2:146.
V008 VEAZEY Bible; pd 1831; eb 1785; em 1834; on McCLURE, HIRONS, GILPIN;
      dep MHS/FCA (127).
V009 VEAZEY Bible; pd 1861; eb 1839; on BRISLER; dep MHS/FCA (127).

INVENTORY OF MARYLAND BIBLE RECORDS

V010 VEAZEY Bible; eb 1851; em 1850; on DUNCAN, KNIGHT; res Cecil Co., MD;
    dep MHS/FCA (127); dep BCGS.
V011 VERMILLION Bible; eb 1889; on COLSON, HAYES, KNIGHT;
    pub PGCGS Bulletin 18-9:151 (May 1978).
V012 VERNAY Bible; pd 1806; em 1788; dep MHS/FCA (127).
V013 VICKARS-JEFFERSON Bible; eb 1794; on WAPLES, JEFFERSON; dep MHS/FCA (127).
V014 VICKERS Bible; eb 1806; em 1841; on NEAL, HACKETT, TURPIN, WRIGHT,
    HILLAND, DAVIS, COULLOURN, HUDSON; res Dor. Co., MD; pub DCGM 4-3:17.
V015 VINCENT Bible; eb 1843; on JONES, CORDDRY, BRATTON; res Snow Hill, MD;
    pub DAR (MdGRC 10:34).
V016 VON KAPFF Bible; pd 1803; eb 1770; em 1804; on RODEWALD, EFFLER, MOTZ,
    MAGRUDER; dep MHS/FCA (127).
V017 VOSHELL-MALCOLM Bible; eb 1807; em 1809; res QA and Caro. Cos., MD; DE;
    pub MDG 23-3:77.

W001 WADDELL Bible; rs 1752-1934; dep MSA (G-412 with G-258).
W002 WAGNER Bible; eb 1879; em 1918; on COCKRAN, HALLOWELL, DRUMMOND, BECKER;
    pub DCGM 1-1:2.
W003 WALKER-CRADDOCK Bible; eb 1705; em 1731; on GARDNER, CRADDOCK;
    res Balto. Co., MD; Peterhead, Scotland; dep MHS/FCA.
W004 WALCHER Bible; eb 1839; em 1863; on PEAK, KINDER; dep BCGS (500).
W005 WALDROP Bible; eb 1879; em 1878; on DAVIS, HENRY; pub MBR 2:150.
W006 WALKER Bible; eb 1768; em 1767; on MORRIS, MORSE, ROBART, BARDWELL;
    pub DAR (MdGRC 8:168).
W007 WALKER Bible; eb 1834; on GASSAWAY; res IN; dep MHS.
W008 WALKER Bible; eb 1866; em 1865; on BOONE, GRIFFIN, TARR;
    res Talb. Co., MD; dep MHS/FCA (Eason).
W009 WALKINS Bible; rs 1689-1957; dep MSA (G-569).
W010 WALL Bible; rs 1770-1887; on ESTEP, WHEATLEY; dep MSA (G-544).
W011 John WALL Bible; eb 1782; em 1781; on COLE, ELLERBEE, COVINGTON, LEAK;
    pub MBR 2:140.
W012 WALLACE Bible; eb 1752; see McKee-Black M084 at BCGS.
W013 S.A. WALLACE Bible; eb 1811; em 1842; on WILSON DAVIS;
    dep MHS (HBFR,4).
W014 WALLACE Bible; pd 1870; eb 1842; em 1868; on HOWLETT, SCARBOROUGH, HEAPS,
    KEARNE, BAY, THOMAS, MICKEL; res Harf. Co., MD; dep BCGS (from DAR).
W015 WALLER Bible; eb 1731; em 1761; on CARR, McGRAW, REDD, KING, COOPER,
    BARKSDALE, DUNCAN, MORRISON, STAPLES; pub MBR 2:134.
W016 Edward WALLER Bible; eb 1754; em 1786; on CALAS; res Stafford Co., VA;
    pub MBR 2:129.
W017 WALLING Bible; pd 1802; eb 1789; em 1809; on WOLTZ; pub DAR (MdGRC 33:95).
W018 WALLIS Bible; pd 1806; eb 1804; em 1799; on COMEGYS, PALMER, THOMAS,
    MAXWELL, BOYER, BILLINGSLEY, SMITH, KENADY, WAFFORD, CREIGHTON,
    LEITCH, PHILLIPS, SCHUTT, RASIN; res Caro. Co., MD; dep MHS/FCA (128).
W019 WALLIS Bible; eb 1850; em 1849; on GIFFIN, MATHER, MEREDITH; dep MHS/FCA.
W020 WALLIS Bible; eb 1865; dep MHS/FCA (128) poor photocopy.
W021 WALSTON Bible; pd 1875; eb 1871; dep MHS/FCA .
W022 WALTER-HINKLE Bible; on HINKLE, DOWNIE; res Bucks Co., PA; dep HCGS.
W023 WALTERS Bible; rs 1777-1833; dep VSL 3240 (acc #20886).
W024 WALTZ-HAEMER Bible; eb 1783; on HAEMER; BCGS (MBR II:131).
W025 WAMPLER Bible; pd 1761; eb 1763; on GARDNER, MILLER, GARRIGUES; res Carr.
    Co., MD; dep CCGS.
W026 WAMPLER Bible; pd 1852; eb 1794; pub MGB 2:18.
W027 WARD Bible; eb 1809; em 1834; on GOVER, WEBB, KEY, WOOD;
    dep MHS/FCA (Jackson, E.W. Chart).

BIBLES

W028 William H. WARD Bible; pd 1871; eb 1813; em 1833; res Mont. Co., MD;
     pub DAR (MdGRC 33).
W029 WARD Bible; eb 1813; em 1879; on POOL; res Carr. Co., MD; dep CCGS (5).
W030 WARD Bible; rs 1834-1900; res AA Co., MD; dep MSA (G-650).
W031 WARD Bible; eb 1849; em 1848; on HOPKINS, MARSHALL; res Dor. Co., MD;
     pub BCGM 3-4:10.
W032 WARD Bible: rs 1882-1962; pd 1882; on ABRAMS, BAILEY, BARLOW, BELL,
     BONEY, CHANDLER, FLOYD, FOSS, GIBB, GLADSTONE, LEWIS, MATHIAS,
     MILLER, MURPHY, PENLAND, REMSEN, ROBINS; res MD; NJ; FL;
     dep VSL (#3261, acc. #30453).
W032 WARD Bible: rs 1882-1962; pd 1882; dep VSL (#3261, acc. #30453).
W033 WARFIELD Bible; rs 1750-1957; res AA Co., MD; dep MSA (G-711).
W034 WARFIELD Bible; rs 1771-1935; dep MSA (G-921).
W035 WARFIELD Bible; pd 1815; eb 1780; em 1792; on THOMAS, GRAY, HOOK, HOFFMAN,
     COCKEY, SNOWDEN, GRIFFITH, DORSEY, pub BMGS 26-2:185;
     dep MHS/FCA; dep BCGS.
W036 Cecilius Edwin WARFIELD Bible; pd 1876; eb 1844; em 1870; res How. &
     Fred. Cos., MD; pub NGSQ 57-1:34.
W037 Rev. Dr. John WARFIELD Bible; pd 1876; eb 1900; em 1932; on MYER, THOMAS,
     SPRAGENS, HAMILTON, BARCLAY; pub NGSQ 57:1:32; pub MDG 8-1:17.
W038 WARLICK Bible; rs 1783-1882; dep MSA (G-334).
W039 WARNER Bible; pd 1830; eb 1834; em 1833; on NACH; pub DAR (MdGRC 13:179).
W040 WASHINGTON Records; eb 1671; em 1691; on TOWNSHEND, STROTHER, HARPER,
     THOMPSON, MAUPIN; res VA; pub DAR (MdGRC 1:79).
W041 WATERMAN Bible; pd 1866; eb 1838; em 1867; on GILBERT, GREENLAND; dep BCGS.
W042 WATERS Bible; rs 1785-1859; res Mont. Co., MD; dep MSA (G-205).
W043 WATKINS Bible; rs 1689-1957; dep MSA (G-569).
W044 Not assigned.
W045 WATKINS Bible; eb 1743; em 1762; pub DAR Mag. Jan. 1967 p.26.
W046 WATKINS-PARSONS Bible; pd 1858; eb 1778; em 1799; on PARSONS, BRYAN,
     CHERRICKS, BRICE, WHEELER, LEE; res Kent Co., MD;
     pub DAR (MdGRC 7:318).
W047 WATKINS Bible; rs 1780-1870; dep MSA (G-570:1).
W048 WATKINS Bible; rs 1803-1930; on CRONMILLER, HARDY, BANSEMER, SMITH,
     HALVERSON, HUTTON, CONNER, MARBURY, STEIGER, GRAVATTE, GARDNER;
     dep HCGS.
W049 WATKINS Bible; pd 1882; eb 1856; em 1882; on FOUNER, ZILE, MYERS, HIGH;
     res Carr. Co., Balto., MD; pub BMGS 11:147.
W050 WATKINS Bible; rb 1862; on PHELPS, YEWELL; res Wilks Co., NC; dep HCGS.
     Note: May be two Bibles.
W051 William WATSON Bible; eb 1806; on NORRIS, AMOSS, HOOPES, BALDWIN, HARLAN;
     pub CMF 2:50.
W052 William V. WATSON Bible; eb 1899; em 1898; on RAWLINGS, FOWLER, BOWEN,
     ARMIGER, GRIFFIN; pub O'Brien p.312.
W053 WALTERS Bible; eb 1751; em 1778; pub NGSQ 28-3:89.
W054 WAUGH Bible; eb 1755; em 1779; on THOMPSON, BOWERS; pub MBR 2:132.
W055 WAYSON Bible; rs 1865-1900; dep MSA (G-607).
W056 Foster WEBB Bible; eb 1735; em 1775; pub MBR 2:147.
W057 WEBB Bible; rs 1816-1900; dep MSA (G-507).
W058 WEBER Bible; eb 1749; em 1805; on WOLTZ; res Wash. Co., MD; Shepherdstown,
     VA (now WVA); pub NGSQ 59-4:302.
W059 WEBSTER-GLOVER Bible; eb 1815; em 1837; on JACOBS, DEEDS; dep BCGS in
     Yingling.
W060 WEBSTER Bible; pd 1845; eb 1845; em 1844; on SMITHSON; dep BCGS.
W061 Not assigned.
W062 WEEMS Bible; pd 1838; eb 1725; em 1777; dep MSA (G-654).

81

INVENTORY OF MARYLAND BIBLE RECORDS

W063 WEIL Bible; cb 1811; em 1842; res Balto., MD; dep MHS/FCA.
W064 WELCH Bible; rs 1753-1942; res Annapolis, MD; dep MSA (G-192:1).
W065 WELK Bible; pd 1860; eb 1800; on GIST; res Carr. Co., MD; dep CCGS.
W066 WELKER Bible; rs 1760-1831; on KORNDORFFEIN, RULE; res MD; PA;
      dep NGSQ (Bible Rec. Coll.).
W067 WELLS Bible; pd 1869; eb 1799; em 1824; on HARROP, HARKNESS, REDDEN,
      HAMILTON, BUTTER; pub MGB 15:47.
W068 WELLS Bible; pd 1611; eb 1723; on GREEN, CLARK; dep MHS/FCA.
W069 WELLS Bible; rb 1790; dep HCGS.
W070 WELLS-DAWKINS Bible; pd 1811; eb 1712; em 1800; on DAWKINS;
      pub DAR Mag., Aug-Sept 1970, p.694.
W071 WELLS (ex-Dupuis) Bible; pd 1712; eb 1752; on GOLD, WHITE, BERNARD;
      res Balto., MD; pub MMG 1-1:9.
W072 WELSH Bible; em 1805; on WATERS, CARR, JONES, DORSEY, EDMONSTON;
      res Hyattsville, MD; pub DAR (MdGRC 25:2); dep MHS/FCA.
W073 WELSH Bible; eb 1812; em 1837; on MUNROE, HAZE, BAUGH; pub MBR 2:133.
W074 WELSON Bible; pd 1811; eb 1773; em 1800; on SEYMOUR, HUTTON, SAKERS,
      FISHER; res Petersburg, WV; dep AAGS.
W075 WELTON Bible; pd 1843; eb 1798; em 1817; on SEYMOUR, HUTTON, SAKERS,
      FISHER; dep AAGS.
W076 Michael WELTY Bible; pd 1827; eb 1840; em 1839; on SOUTH; res Wash. Co.,
      MD; pub MDG 7-2:31.
W077 WENTZ Bible; eb 1717; res Carr. Co., MD; York and Adams Cos. PA;
      dep MHS/FCA (typed copy).
W078 WENTZEL Bible; rb 1850; res Balto. Co., MD; dep HCGS.
W079 Rev. William WEST Bible; eb 1795; em 1725; res Balto., MD; pub GKF 2:613.
W080 WEST Bible; eb 1704; em 1725; on WALKER, GARDNER, HARRISON, HALLEY,
      HOWARD; res St.M. & Harf. Cos., MD; dep MHS/FCA (Howard-Sears Coll).
W081 WEST Bible; pd 1680; eb 1677; res VA; pub DAR (MdGRC 1:106) typed copy.
W082 WEST Bible; pd 1680; eb 1707; em 1711; pub MMG 2:477.
W083 WEST Bible; pd 1874; eb 1837; em 1869; on BLAMIRE, MARR, CLARKE, WASBORN;
      res Balto., Co., MD; dep AAGS; dep MHS/FCA.
W084 WEST Bible; dep MHS/FCA.
W085 WEST-OREM Bible; pd 1857; eb 1884; em 1870; on OREM; res Balto., Co., MD;
      dep MHS/FCA (transcript).
W086 WETHERILL Bible; rb 1804; on BROWN, PENNINGTON, MacLEAN, WEBBER, MATTHEWS,
      SORBOUGH, MAGNESS, FRANCIS, BLACKBURN, HESS, MURDOCK, GLADDEN, KIRK,
      MYERS, AMOSS, SEWELL, BOSLEY; WATTERS, RICHARDSON, JOHNSON, DUFF,
      SCHMIDT, THOMPSON; res MD; dep HCGS.
W087 Not assigned.
W088 WHAYLAND Bible; pd 1844; eb 1811; em 1829; on BRICE, CAMP, CARILLE,
      CALLEN, WELCH, WICKES; dep BCGS (#505).
W089 WHEATLEY Bible; eb 1837; em 1861; on MESSICK, LAMBDON, LLOYD;
      res Som. Co., MD; pub MDG 1-1:19.
W090 WHEELER Bible; pd 1890; eb 1840; em 1891; on ARMACOST, NEUSSINGER, WELSH;
      res Balto. Co., MD; IN; dep MHS/FCA (132); dep BCGS (in Yingling).
W091 WHEELER-BIXLER Bible; pd 1858; eb 1792; em 1837; on BIXLER, SHAMBERGER;
      dep MHS/FCA (Box 132); dep BCGS (in Yingling)
W092 WHIPS Bible; pd 1816; eb 1670; em 1825; on SHIPLEY, BRENGMAN, HALL, RUDY,
      FISHER, HANEY, GRUSE; res Calv. Co., MD; KS; England;
      pub BCGS 17-3:165-166.
W093 WHIPS Bible; pd 1813; eb 1814; em 1812; on DAVIS, WIFORD, LACEY, FRANCE,
      GOODIN, BENNET, FRANTY, EBERLY, ANKENY, DEXTER, STOHLER, HOFFMAN;
      res MD; OH; IN; pub BMGS 17-3:167.

W094 Joseph WHITAKER Bible; eb 1790; em 1844; on WAGEMAN; res Hamilton Co., OH;
     pub DAR (MdGRC 8:19).
W095 WHITE Bible; eb 1745; res Calv., Cecil Cos., MD; pub NGSQ 2-1:6.
W096 WHITE-GOLD Bible; pd 1798; eb 1760; em 1762; on GOLD; res Balto. MD; MA;
     NY; pub MGB 7:16.
W097 Zachariah WHITE Bible; eb 1794; em 1814; on BLACKWOOD, BUCHANAN, WOOD,
     COPELAND, KELLY, GAINES; pub MRB 2:156.
W098 WHITE Bible; rs 1795-1901; MSA (G-345).
W099 John WHITE Bible; eb 1798; em 1824; on HALL, STEEL, CURRIER, BEJAMIN,
     BURNER, EAGLSTON, PRESTON; dep BCGS.
W100 WHITE Bible; pd 1843; eb 1854; em 1847; on GIBSON, BAILY; res Kent Island,
     MD; dep CCGS (#17).
W101 Jame F. WHITE Bible; pd 1872; eb 1861; em 1860; on EAGLESTON; dep BCGS.
W102 WHITNEY Bible; inss 1790; eb 1714; on TULL; res Som. Co., MD; pub MGB 17:37.
W103 WHITSON Bible; rb 1825; on HUNTSBERRY, CLOUGHLIN, ANDERSON; dep HCGS.
W104 WHITSON Bible; rb 1838, on GODFREY, HAYDEN; dep HCGS.
W105 WHITTINGHAM Bible; pd 1853; eb 1843; em 1841; on BEALE, JAMESON, NEWLEET,
     JONES, KELLY, GEAREY; res Phila., and Bucks Co., PA;
     dep MGS Library (typed copy).
W106 WHITTINGTON-JONES Bible; eb 1865; on JONES, CUNNINGHAM, ENGERLITH, THOMAS,
     GRADNER; dep MHA/FCA.
W107 John WHORLEY Jr. Bible; pd 1824; eb 1832; em 1830; on KENNEDY, SHAGGS,
     DALEY, GREENWALT, CAUFFMAN, JOHNSON; pub DAR (MdGRC 6:203).
W108 WHORLEY Bible; pd 1811; eb 1808; em 1808; on TICE; res Phila. PA;
     pub DAR (MdGRC 6:203).
W109 Solomon WIATT Bible; pd 1803; eb 1744; em 1778; on NORTH, NEADELS,
     BRANSON, WARNER, MARTIN, BOWEN, BARNHART, FISHER, WOOD; res DE;
     NJ; pub MGB 13:23; 14-1,23.
W110 Simon WICKES Bible; pub CC 10-1:16 (1983-84).
W111 WICKES Bible; pd 1850; eb 173(?); em 1755; on ADAMS, BLAKE, BRANHAM,
     de FLOUW, FREEMAN, GILL, HUTCHISON, HURTT, MERRITT, NICHOLS, ROGERS,
     SAYER, SPENCER, STERN, WESTCOTT, WETHERED; dep BCGS (#506).
W112 WICKES Bible; eb 1862; em 1821; on CHAMBERS, GREEN, TILGHMAN, GRIFFIN,
     WELSH; res Kent Co., MD; PA;
     pub DAR (MdGRC 12:90); pub KBT p.1.
W113 WIER Bible; pd 1849; eb 1811; em 1841; on CUSHING, WAYLAND, JOHNSON,
     McMANUS, ELLICOTT, BOYD, MAYNARD, YATES; res Balto., MD; Ireland;
     dep MHS/FCA.
W114 John WILCOX Bible; eb 1728; em 1771; on BUTTLER, LEA; pub MBR 2:142.
W115 WILCOX Bible; eb 1830; em 1829; on ROSE, STRIBLE; dep MHS/FCA.
W116 WILCOXEN Records; eb 1723; em 1769; res PG Co., MD; pub NGSQ 6:(?).
W117 WILEY Bible; pd 1801; eb 1769; em 1796; on McNEIL, TINSDALE, MORRELL,
     ESTEP, KEECH; dep MHS/FCA.
W118 WILEY-EVANS Bible; rb 1819; on EVANS, SMITH, KITTERWWILL, GALBREATH,
     McCONKEY, DONNAN, ALEXANDER, WHITE, COLE, DUNNUCK, KAUFFETT;
     res York Co., PA; dep HCGS.
W119 WILHIDE Bible; eb 1854; em 1875; on DEVILBISS, GAUGH; res Creagerstown, MD;
     dep MHS/FCA (has clippings).
W120 James F. WILKINS Bible; eb 1810; em 1831; on TUXWORTH, TREW, WALLIS,
     SIMPERS; pub DAR (MdGRC 7:279).
W121 Thomas WILKINS Bible; pd 1816; eb 1803; em 1802; on FRAZIER, BECK,
     WILKINS; res Kent Co., MD; pub DAR (MdGRC 7:276).
W122 WILKINESS Bible; eb 1753; em 1782; on KEMP, SHIELDS, JONES, JOINER;
     res Kent Co., MD; pub KBG1 p.16.
W123 WILKINS Bible; pd 1848; eb 1764; em 1831; on TUXWORTH, TREW, WALLIS,

W123 WILKINS Bible, contd.; on SIMPERS, FRAZIER; res Kent Co., MD; KBT p.18.
W124 WILKINS Bible; pd 1812; eb 1803; em 1802; on FRAZIER, BECK; res Kent Co., MD; KBG1 p.15.
W125 James WILKINSON Bible; eb 1739; em 1760; on BURNETT; pub MBR 2:129-130.
W126 WILKINSON Bible; eb 1784; em 1807; pub NGSQ 10-2:94.
W127 WILKINSON Bible; eb 1794; em 1819; on NANCE, ATWELL, HAMMET; res Calv. Co., MD; dep MHS/FCA.
W128 WILKINSON Bible; pd 1873; eb 1835; em 1871; on HOLLYDAY; res MD; MO; dep MHS/FCA.
W129 WILKINSON Bible; pd 1842; eb 1844; em 1843; on CHIPLEY, GREENLEE, BEAVEN, ANDERSON, FRAZIER, RICHARD; res QA and Balto. Cos., MD; dep MHS/FCA.
W130 WILKINSON Bible; pd 1848; eb 1884; em 1849; on DEROCHEBRUNE, BUSTEED, PERRY, McFEELEY; res QA Co., MD; dep MHS/FCA.
W131 William D. WILLARD Bible; pd 1879; eb 1821; on SCANLAND, COFFEY, HILL, KREH; res Fred. Co., MD; VA; MO; pub DAR (MdGRC 33:124).
W132 WILLERT Bible; pd 1773; eb 1784; dep MHS/FCA.
W133 WILLHAM Bible; rs 1740-1957; dep MSA (G-711).
W134 WILLIAMS Bible; eb 1708; em 1732; on HOWELL, MAY, DAVIS, BURNAP, HAWKINS, BONAPARTE; dep MHS/FCA.
W135 WILLIAMS Bible; pd 1841; eb 1825; em 1779; on STUMP, WILSON, COSTEN, NEILSON, McFADON; dep MHS/FCA.
W136 WILLIAMS Bible; eb 1780; em 1802; on DUVALL, STALEY, SHEPHERD, ANDREW; dep MHS/FCA.
W137 WILLIAMS Bible; eb 1782; em 1809; on BARNEY, DALRYMPLE, REMINGTON; res MD; Roxbury, MA; dep MHS/FCA.
W138 WILLIAMS Bible; eb 1814; pub QMF 2:44.
W139 WILLIAMS Bible; inss 1866; eb 1796; on TOWNSEND; dep MHS/FCA.
W140 WILLIAMS Bible; pd 1866; eb 1839; em 1839; on TOWNSEND, WHITE, WAPELS; dep MHS/FCA.
W141 WILLIAMS Bible; eb 1844; em 1842; on KENSEY, STOREY; dep MHS/FCA.
W142 Lloyd W. WILLIAMS Bible; pd 1845; rs 1787-1893, on BROCKENBROUGH, HIRLINGS, PORTTICK; res Balto. MD; PA; dep VSL (#3414, acc. #30453).
W143 Thomas J. WILLIAMS Bible; rb 1843; on SCARBOROUGH, WILSON, THOMAS, NIGHTENGALE, OLFIELD, JOHNSON, BURGER, HUBEL, LINDSTROM, JORDEN, BUTTON, DEMPSEY, MACOMBER, HEPFORD, MAKAN, FISHER, NORTON, SIMS, SEIBERS, BOSS; res Delta, PA; dep HCGS.
W144 Elijah WILLIAMSON Bible; eb 1754; em 1782; on BIRD; pub MBR 2:151.
W145 WILLIAMSON Bible; eb 1865; em 1836; on SEEKAMP, YOUNG, TROUP, MULLAN, SPENCER, MONTGOMERY; res Balto. MD; dep MHS/FCA.
W146 WILLING Bible; eb 1810; em 1835; pub DAR Mag. March 1981.
W147 WILLIS Bible; pd 1749; eb 1754; on COLLINS; dep MHS/FCA.
W148 WILLMOT Bible; pd 1773; eb 1785; em 1777; on BOWEN, TALBOTT; dep MHS/FCA.
W149 WILLSON Bible; pd 185(?); eb 1738; em 1762; on PERRY, MAGRUDER; pub DAR (MdGRC 10:272).
W150 WILLSON-SAPPINGTON Bible; pd 1911; eb 1864; em 1865; on WIKES, CHANCE, MORRIS, BLACKISTON, SAPPINGTON; res Kent Co., MD; pub MDG 25:118.
W151 WILLSON Bible; pd 1876; eb 1865; on SAPPINGTON, WICKES, CHANCE, MORRIS; pub DAR (MdGRC 11:123).
W152 WILMER Bible; pd 1809; eb 1787; on COOMBE, THOMAS, FARRON, MEGREDY, WILSON, HOLLIDAY; res Cecil Co., MD; dep MHS/FCA.
W153 WILMOT Bible; rs 1753-1798; dep MSA (D-553).
W154 James WILSON Bible; pd 1768; eb 1744; em 1766; on GLASGOW, ELZEY, POLK, McCLEMMING; dep MHS/FCA.

BIBLES

W155 Benjamin WILSON Bible; eb 1747; em 1770; on RUDDELL, DAVISON;
        pub MBR 2:154.
W156 John Kidd WILSON Bible; eb 1748; em 1778; on GITTINGS, MARLE, EDWARDS,
        SLEE, FERGUSON; dep MHS/FCA.
W157 John WILSON Bible; eb 1756; em 1783; on ROBERTSON; pub MBR 2:137.
W158 WILSON Bible; eb 1763; em 1787; on PICKETT, LONG; res Caro. Co.;
        pub MBR 2:152.
W159 WILSON Bible; eb 1771; em 1801; on MANIFOLD, GLADDEN, ANDERSON, WILEY,
        WALLACE, KILGORE, GALBREATH, JAMES; res York Co., PA;
        dep MHS (HBFR,8).
W159A WILSON Bible; on MANIFORD, GLADDEN, ANDERSON, WILEY, WALLACE,
        KILGORE, GALBREATH, ALEXANDER, WETHERILL, FORD, FREDERICK,
        PENNINGTON, JAMES; res York Co., PA; dep HCGS.
W160 Hezekiah WILSON Diary; eb 1785; em 1784; res Mont. Co., MD; pub NGSQ 6:27.
W161 WILSON Bible; eb 1804; em 1893; on WHALEY, THOMAS; res Balto. MD, VA;
        pub BMGS 19-1:25; dep MHS/FCA.
W162 WILSON Bible; rs 1816-1943; res Cecil Co., MD;
        dep MSA (G-205:16, with D-150).
W163 WILSON Bible; rb 1821; on SCARBOROUGH, CURTIS, FOARD, DAVIS;
        res Balto. Co., MD; dep HCGS.
W164 Simeon WILSON Bible; eb 1822; em 1848; on WARREN; res Clark Co., KY;
        pub MBR 2:152.
W165 WILSON Bible; eb 1822; em 1851; on DEAVERS; pub MBR 2:149.
W166 WILSON Bible; pd 1857; eb 1835; em 1863; on RISTEAU; dep MHS/FCA.
W167 WILSON Bible; eb 1847; res Cecil Co., MD; dep MHS/FCA (6).
W168 WILSON Bible; eb 1851; em 1848; on APPLETON, WADE; res Balto., MD;
        Portland, ME; dep MHS/FCA.
W169 John WILT Bible; eb 1775; on MAYHUE, BROWN, JONES, McFATHON, MILLER,
        HOOVER, HOOK, HOWELL; res Garrett Co., MD; pub MGB 8:31.
W170 WINDER Bible; pd 1838; eb 1798; em 1820; on LLOYD, THOBURN, BECHANAN,
        PENNINGTON; res Talb. Co., MD; dep MHS/FCA.
W171 WINDER Bible; pd 1841; eb 1821; em 1820; on LLOYD, THOBURN, BUCHANAN,
        STUMP, PENNINGTON; res Talb. Co., Balto., MD; dep MHS/FCA.
W172 WINEBURGER Bible; eb 1772; em 1803; on BOOSE, FLENNER, WILLIAMS, MYERS,
        LUSBY, HAWKINS, ALDRIDGE, STORM; dep MHS/FCA.
W173 WINGATE Bible; eb 1802; em 1823; on TREGOE; res Dor. Co., MD;
        pub DCGM 3-3:7.
W174 John WINGFIELD Bible; eb 1723; em 1744; res Hanover Co., VA;
        pub MBR 2:146.
W175 WISE Bible; eb 1808; em 1834; on FLOYD, EVANS, JACOB; dep MHS/FCA.
W176 William WITHERS Bible; eb 1731; em 1761; on WRIGHT; pub MBR 2:145.
W177 WITHERS Bible; eb 1828; em 1851; on COLLIER, PEEBLES, HOWELL, SCULL,
        TRIMBLE, RICHARDSON; pub MBR 2:143.
W178 WITT Bible; eb 1775; dep MHS/FCA (original in German).
W179 WOLF Bible; eb 1760; res Wash. Co., MD; pub NGSQ 25-3:93.
W180 Conrad WOLF Bible; pd 1817; eb 1814; em 1812; on SNYDER, McCLAIN;
        pub DAR (MdGRC 33:115).
W181 WOLFE Bible; eb 1872; on WRIGHT, CHANEY; res Fred. Co., MD;
        pub BMGS 23-3:258.
W182 WOMBLE Bible; eb 1807; on AVERT, LAWRENCE, BOOTHE, GRIFFIN;
        dep MHS/FCA (Box 44 "Eldridge").
W183 WOOD Bible; eb 1818; em 1848; on LEFINBY, DILL, HAGUE, BRAMBLE, DUYER,
        NEWTON; pub DAR (MdGRC 11:78).
W184 Henry Hobbs WOOD Bible; pd 1829; eb 1771; em 1813; on BARTON, MERRIKEN;
        res Balto., MD; pub MGB 11:23.

85

W185 John Wesley WOOD; eb 1854; em 1949; on ROBINSON, HUTCHINS, LERT, LANKFORD; pub O'Brien p.313.
W186 Lewellen WOOD; rs 1843-1973; pd 1872; on PARKINSON; res MD; VA; GA; dep VSL (#480, acc. #30434).
W187 WOOD Bible; eb 1867; em 1872; res Germantown, PA; dep BCGS (transcript).
W188 WOODLAND Bible; eb 1738; em 1813; on MOODY, TOBIN, HURLEY; pub DAR (MdGRC 13:112).
W189 James WOODS Bible; eb 1743; em 1779; on GARLAND; pub MBR 2:138.
W190 William WOODS Bible; eb 1784; em 1817; on WILSON, JOHNSON; pub MBR 2:139.
W191 WOODS Bible; rs 1815-1909; on CREIGH, DORSEY, LUPTON, MORRIS, WATTS; res MD; WV; AL; dep VSL (#3491, acc.#30414).
W192 WOODWARD Bible; eb 1786; em 1809; on TOMPKINS, SWEENY, BANGS, KNOTT, LYMAN, GASKINS, BALLARD, HARRY, MITCHELL, McPHERSON, BARBER, WILLIAMS, GRIFFIN, TAYLER, SOMERVILLE; res Georgetown, Mont. Co., MD, (now DC); dep AAGS; dep MHS/FCA.
W193 Abner WOOLARD Bible: rs 1852-1924; VSL (#3508, acc. #30315).
W194 WOOLFORD Bible; pd 1833; eb 1802; em 1837; pub MDG 20-4:123.
W195 WOOLSEY Bible; rs 1812-1888; res NY; IO; MA; Nova Scotia; dep MSA (G-560:107 with D-150).
W196 WORTHEN Bible; eb 1804; pub DAR (MdGRC 5:8) typed copy.
W197 WORTHINGTON Record; pd 1729; eb 1713; em 1728; pub BMGS 23-1:73.
W198 WRIGHT Bible; eb 1756; em 1756; on McCOTTER; res Dor. Co., MD; pub DCGM 1-4:10.
W199 WRIGHT Bible; eb 1793; em 1781; on TURPIN, ALLEN; res Dor. & Som. Cos., MD; pub DCGM 4-3:18.
W200 WRIGHT Bible; eb 1818; em 1836; res Chas. Co., MD; pub NGSQ 69-4:250.
W201 John WYATT Bible; eb 1744; em 1772; on SUMMIT; res Spotsylvania Co.,VA; London, England; pub MBR 2:135.
W202 WUNNE Bible; eb 1788; em 1813; on JEFFREYS, FURMAN; res NC; GA; dep MHS.

Y001 YODER Bible; rb 1871; res IN; dep HCGS.
Y002 YINGLING Bible; eb 1852; em 1889; on BUSH, GRAYBILL, GREEN, EYLER, THOMAS, BAINBRIDGE; res Carr. Co., MD; PA; dep BCGS (in Yingling).
Y003 Richard YOUNG Bible; eb 1816; em 1815; on BERRY, MAGRUDER, WALKER, COX, MANNING; pub DAR Mag., Oct. 1980 p.1034.
Y004 YOUNG Bible; pd 1747; eb 1735; on WESTON, LEWIS, MONKS, LONEY; res Harf. and Calv. Cos., MD; pub MGB 16:15, 24, 52, 61.
Y005 James YOUNG Bible; inss 1883; eb 1863; on FERGUSON; res MD; Peterhead, Scotland; dep BCGS.
Y006 YOUNG Bible; pd 1794; eb 1714; on BEDFORD, BUCHANAN, COUCHER, PURCELL, SANGER; dep MHS/FCA (137).
Y007 YOUNG Bible; eb 1850; em 1847; on GREEN; res Balto., MD; dep MHS/FCA.
Y008 YOUNG-BAKER Bible; pd 1816; eb 1792; em 1791; on MOSER, WHEELER, WOOLFORD, BAKER, FEARSON, PICKERSGILL; dep MHS/FCA (137).
Y009 YOUNG-BEDFORD Bible; pd 1786; eb 1714; on FLOWER, THOMPSON, RENSHAW, SMITH, COULSON, GILBERT; res Balto., MD; Phila., PA; pub GPF 3:433.
Y010 YOUNG Bible; eb 1764; em 1737; on WOODWARD, HESSELIUS; pub MGB 2:510.
Y011 YOUNKIN Bible; pd 1871; em 1868; on HORNER; res Meyersdale, PA; dep AAGS; dep MHS/FCA.
Y012 Not assigned.
Y013 James YULE Bible; eb 1755; em 1779; on CHRISTMAN; res Balto.,MD; Ireland; pub NEHG Reg 88:92.

Z001 ZAISER-MAISEL Bible; rs 1865-1978; pd 1895; eb 1865; em 1891; on WADDELL, MAISEL, BAUERNSCHMIDT, BROOKS, FEHRMEN, SPARHAWK; res Catonsville and Glenelg, MD.; pub HCMR 5:80-81.

Z002 ZELLER Bible; eb 1819; em 1834; on CUNNINGHAM, KOHR, WILKES; res Wash. Co., MD; Winchester, VA; dep BOGS (526).

Z003 ZENTZ Bible; pd 1852; eb 1800; em 1845; on YEAGERLINE; res Silver Run, MD; Littlestown, PA; dep COGS (35).

Z004 J.E. ZIMMERMAN Bible; rs 1852-1946; on BEAUMONT, KAISER; dep VSL (#3579, acc. 30453).

Z005 ZOUCK Bible; pd 1850; eb 1835; em 1883; on DIVAN, WILMA, ARMACOST, SCHULTZ, ALBAN, HALE; res Balto. Co., MD; pub BMGS 23-3:256; dep MHS/FCA.

Z006 ZUG Bible; eb 1760; res Wash. Co., MD; PA; pub NGSQ 25-3:93.

Surname	Bibles			
AARON	A010			
ABBEY	C030			
ABBOT	G093	N016		
ABBOTT	G139	H115	S043	
ABEL	C045	P064		
ABELL	B141	H291	H294	
ABLE	F020			
ABRAMS	W032			
ABREHLER	S115			
ACTON	B271			
ADAMS	B028	B123	B153	
	B217	B225	B273	C200	CO73
	D085	D100	F003	G082	G100
	G113	H004	H125	H127	H173
	H283	H293	K039	K064	S068
	S105	U005	W111		
ADAMSON	F070			
ADDISON	H164			
ADEMS	F019			
ADKINS	N004			
ADREAN	B033			
ADRIAN	A069			
ADY	K003			
AFFLICK	M010			
AINSWORTH	D114	D115		
AIREY	G041			
AITKEN	H076			
AKEHURST	N001			
ALBAN	B052	Z005		
ALBAUGH	D012	M122	M181	
	S125	S127	S128	
ALBERT	B042	B043	S008	
	S162			
ALBOUGH	C046			
ALDERMAN	J002			
ALDRIDGE	C054	F048	W172	
ALEINE	R016			
ALER	A037	H246		
ALEXANDER	C001	F040	R015	
	T045	W118	W163	
ALFORD	B132	M030		
ALKER	O003			
ALKIN	K023			
ALLBEE	F019			
ALLEIN	F071	F072		
ALLEN	B336	D011	E032	
	G031	G093	H246	M030	M067
	R014	S079	U005	W199	
ALLERDICE	M098			
ALLISON	E008	J056		
ALLMAND	T001			
ALLNUT	B004	M146		
ALLNUTT	F070			

Surname	Bibles			
ALLUISI	G129			
ALMY	B323			
ALVAN	F083			
ALVERDA	E033			
ALVIN	P039			
AMBERG	S170			
AMOS	K035	R094		
AMOSS	H288	R045	S118	
	WO51	W086		
ANDERSON	B075	C102	D050	
	D133	D171	H079	H148	L075
	M135	P006	P052	R078	T008
	U001	W103	W129	W159	W159A
	N024A			
ANDERTON	H065			
ANDREW	J047	W136		
ANDREWS	E073			
ANES	H112A	H161		
ANGELL	C048			
ANGIER	C103			
ANKENY	W093			
ANNEN	M081			
ANTHONY	A097	B129	E073	
ANTRAM	L031			
APPLETON	W168			
APPLING	L003			
APPOLD	D160			
APRINTIEL	N025			
ARCHER	C104	C105	E057	
	E058	G004	J048	
ARCHIBALD	G082			
ARDENGER	M074			
ARDINGER	G017			
ARGY	B229			
ARLUCEL	M062			
ARMACOST	P076	W090	Z005	
ARMAT	G120			
ARMIGER	H048	W052		
ARMOR	G029			
ARMSTRONG	B158	B340	B341	
	B343	C215	G020	J022	U006
ARNETT	N001			
ARNOLD	B129	J016	M164	
AROSEMENA	C158			
ARTHUR	H024	R016	R049	
ASBURY	J056			
ASH	E056	H274		
ASHCRAFT	T084			
ASHLY	C221			
ASHMAN	O007			
ASKEW	B002			
ASMUS	H141			
ATCHISON	C151	C152		
ATHEY	H090	H091	H092	

Surname	Bibles		
ATKINS	B015		
ATKINSON	B245	C117	P008
	T062		
ATTEE	J037		
ATTEWAY	M061		
ATWELL	W127		
AUGHENBAUGH	G100		
AUBLE	B121		
AULD	C164		
AULD	H084		
AURT	S134		
AUSTIN	C058	H218	
AVERILL	C047		
AVERLY	R086		
AVERT	W182		
AVERY	S063		
AXE	W053		
AYDELOTT	H260		
AYERS	A022		
AYRES	N017		
BABCOX	D061		
BABYLON	M178	M180	
BACHER	F063		
BACON	A059	B056	B134
	S178		
BAER	D119		
BAGGS	C109	N032	T021
BAGLEY	B257B	B258	
BAILE	D082	E044	
BAILEY	B323	H112A	H207
M113 M177	S008	S162	T035
	W032		
BAILY	W100		
BAINBRIDGE	Y002		
BAINES	H218		
BAINNER	B116		
BAINTER	M080		
BAKER	B176	B339	D062
E039 G008	G090	H197	H312
M121 P038	R079	S073	T041
	Y008		
BALDNER	P039		
BALDURN	E025		
BALDWIN	B150	B269	B297
C048 G142	H115	P032	R038
S011 T009	T030	W051	W053
BALKENS	M162		
BALL	CO83	E003	R054
BALLARD	C133	C230	W192
BALLES	F072		
BALLOU	P085		
BALTZELL	L077		
BANDEL	H200		

Surname	Bibles		
BANDER	N025		
BANE	H226	H232	
BANGS	B247	S119	
BANGS	W192		
BANKEN	K045		
BANKERT	C128	R020	
BANKS	M034	H258	
BANNER	S039	T061	
BANNING	T017		
BANNISTER	H135		
BANSEMER	C210	W048	
BARBER	F063	S173	T035
	W192		
BARBOUR	N025		
BARCLAY	C144	W037	
BARD	S082		
BARDWELL	W006		
BARE	W053		
BARGER	H120	S104	B058
BARKER	M070		
BARKSDALE	W015		
BARLEY	M116		
BARLOW	C151	C195	W032
BARMORE	M050	M051	
BARNARD	K064		
BARNES	A055	B028	B127
C076 D054	D082	E008	E045
G107 J002	K046	K047	L018
P014 P059	S059	S184	S185
S186 T040			
BARNETT	R048	S063	S067
BARNEY	C070	H245	W137
BARNHART	W109		
BARNHISER	G132		
BARNS	D001	H112A	L081
BARR	D139	D171	
BARRACKMAN	B107		
BARRATT	H283		
BARRETT	G143		
BARRICK	S047		
BARRON	C045	H237	
BARRY	H281		
BARTHOLOW	U005		
BARTLETT	B307	C007	
BARTLEY	C226		
BARTON	B348	E073	K027 W184
BARWICK	S179		
BASCOM	T076		
BASFORD	I005		
BASTER	C210		
BATCHER	R031		
BATES	C089	C197	D181
J039 N016	P017		
BATTEN	F060		

Surname	Bibles		
BATTLE	G047		
BAUBLITZ	E010	L032	
BAUCHTEL	H290		
BAUER	B219	L037	
BAUERMAN	S091		
BAUERNSCHMIDT	Z001		
BAUGH	S047	W073	
BAUGHER	R049		
BAUMGARDNER	D076		
BAXTER	B021	B036	B353
	0020		
BAY	C022	W014	
BAYARD	L044		
BAYLESS	B048		
BAYLEY	A055	B048	H161
	L017		
BAYLIE	B298		
BAYLOR	B350		
BAYLY	H126		
BAYNARD	B173		
BAYSINGER	T015		
BEACH	S001		
BEACHTEL	L045		
BEADENKOPF	G075		
BEAL	E070		
BEALE	W105		
BEALL	H209	M014	M136
BEAMAN	H286		
BEAR	S106		
BEARD	B186	C221	C222
	F019	K046	R074
BEARDSLEY	T054		
BEARY	B310		
BEASMAN	B120		
BEATLEY	S159		
BEATTY	B320	G063	H010
BEATY	G043	P078	
BEAUCHAMP	S016		
BEAUMONT	C195	Z004	
BEAVANS	L056		
BEAVEN	P018	W129	
BECHANAN	W170		
BECHTOLD	B219		
BECK	B089	C225	E039
J007	L005	S015	W121	W124
BECKER	G132	S001	W002
BECKETT	B088		
BECKLEY	S043		
BECKMAN	S112		
BECKWITH	B257B	B258	H265
BEDELL	S164		
BEDFORD	Y006		
BEDLOW	H218		
BEECHLEY	E012		

Surname	Bibles		
BEEKMAN	C144		
BEEKS	A009		
BEEMAN	R058		
BEJAMIN	W099		
BELL	B034	D148	H253
H260	L081	N003	P020	P028
P074	S015	S022	W032
BELLINGER	M001		
BELT	B007	D064	
BENNANZER	B146	H144	H144
BENNET	W093		
BENNETT	A058	A069	B333
C113	H054	M129	N016	S184
BENSON	B217	D154	E046
F074	G030	G082	G102	H125
H295	P036		
BENT	0014		
BENTON	K048	K049	K050
BERESFLOYD	J028		
BERGSGESSER	M088		
BERNARD	C125	W071	
BERRY	B242	B343	C187
D019	G097	H127	H305	Y003
BERSCH	S068		
BETTERTON	P075		
BETTES	B089		
BEVAN	C018		
BEVANS	T056		
BEVYLEY	T029		
BEYER	P075		
BIANCAVILLA	H141		
BIBB	C158	E017	
BIDDINGER	M038		
BIDDISON	B288		
BIDDLE	C229	E051	H274
	H282	T040	
BIGELOW	N020		
BIGGER	B134		
BIGGS	K060		
BILLINGS	M063	R042	
BILLINGSLEY	W018		
BILLUPS	B236		
BINGHAM	D128		
BINNANZER	H144		
BIRCH	0014		
BIRD	B338	K014	W144
BIRDAEL	C199		
BIRDSALL	M097		
BIRDWELL	D156		
BIRELY	G032		
BIRLEY	D065		
BIRT	B117		
BISBEE	D104		
BISCOE	D111		

Surname	Bibles		
BISHOP	D115	L056	S119
	T057		
BISPHAM	B320		
BITZBERGER	H151		
BIXLER	W091		
BLACK	C099	G104	G108
	L033		
BLACKBURN	H010	W086	
BLACKISTON	W150		
BLACKISTONE	B178		
BLACKLOCH	D177		
BLACKMAN	B297		
BLACKMORE	F012		
BLACKSHIRE	G114		
BLACKWELL	C074	C082	C136
	CO83	D148	H122
BLACKWOOD	W097		
BLADES	B181	L033	
BLAKE	A039	B004	B039
	L033	W111	
BLAKESLEE	S077		
BLAMIRE	W083		
BLANCHARD	E025	R064	
BLAND	D019	L012	
BLANDING	U006		
BLASS	S159		
BLEDSOE	T081		
BLENK	P079		
BLOCK	F018		
BLOODSWORTH	L070	P083	
BLOOM	B272		
BLOUNT	L041		
BLOW	B243		
BLOXOM	B148	D100	
BLOXSOME	H149		
BLUE	P052	P052	
BLUNT	B011	D059	H277
	S130		
BLYTHWOOD	B153		
BOARDLEY	D136		
BOESHAL	E036		
BOGGS	A031	B265	
BOHANNON	H010		
BOHANON	F024		
BOLES	B147		
BOLGIANO	B173	J060	
BOLTON	H196		
BOLVILL	J055		
BONAPARTE	W134		
BOND	G027	G093	K054
	R014		
BONEY	W032		
BONN	M135		
BONNAWILL	J045		

Surname	Bibles		
BONNER	A054	B075	M062
	R047	R048	
BONNETT	B219		
BONSAL	J015		
BONSELL	H026		
BOOKER	B134	H106	
BOOKHART	B171		
BOOKMAN	H162		
BOONE	B115	H063	J015
	N027	S153	W008
BOOSE	W172		
BOOTH	P093		
BOOTHE	W182		
BORASTON	B252		
BORCHERDING	D065		
BORDLEY	C078	F032	
BORING	H093		
BORMAN	B339		
BORROWS	C144		
BOSLEY	G027	K007	W086
BOSS	D128	W143	
BOSSEN	H214		
BOSTON	B111		
BOSWELL	P053		
BOTELER	M146		
BOUCHELLE	E051		
BOUGHAN	M034		
BOUGHERT	C144		
BOULDIN	C136	E016	M161
BOUNDS	B280	H207	L017
BOVEN	M146		
BOVEY	F090		
BOWDIN	B344		
BOWDLE	C040		
BOWDOIN	J005		
BOWE	C089		
BOWEN	D027	D066	D091
	D120 D134	E027	F007 G077
	G094 H133	H223	H309 H310
	M143 R038	S153	W052 W109
	W148		
BOWER	M081		
BOWERS	C059	G011	M026
	R037	W054	
BOWIE	C191	P032	
BOWLAND	H125		
BOWLES	L090		
BOWMAN	B153	D066	T027
BOWNESS	A005		
BOYD	A049	B176	G089
	H282 K056	L031	M036 S079
	S116 T057	W113	
BOYER	W018		
BOYERMAN	E064		

Surname		Bibles			Surname		Bibles		
BOYLE	H218	J056	S009		BRIEN	PO72			
BOYLEN	B021				BRIGG	E058			
BOYLES	S171				BRILEY	H006			
BOYS	T039				BRILHART	B001			
BRACH	F037				BRILL	S094			
BRACKER	S085				BRILLINGHAM	C195			
BRADFORD	G135				BRINKLEY	B265	G136		
BRADLEY	C123	C124	F089		BRINSFIELD	H007	J053		
HO10 H304	N008	S053			BRISCOE	B040	B117	B141	
BRADLIE	B142				C149 D033	G020	K026		
BRADSTREET	B162				BRISLER	V009			
BRADY	B074	J015	N005		BRISOCE	D032			
P034 T057					BRITE	PO39			
BRAGG	L063				BRITT	S113			
BRAILSFORD	L029				BRITTINGHAM	B118	P007		
BRAITHWAITE	M014				BRITTON	H103			
BRAKE	F070				BROADAWAY	G114			
BRAMBLE	M167	M168	P081		BROADWATER	H029	S137	T031	
	W183				BROCK	B063			
BRANCH	C098				BROCKENBROUGH	E047	E049	W142	
BRANDENBURG	M175	S059			BROGDEN	G049			
BRANHAM	W111				BROHANN	K007			
BRANNAN	R038				BROHAWN	B195			
BRANNOCH	L052				BROOKE	B128	B256	G033	
BRANSON	W109					G093	J037		
BRASHEARS	B241				BROOKS	B255	B257	D119	
BRASHER	C103				E039 M056	M145	Z001		
BRATTEN	D004	D005	D072		BROOME	D166			
BRATTON	G082	V015			BROOMELL	H229			
BRAUER	F003				BROTHERTON	H289			
BRAWNER	B028	J015			BROUGHTON	B047	B096		
BRAY	M109				BROWER	C113			
BRECKENRIDGE	B271				BROWN	A038	A069	B006	
BREED	H110				B074 B211	B267	B305	B309	
BREEDON	G047				B355 B359	C028	C043	C047	
BREIDENHARDT	F083				C135 C144	D018	D053	D065	
BREIDENHART	F082				D119 D120	D154	E032	E059	
BREITENBACH	L062				G009 G092	G119	H116	H148	
BREMMER	G081				H170 H188	H189	H212	H282	
BRENGMAN	W092				J004 J016	K042	L017	M038	
BRENNISEN	B049				NO24A R057	S007	S091	S130	
BRENT	M045	M147			T001 T029	W086			
BRETT	0003					W169			
BREVARD	M053				BROWNE	C102	C120	C126	
BREWBAKER	L057					R051	R069		
BREWER	B228	D043	F001		BROWNING	R012			
	G119	G120	K063		BROWNLEY	F062			
BREWSTER	M028				BROYES	N024a			
BREYMAIER	U003				BRUCE	B019			
BRIAN	G006				BRUCHEY	M103			
BRICE	H271	H085	J060		BRUFF	D073	L033		
	K009	W046	W088		BRUNE	A038	C117		
BRICKER	A084	M077			BRUNER	H067			
BRIDGES	N004	R001	R007	T057	BRUNNER	R025			

INVENTORY OF MARYLAND BIBLE RECORDS

Surname	Bibles			Surname	Bibles		
BRUNT	D179			BURTON, contd.	H091	H260	K058
BRYAN	B361	C119	C211		O017	T065	
F075 H239	M033	S098	W046	BURWELL	H105		
BRYANT	H174			BUSH	C015	C016	G035
BUCHANAN	A038	B035	C117		L040	Y002	
F087 L067	W097	W171	Y006	BUSHEY	M088		
BUCHER	R073			BUSHWALLER	R066		
BUCKEL	H286			BUSTEED	W130		
BUCKEY	E042	E043	J001	BUTLER	B075	B128	B302
	K060			D108 L014	M053	M080	O020
BUCKINGHAM	B075	L085	P031	W067			
BUCKLER	G077	G078		BUTTLER	W114		
BUCKLEY	A024	C163	K003	BUTTON	W143		
BUCKMASTER	B181			BYELL	G133		
BUCKNER	B257	T044		BYERS	D143	E059	
BUDD	D068	D104	H193	BYNE	T009		
	M141			BYRD	B148	D031	F079
BUEL	S001			K033 N036	N037		
BUFFINGTON	D108	E046	G027	BYRENS	L059		
	G066			BYRON	R090		
BUGG	L003			BYURGEON	H288		
BUHRMAN	B285	B286					
BUIER	F036			CABURN	R014		
BULL	B184	D175	H053	CADE	D099		
H216 H291	H294	M054	S039	CAIN	A024	C074	K003
	T061				M135	R057	
BULLOCK	H155	T008		CAIRNES	B074	C022	
BUMBAUGH	G085			CALAS	W016		
BURCKARET	R093			CALDER	C016		
BURDICK	C090			CALDWELL	A044	D179	G019
BURFORD	R082				R057		
BURGER	W143			CALHOUN	C049	G082	H022
BURGES	E064				H173		
BURGESS	B134	B216	B338	CALLAHAN	M052	N001	
D032 D148	D149	K024	T040	CALLEN	W088		
	U001			CALLIS	A017	A018	A019
BURGNER	G100			CALLOWAY	H122		
BURGOYNE	A068			CALVERT	D133		
BURK	G067			CAMBELL	F006		
BURKE	P038	S063		CAMBLESS	B320		
BURLEY	H138			CAMBURN	D056		
BURNAN	J035			CAMERON	G099	N006	
BURNAP	W134			CAMP	H101	W088	
BURNER	W099			CAMPBELL	B108	B160	C144
BURNESTON	B018			G038 H110	H224	H232	H249
BURNETT	D085	E004	W125	K022 M099	M125	P038	P068
BURNHAM	C181			CANNON	A005	C171	F069
BURNLEY	T010				G068	P081	P082
BURNS	G019	I003	J053	CAPITO	F032		
	M054			CAPLES	G070		
BURR	B320			CARDWELL	M010		
BURRESS	C096			CAREINS	B019		
BURROUGHS	H094			CAREY	H205		
BURTON	C022	C097	H090	CARICO	B219		

Surname	Bibles			Surname	Bibles		
CARILLE	W088			CAYTON	P092		
CARLE	E065			CAYWOOD	C035		
CARLISLE	C120			CAZIER	F048		
CARLSON	B117			CENER	M154		
CARLTON	B162			CHABROUGH	L023		
CARMACK	L010			CHADSEY	T068		
CARNAN	V001			CHALMERS	K023	P037	
CARNES	G082			CHAMBERLAIN	B325	H210	
CARPENTER	D056	D120	M088	CHAMBERS	B160	H245	J030
CARR	D182	F003	M081		W112		
	N024	W015	W072	CHAMPAYNE	C210		
CARREN	R011			CHAMPERLAIN	P034		
CARRICO	H286			CHAMPLAIN	F004		
CARRINGTON	C132			CHANCE	W150	W151	
CARRIS	G115			CHANDLEE	T077		
CARROLL	A028	A053	A054	CHANDLER	D023	H129	W032
A086	B195	F039	G098 G122	CHANEY	W181		
H198	H281	R050		CHANNELL	P034		
CARSINS	M065			CHAPEL	B026		
CARSON	L079			CHAPIN	A042		
CARTER	B349	D029	D136	CHAPMAN	B211	F029	H278
G065	H072	L030	P035 R021		0001		
S150	T029	T076		CHAPPELL	F004		
CARTY	G114			CHARBONNIER	B069		
CARTZENDOFNER	F085			CHASE	M166		
CARVER	A011	C076	C089	CHAVANNES	D127		
CARVILL	H210			CHAVER	B237		
CARY	E017	H035		CHEELEY	K030		
CASE	B278	S187		CHENEY	B225	M176	
CASH	B100			CHENOWETH	B075	D135	
CASHO	H274			CHERRICKS	W046		
CASON	M157			CHERRY	B006		
CASSARD	L062			CHESNEY	T038		
CASSELL	B013	B014		CHESTER	A042	B355	
CASTATOR	S179			CHESTNUT	M063		
CASTLEMAN	J051			CHEW	H266	H267	
CASWELL	C126			CHICHESTER	R064		
CASTON	D080			CHILCOAT	M169		
CATESBY	B269			CHILDRESS	C060		
CATHCART	T035			CHILDS	H291	N006	
CATHELL	H079			CHILTON	H231	L043	R010
CATLIN	N018	S182			S175		
CATMAN	A088			CHILTUM	H289		
CATON	P092			CHIPLEY	W129		
CATTELL	C003	H022		CHISWELL	D167		
CATTERTON	H032	R032		CHOATE	H095		
CAUFFMAN	W107			CHRISISENSEN	B064		
CAULDER	G125			CHRISMAN	L077		
CAULFIELD	H121			CHRISTIAN	R083		
CAUSEY	C181	F046		CHRISTMAN	Y013		
CAUTHORNE	V001			CHROSWELL	C073		
CAVANAUGH	B236			CHURCH	G122		
CAVENDER	B043			CHURCHILL	P068		
CAYLOR	B092			CIPRIANI	H220		

Surname	Bibles		
CLAGETT	B057	D032	D180
F070 H019	H024	P053	
CLAIRE	A074		
CLAPHAM	D106		
CLARK	A089	B107	B133
B147 B238	B257	B288	C012
C055 C148	C229	D142	G084
H115 H118	H218	J016	L013
M039 M135	S091	T030	W068
CLARKE	B036	C089	C103
F054 F056	W083		
CLARVOE	C073		
CLAWSON	C088		
CLAY	B105	P038	P079
CLAYBROOK	T001		
CLAYLAND	R093		
CLAYTON	B106	B326	B353
C029 C225	H229	H230	R030
S063			
CLEAVER	B237		
CLELAND	M105		
CLEMENS	G031		
CLEMENT	D029	S162	
CLEMENTS	B034	C103	N032
S008			
CLEMSON	P030		
CLEVIDENCE	C088		
CLIFTON	S053		
CLINE	A028	B298	G088
CLOSE	F031	K060	
CLOTHEIR	T025		
CLOUGHLIN	W103		
CLUTTER	B297		
CLUTZ	H197		
COAKLEY	T057		
COALE	B252	C210	C225
R036			
COANE	B290		
COARD	E067	M092	
COATES	E015	O013	
COBB	B117	B231	H160
COBLE	H231		
COCHRAN	S148		
COCK	S173		
COCKEY	B305	G043	G044
G045 H286	M068	W035	
COCKRAN	F075	W002	
COCKRUM	B297		
CODLING	E032	E033	
COE	G130		
COFER	H300		
COFFEY	W131		
COFS	K007		
COGSWELL	B058		

Surname	Bibles		
COHAGAN	C189		
COKER	M061		
COLE	A072	B119	C070
H056 H265	M089	P037	R011
R016 W011			
COLEMAN	B105	C125	C153
E057 E058	H275	H276	J048
N002 G113			
COLESCOTT	S052		
COLGATE	G089		
COLL	S094		
COLLIER	E070	M161	W177
COLLIFLOWER	H074		
COLLINGSGROVE	K058		
COLLINS	A059	B307	C102
E002 G035	G136	L056	M036
M127 S178	W147		
COLLINSON	B186	J060	
COLLISON	E015		
COLQUITT	J011		
COLSON	L029	V011	
COLSTON	C143		
COLT	S063		
COMAN	A004		
COMEGYS	G084	W018	
COMPTON	B263	C142	
CONARD	K045		
CONAWAY	B120	B315	
CONGER	M062		
CONN	P080		
CONNALLY	C020		
CONNELL	T040		
CONNER	C210	D011	W048
CONRAD	J002		
CONSTANT	S171		
CONTEE	O002		
CONWAY	D185		
COOK	B233	B302	C151
D186 F076	G084	H142	H179
H221 H291	P059		
COOKE	G041	P017	
COOKER	E072		
COOKERLY	M179		
COOKSON	G119		
COOLEY	H293		
COOMBE	W152		
COOMBS	B216		
COOMS	S015		
COOPER	A086	A088	B217
C004 C065	G096	H001	H084
H173 J001	J002	K017	L087
M180 P001	P057	S118	S119
W015			
COPELAND	W097		

Surname	Bibles			Surname	Bibles		
COPENHAVER	T061			CRAIG, contd.	F089	K008	L065
COPPAGE	D168			CRAMER	S054		
COPPERS	P086			CRAMMER	J047		
CORBIN	C082	C083	C084	CRAMPTON	H290		
	F009	M174	T067	CRANDALL	G016		
CORBLEY	M177			CRANE	D052	M111	M112
CORD	B245			CRANFORD	D127	D134	F079
CORDDRY	V015			CRANOR	A012		
CORDRAY	L033			CRAUMER	G098		
CORE	D171			CRAWFORD	B143	C098	H209
CORILLOURN	V014				L027	O002	R068
CORKRAN	A054	J047		CREACY	M039		
CORKREN	G137			CREAGER	E046		
CORKRILL	C037			CREELY	S181		
CORNEL	H091			CREGAN	F035		
CORNER	R058			CREIGH	W191		
CORNETT	P085			CREIGHTON	B268	J038	L062
CORNISH	K007				M101	S105	W018
CORRELL	M014			CRESWELL	D031		
CORRIE	G052			CREVENSTEN	G103		
CORRIGAN	S013			CREW	S134		
CORSON	C020	G125		CRIDLER	M144		
COST	B236	S061		CRIST	M176		
COSTEN	W135			CROCKETT	B066	H124	U006
COSTIN	H061			CROFT	B339		
COTTER	B297			CROMWELL	B236	B333	D058
COTTINGHAM	M092			D127 HO72	H110	H118	
COTTRELL	R071			CRONEN	M113		
COUCHER	Y006			CRONISE	S061		
COULBOURNE	G060	K013		CRONMILLER	W048		
COULSON	Y009			CROOK	B307		
COULTER	P003			CROOKS	M176		
COUNCILMAN	O014			CROPPER	B355		
COUNTERS	E070			CROSS	B133	F044	
COUNTISS	C135			CROSSGI	H163		
COUNTS	B213			CROUSE	K060		
COURTNEY	E073	H056	M113	CROUT	R073		
	M116			CROWDER	B270		
COURTRIGHT	J055			CROWTHER	M169		
COUTURIER	L029			CROXALL	B024		
COVER	H297	H298		CRUIKSHANK	D052		
COVERDALE	T027			CRUMP	C014	T001	
COVINGTON	D181	G074	G114	CRUMPECKER	L047		
MO27 MO90	M127	R037	W011	CRUMSON	C113		
COWAN	U006			CRUNLISH	S010		
COWEN	B060			CRUTCHER	S104		
COWGILL	R037			CUBBAGE	D154	T027	
COWMAN	N030			CUFF	F036		
COX	B079	D012	D158	CULBERTSON	K056		
G094 I005	J017	J060	K016	CULBRETH	H061	H238	
M169 S008	S173	W053	Y003	CULLARS	M080		
CRABBS	B321			CULLEMBER	G078	G079	
CRADDOCK	W003			CULVAN	M044		
CRAIG	B031	B117	B181	CULVER	K030		

Surname	Bibles			Surname	Bibles		
CUMMING	F055			DAVIES	L027		
CUMMINS	F057			DAVIS	A015	B076	B217
CUMP	G100			B355	C015	C016	C158	D161
CUNNINGHAM	B074	G137	M067	D182	F003	G004	H043	H129
	W106	Z002		H168	H184	H186	H231	H288
CURLLEY	H157			J015	P068	P085	R011	R038
CURRIER	G131	W099		R039	S010	S145	S177	T037
CURRY	F030	S119	T024	T084	W005	W093	W134	W163
CURTIS	B032	B209	W163	DAVISON	W155		
CUSHING	W113			DAW	G115		
CUSICK	G064			DAWSON	B105	B276	D180
CUSTIS	H252			H010	K017	L065	M015	R055
CUTLAR	S168			R054	S019		
CUTSAIL	B355			DAY	F003	K030	S112
					T010		
DAGGETT	F019			DAZEY	M061		
DAHLGREEN	M182			DEADY	U001		
DAIL	B195			DEAKYNS	R037		
DAILEY	H170	M144	S091	DEAL	L008		
DAILY	S181			DEAN	S112		
DAINGERFIELD	K027	L053		DEARDORFF	E047		
DAKES	B123			DEATRICH	T082		
DALE	H035			DEAVERS	W165		
DALEY	B065	G098	L040	DECKER	C184		
	W107			DeCAMP	T054		
DALLAM	B355	H271	J015	DeFORD	A076		
DALRYMPLE	F079	W137		DeGRANGE	H054		
DALY	G129	H173		de GRAFFENREID	B105		
DAMERON	B357			DeHART	C174		
DANBY	L009			DELANY	D007		
DANDY	H192			de JARNETTE	R057	R059	
DANGIRARD	D064			de la ROCHE	P017		
DANIELL	L029			DELWORTH	S010		
DANIELS	A074			DeMARCELLIN	D104		
DANSON	R036			DEMARCO	H053		
DARBY	B247			DeMOSS	H237		
DARDEN	B034			DEMOTT	C174		
DARLY	H004	S100		DEMPSEY	T039	W143	
DARNALL	C036			DENDLER	J010		
DARNELL	S145			DENISON	R065		
DARROW	H186	H270		DENLY	F003		
DARRS	K007	M095	V014	DENNINGS	H014		
DARWIN	H237			DENNIS	B096	C191	C203
DASHIELD	G093			C230	H072	M022	M105
DASHIELL	A079	B079	D072	DENT	C156	D168	H019
	J040	N018		DERBYSHIRE	G100		
DATTON	E030			DERECKSON	M036		
DAUGHTERS	E030			DEROCHBRUNE	L035	W130	
DAUGHTERY	H118			DERR	M103		
DAVE	P035			DESHAROON	D144		
DAVENPORT	C215			DEVALL	G117		
DAVEY	L009			DEVEREUX	J014	J015	
DAVID	G085			DEVERS	B357	G078	
DAVIDSON	C063	L031	S116	DEVILBISS	B013	B050	G107

Surname	Bibles			Surname	Bibles		
DEVILBISS,contd.	H165	M136	W119	DORSEY, contd.	J051	L008	L014
DEVILLBISS	E042			M080 0026	W035	W072	W191
DEVINE	T024			DOUB	F090		
DEVOE	G007			DOUCH	G098		
DeVRIES	B120			DOUGHTY	C062		
DEWEY	S041			DOUGLAS	L027	M039	T084
DeWOLD	H218			DOUGLASS	H149	J009	
DEXTER	W093			DOVAY	R066		
DICK	B270			DOWELL	B128	D112	D166
DICKENSHUT	M110			DOWLEY	B300		
DICKERSON	G082	H044	T054	DOWNE	C140		
DICKEY	E012	R029		DOWNES	D077	D186	
DICKINSON	M061			DOWNEY	A082	H045	J037
DICKSON	L081	0001	0010	DOWNIE	L005	W022	
	S091			DOWNING	P078		
DIDIER	D016			DOWNS	H118	S036	
DIEHL	H197	H301	K012	DOYLE	B236		
	S165			DOZIER	H010		
DIETRICH	R075			DRAKE	C181	G135	
DIGES	K020			DRAY	T053		
DIGGES	B349			DREGHORN	L084		
DIGGS	C125			DRESSER	G079		
DILL	B219	W183		DREW	C014		
DILLEHUNT	B237			DRIVER	H288		
DINGES	J062			DROGESON	B117		
DISAROON	D021			DRUMMOND	W002		
DISHAROON	G136			DRYDEN	H076		
DISNEY	A047	A048	H090	DUBBER	S085		
	H091			DUCKETT	G059		
DITMARS	R073			DUDDERAR	P030		
DIVAN	Z005			DUDLEY	D052	R057	
DIXON	B052	B061	C224	DUER	F028	H133	
	M061	R078	R079	DUFF	B137	C011	W086
DOBBIN	A038	B184		DUFFY	0007		
DOBBINS	B320			DUKE	D177	I008	M146
DOCKERY	H010			DUKEHART	B272		
DOD	R064			DUKHART	G032		
DODD	C056	S110		DULANEY	H310		
DODGE	B297	C063		DULANY	A017	A018	A048
DOLLY	R076				C078	D181	
DONAHUE	K014			DUN	P006		
DONALDOSN	C117			DUNBAR	C157		
DONE	H126			DUNCAN	B271	E022	H029
DONELLAN	B066			L031 S171	V010	W015	
DONNAN	W118			DUNGAN	K043	L009	
DONNELO	K016			DUNICAL	B297		
DOOMES	G027			DUNLAP	H134		
DORAN	D177			DUNN	S112		
DORMAN	B033			DUNNOCK	S051		
DORSEY	B131	B143	B274	DUNNUCK	W118		
C098 D180	E072	F085	G002	DUPONT	B153		
G003 G041	G043	G046	G102	DUPRE	H127		
G119 G122	H057	H076	H117	DURANT	S094		
H218 H221	H257	J005	J022	DURBIN	J036		

Surname	Bibles			Surname	Bibles		
DURENT	D168			EGGLESTON	S063		
DURHAM	H053	H286		EHLERS	M028		
DURRUM	M081			EICHELBERGER	B348		
DURSILL	P037			EICHOLTZ	K012		
DUTTERA	D076			EICHORN	J004		
DUTTON	D177			ELBURN	A076		
DUVALL	A045	B166	F070	ELDER	B024	H223	
	G124	S083	W136	ELDRIDGE	B034		
DUYER	W183			ELIASON	F060		
DWYER	S170			ELLCOTT	S173		
DYER	F052			ELLENDER	B179	B180	
DYKES	J058			ELLERBE	B132		
DYKMAN	D056			ELLERBEE	W011		
				ELLICOTT	W113		
EADER	K012			ELLIOT	F019		
EAGER	H266			ELLIOTT	A053	C137	G026
EAGLESTON	W101			G068 H148	L039	S083	S095
EAGLSTON	W099			T017			
EAMES	H087			ELLIS	K040	S178	
EARHART	B071	L040		ELLISON	P004	R048	
EARICKSON	H107			ELLZEY	G092		
EARLE	F019	M053		ELSON	B074		
EARLY	A042	B152		ELY	R068		
EARP	B257A	B257B	B258	ELZER	S085		
EASON	M148			ELZEY	G091	W154	
EASTBORN	H284			EMERSON	B155	C186	H245
EASTER	C210				L062		
EASTMAN	G065			EMICH	G071		
EASTON	H225			EMMERT	K025	N014	
EATON	A055	K045		EMMON	B105		
EBAUGH	A068	H299		EMORY	L092		
EBERLY	W093			EMRICH	J062		
EBERT	S115			ENGEL	E042		
EBY	B013			ENGERLITH	W106		
ECCLESTON	B363			ENGLAND	S010		
ECKER	G107	O001		ENGLAR	M088		
ECTON	S171			ENGLE	B092	D081	D167
EDDINGTON	U002			ENGLER	B152	D081	E012
EDE	C159			H299 R072			
EDGE	M039			ENGLISH	R010		
EDGELL	A012	H203		ENNALLS	B365		
EDGEN	A012			ENNALLY	H227		
EDGER	B034			ENNALS	C191	C199	
EDMANDS	C048			ENNELS	B364		
EDMONDSON	H281			ENNIS	M036		
EDMONDSTON	O009			ENOCH	N007		
EDMONSTON	B242	W072		ENROUGHTY	S185		
EDMUNDSON	P019			ENSMINGER	S141		
EDWARDS	D148	I004	K030	ENSOR	B050		
	W156			EPES	P006		
EFFLER	V016			EPPERLY	H067		
EFFORD	M015			EPPES	C133		
EGAN	M055			ERB	L040		
EGERTON	B240			ERDMAN	L068	L069	

Surname	Bibles			Surname	Bibles		
ERK	B288			FEATHERSTON	D061		
ERNST	B100			FEDDON	M136		
ERWIN	A020	M084		FEHRMEN	Z001		
ESTEP	W010	W117		FEINOUR	C097		
ESTES	G035			FELL	R014		
ESTILLE	C089			FENDALL	B355		
ETER	S043			FENDER	H053		
ETTING	C127			FENLY	B065		
EUBANKS	D148			FENWICK	B249	B250	F054
EUSTIS	H101			FERGUSON	C225	D156	J015
EUSTON	L059				L079	W156	Y005
EVANS	A059	B079	D179	FERLL	D171		
G016	G038	H010	H118	J005	FESSLER	B006		
L012	J043	M003	T069	W118	FEYE	B305		
W175				FICKEY	L081		
EVELER	H162			FIELD	B143		
EVELINE	J008			FIFE	H112A		
EVERETT	B080	C135	T019	FILLER	B050		
EVERIST	G103	M111	M112	FILLESON	C164		
EWING	H026	M060		FILLISON	H084		
EY	M036			FINCH	M161		
EYERS	C133			FINCHAM	B340	B341	
EYLER	Y002			FINK	A070		
				FINKS	B357		
FADE	S073			FINLEY	C203	S152	
FADELEY	M144			FISHBACK	P034		
FAGUE	N027			FISHER	A051	B041	B042
FAHNESTOCK	E047	G085		B043	B052	C018	C183	D082
FAIN	N029			F085	H072	H157	M078	W074
FAIR	R057			W075	W092	W109	W143
FAIRALL	H118			FISTER	M090		
FAIRBAIRN	G115			FITCHETT	H168		
FAIRBANK	C171	F075		FITZELL	S043		
FAIRCLOTH	H029			FITZGERALD	G004	H039	H124
FAIRLAWN	H123				S145		
FALK	I005			FITZHUGH	M095	T044	
FALLEY	M050			FITZSIMMON	L018		
FANNING	C164	H084		FITZSIMMONS	D118		
FARBER	C151			FIZZEL	B333		
FARIS	E016			FLADGER	H127		
FARLEY	M022	M105		FLANAGAN	S106		
FARMER	B074	C157	H010	FLATER	A071		
FARN	H031			FLAYHARDT	H118		
FARRON	W152			FLEMING	C014	H044	L012
FARVEL	G111				M092	M142	
FARVER	S059			FLENNER	W172		
FATHERLY	D142			FLENNIKEN	L001		
FAUCETT	P036			FLETCHALL	C085	C086	C089
FAUNTLEROY	T076			FLETCHER	A053	B255	C076
FAUTH	C153				F047	T040	
FAVORITE	E024			FLOWER	Y009		
FAY	B143	D048	V001	FLOWERS	A010	C200	
FEAGO	E046			FLOYD	J028	N036	N037
FEARSON	Y008				W032	W175	

Surname	Bibles			Surname	Bibles		
FOARD	F038	S008	W163	FREDRICH	B290		
FOGERTY	H286			FREEBORNE	G102		
FOLK	B213			FREEHAN	T056		
FOLTZ	H290			FREELAND	I005		
FONVILLE	F017			FREELMYER	P065		
FOOKES	C052			FREEMAN	B260	F054	W111
FOOKS	H206	P008	S178	FREENY	M127		
FORBES	G085			FRELINGHUYSEN	H094		
FORCAN	H284			FRENCH	C043	J017	L037
FORD	B035	B230	C048	FRESHOUR	J051		
C054	D054	D150	J014	J015	FREY	C004	F086	K052
M022	T017	W163			FRIFEGLE	S012		
FORE	B132			FRISBY	S120		
FOREMAN	H048			FRITCHIE	H054		
FOREST	B072			FRITZ	G108		
FORMAN	C059	J030	S171	FRIZZELL	S118		
FORNER	R055			FROCK	H188	H189	
FORREST	C063	D076	L020	FROST	D068		
	O002			FRUSH	E010		
FORSHEY	BO73			FRY	B117	B117	H117
FORWARD	H119				R053		
FORWOOD	A051	B041	B042	FRYE	P057		
	B043	E036	H119	FRYMILLER	G083	G084	
FOSKET	S048			FULFORD	H131		
FOSS	W032			FULKERSON	S085		
FOSTER	A040	C007	C054	FULLER	G128	G136	S072
C076	F048	M054	M120	N019	FULTON	B107	H265	
P015	S167			FUNK	B193	M084	S094
FOUDRAY	O018			FURLOW	H206		
FOUNDS	L065			FURMAN	M040	W202	
FOUNER	W049			FURTZ	C077		
FOUNTAIN	S127	S128					
FOWBLE	H179			GABLER	T052		
FOWLER	B169	B265	C042	GABY	P039		
	F063	H079	W052	GADDIS	M084		
FOX	F086	L009		GAGE	L029		
FOXWELL	G114			GAINES	B129	M174	W097
FOY	D099			GAITHER	C042	G018	G122
FRAILEY	D064	M030			H218	J056	P058
FRAIZER	L025			GALBREATH	W118	W159	W163
FRALEY	S075			GALE	D111		
FRAME	S155			GALL	D065		
FRANCE	D062	W093		GALLAHER	H122		
FRANCIS	G027	M173	W086	GALLION	C009		
FRANK	F057			GALLOWAY	U001		
FRANKLIN	C180	N003	N030	GALPIN	C153		
FRANTY	W093			GALT	S047		
FRANZON	R039			GAMBELL	M061		
FRASER	M004			GAMBLE	L024		
FRAY	L005			GAMBRIEL	M093	S053	
FRAZIER	G085	H045	S155	GAMBRILL	C171	J037	J051
W121	W123	W124	W129		D056		
FREDEKING	S106			GANT	M090		
FREDERICK	B287	W163		GANTT	L029		

Surname	Bibles				Surname	Bibles		
GAPPAN	R079				GILBERTHORP	H160		
GARDE	R001				GILCHRIST	B028		
GARDENER	D182				GILDER	K023		
GARDINER	F084	J015	L043		GILES	S083		
	L073				GILL	A033	B035	B043
GARDNER	B052	B172	C210		J038 M097	T075	W111	
G073	K052	P018	R047	S008	GILLEN	A085		
W003	W025	W048	W080		GILLESPIE	M060	S182	
GAREY	D142				GILLETT	C215	M092	
GARLAND	J014	J015	W189		GILLIAN	J058		
GARNER	G079	M181	T016		GILLILAND	D156		
GARRARD	B105				GILLINGS	B305		
GARRET	M147				GILLION	B116		
GARRETT	G135	H294	R012		GILLIS	D117	N018	R053
GARRETTSON	B189	G103	H056			S059		
	M044				GILLISPIE	C193		
GARRIGUES	W025				GILMOR	H266	H267	
GARRISH	A064	A065			GILPIN	H229	U008	
GARRISON	C098				GILSON	C082		
GARY	A040				GIMPER	P039		
GASKINS	B030	W192			GIRDLETREE	B118		
GASSAWAY	B091	J051	W007		GIST	C119	E064	F028
GATCHELL	C201	H228				H265	H268	W065
GATES	B064	C063	S061		GITTINGS	B024	W156	
GATEWOOD	S020				GIVANS	D161		
GATTIS	P006				GLACOCK	M053		
GAUGH	W119				GLADDEN	D041	D047	D175
GAULT	D082					W086	W159	W159A
GAVER	G108	H249	H249		GLADSTONE	W032		
GAWTHROP	C018				GLANVILL	S153		
GAYER	B075				GLASCOW	C096	H051	W154
GEAREY	W105				GLASS	G092		
GEBHARD	D066				GLENN	B211	H074	
GEDDES	H121				GLIDEWELL	E057	E058	
GEIB	J007				GLOVER	B257B	B258	
GEIST	A028				GNAGEY	H251		
GEMMILL	H036				GODDALL	R057		
GENKINS	D015				GODFREY	T064	W104	
GEORGE	A051	B041	G137		GODWIN	H001		
	G139	N007	R090		GOEBEL	D048		
GERMAN	B078				GOETZE	F029		
GESH	B296				GOFFIGON	H300		
GETTY	B340	B341			GOLANDER	S119		
GIBB	W032				GOLD	W071		
GIBBONS	B333	D141	J030		GOLDSBOROUGH	C191	E005	K013
GIBBS	B035	R012				L067		
GIBSON	B168	C020	I005		GOLDSMITH	D066		
	W100				GOLDWITH	S077		
GIFFIN	W019				GOLDY	D025		
GIFFORD	B162				GONDER	S015		
GILBER	H043				GONSO	E010		
GILBERT	B013	B019	B048	B240	GONTEE	S050		
C221	E012	F036	H301	M065 M113	GOODE	M161		
N028	P039	R002	W041	Y009	GOODEN	M070		

103

INVENTORY OF MARYLAND BIBLE RECORDS

Surname	Bibles			
GOODIN	B117	W093		
GOODMAN	P064			
GOODWIN	H098			
GOODYEAR	B039			
GOORE	D013			
GORDON	F029	H216		
GORDY	C052			
GORE	H227	J047		
GORMAN	E049			
GORRELL	C076	R016		
GORSUCH	B307	B359	D082	
	G037	H258	M080	
GOSNELL	G108	S059		
GOSSETT	M105			
GOTT	C086	C089	R032	
GOUGH	M065			
GOULD	H123	M051	P037	
GOVANE	H271			
GOVE	I008			
GOVER	W027			
GOWAN	C074			
GOWING	G106			
GRABILL	A073	R049		
GRABLE	M084			
GRACE	B129			
GRADNER	C210	W106		
GRAFF	D142			
GRAHAM	H299	P049	T021	
GRANER	C133			
GRANT	G041	G138	M030	
GRARATLE	C210			
GRASON	R093			
GRAVATTE	W048			
GRAVEN	D158			
GRAY	A071	B211	B356	
C056 G128	H048	H072	M028	
R078 W035				
GRAYBEEL	O011			
GRAYBILL	B152	B296	S003	
	Y002			
GRAYSON	B153			
GREATHOUSE	S083			
GREELEY	J016			
GREEN	A071	B226	B270	
D180 G008	G050	L009	M161	
M182 T037	W068	W112	Y002	
Y007				
GREENAWALT	A085	W107		
GREENBURY	K016			
GREENFIELD	C202	H019	H209	
GREENLAND	B019	W041		
GREENLEAF	P017			
GREENLEE	W129			
GREENWALL	B005	B004		

Surname	Bibles			
GREENWELL	B004	R052		
GREENWOOD	H014	H127	R090	
GREER	M039			
GREGG	M177			
GREGOR	B209			
GREGORY	B269	H181		
GREIMAN	T017			
GRESSILT	L009			
GRICE	T043			
GRIENDFIELD	H226			
GRIER	B174	C105		
GRIFFIN	B030	B217	C142	
C226 F009	H123	W008	W052	
W112 W182	W192			
GRIFFITH	A045	B191	C085	
C086 C089	C093	M011	M062	
S162 W035				
GRIGG	E057			
GRIGSBY	M053	N024		
GRIMES	R085			
GRISCOM	C128			
GRISE	B355			
GRISWALD	C195			
GRISWOLD	D105			
GROFF	A041			
GROMAN	H286			
GROSS	G067	S118	S119	
GROVE	E010	F044		
GROVER	G134			
GROVES	G011	L005		
GROVINE	P003			
GRUBB	K051			
GRUNDEN	D078			
GRUNDY	D120			
GRUNER	G096			
GRUSE	W092			
GRYMES	B350	H288	T044	
GUDLER	C140	D146		
GUE	P053			
GUERARD	L029			
GUFERIA	B116			
GUNBY	L018	S016		
GUNN	D156			
GUNNELL	P005			
GUY	A013	A069		
GUYER	C001			
GUYTHER	L043			
GUYTON	B121	H148		
GWALTNEY	L092			
GWYN	F009			
HACEDY	D095			
HACH	J005			
HACKETT	A015	G052	G068	R037

104

Surname	Bibles
HACKNEY	B247 D079
HADDAWAY	A086
HADSKIN	H173
HAEMER	W024
HAGAN	F063
HAGERTY	B348
HAGLE	R069
HAGMEIR	B101
HAGUE	W183
HAHN	H297 H298
HAIGHT	G078 G079 N006A
HAILE	H015
HAINES	B013 B281 B321 C113 C114 E010 E013 E046 G032 H308 S059 S076
HALBERT	B129
HALE	J023 Z005
HALES	C017
HALEY	L090
HALL	B034 B042 B043 B216 B321 C003 C049 D108 D136 D148 F007 G051 G082 G134 H087 H168 H209 H239 J049 K008 L018 L029 M081 M128 P049 P078 R032 S100 S134 T069 T076 W092 W099
HALLER	H043 S015 S113
HALLETT	C144 N006
HALLEY	W080
HALLING	C123
HALLOWELL	W002
HALTON	N024
HALVERSON	C210 W048
HAM	K026 N015
HAMBLETON	A097
HAMILTON	A004 B334 B338 C002 F018 H160 H173 J015 M062 T034 W037 W067
HAMMAKER	K061
HAMME	T057
HAMMET	W127
HAMMETT	D168
HAMMOND	C011 C098 D106 D119 D129 G043 G044 G102 J037 M095 P001
HAMPTON	P035
HANBY	M081
HANCOCK	J045 L040
HANDLEY	M028 M062 R009 S040
HANDY	B047 J028
HANEY	B075 W092
HANN	C172
HANNA	H240 S095 T019
HANNON	G129
HANS	P037
HANSON	B040 C063 M111
HARD	D012
HARDEBECK	C186
HARDEE	M136
HARDEN	B120
HARDESTY	C030 G016 G083 H019 H064
HARDING	B147 H068 K054 S015
HARDY	D144 H129 W048
HARE	M180 S054
HARFORD	P001
HARGET	F070
HARKNESS	W067
HARLAN	H059 W051
HARLOW	B096 L003
HARMAN	A088
HARNES	H243
HARNINGTO	H103
HARNNETT	G094
HARP	K041 M172
HARPER	A097 B338 C042 F015 F075 H210 H218 J033 K044 M063 S168 T036 V004 W040
HARRINGTON	C006 D001 D019 N008 S098
HARRIS	B159 B302 C042 C091 D160 F071 F072 H010 H137 H195 K026 L025 M021 M036 M081 M136 P035 R088
HARRISON	A088 B173 B185 B325 B363 C029 C102 C164 D058 D180 G075 G130 H285 M070 M077 P038 R001 R079 S052 W080
HARROP	W067
HARRY	B030 D047 W192
HARRYMAN	R093
HARSHMAN	A070
HART	B337 G016 S083
HARTLEY	F036
HARTMAN	D014 H197
HARTSOOK	B050
HARTUP	Ro54
HARTWELL	E047 E049
HARVEY	B043 C030 G035 G043 H156 J055 P015 R071 S078
HARVYE	H103
HARWOOD	H016 H277 K016
HASELDEN	B132
HASELTINE	A055

Surname	Bibles			Surname	Bibles		
HASLEM	H273	H279		HELFRICH	R034		
HASSON	P018			HELLEN	I008	S114	
HASTINGS	D005			HELM	A029		
HATTO	T077			HELMS	H108		
HATTON	B178			HELMUTH	B115		
HAUGHTON	P035			HELTIBRIDLE	B214		
HAUSE	A057			HEMLING	H144		
HAVELL	C062			HEMPSTEAD	N016		
HAVNER	D171			HEMSLEY	C059	F053	
HAWKES	H125			HENDERSON	B259	S016	S119
HAWKINS	C076	D180	H020	HENDON	H181		
	M014	W134	W172	HENDRICKS	B074		
HAWTHORNE	P004			HENDRICKSON	M158		
HAWTHRONE	M149			HENDRIX	S018	S039	
HAWYER	C159			HENDRY	S141		
HAYDEN	K044	W104		HENKLE	C183		
HAYDON	H173			HENLEY	F089		
HAYES	B304	B343	B343	HENNESSEY	H010		
	C065	V011		HENNYS	P038		
HAYMAN	B217	H206	R016	HENRY	B049	C222	F001
HAYNES	M063	M066			W005		
HAYNIE	D111			HENSCHEL	B272		
HAYS	G115	H278	S052	HENSHAW	B150	B151	
HAYSE	J040			HENTY	F043		
HAYWARD	B209	N026	B325	HEPFORD	W143		
	J023			HERBERT	B236		
HAYWELL	H155			HERGENRATHER	G075	G076	
HAZE	W073			HERITAGE	C119		
HAZELLWOOD	A020			HERNDON	M161		
HAZTWELL	E047			HERR	B333		
HEACOCK	G008			HERRICH	M150		
HEADLEY	K058			HERRING	D181	G083	G084
HEADON	D079			HERRMANN	E010		
HEANY	D095			HERSHEY	S106		
HEAPS	B043	W014		HERSPERGER	P052		
HEARD	S015			HERUE	P075		
HEARDY	O013			HESLETINE	B263		
HEARN	F076	H207		HESS	M088	W086	
HEARNS	D005			HESSELIUS	Y010		
HEART	G026	P064		HESSER	M014		
HEARVE	H206			HETRICH	H240		
HEATH	B021	C210		HEVALON	D011		
HEATON	B323			HEWITT	M102		
HECKMAN	H142			HEWLETT	J036		
HEDGES	B107			HIATT	B129		
HEFFNER	D171	R003	R025	HIBBS	M177		
HEGE	S115			HICKEY	C226	C227	
HEGLEHURST	L024			HICKLEY	J014	J015	
HEIDLER	B126	B127	K049	HICKMAN	H149	R011	
HEINICKEN	C045			HICKS	B034	B364	B365
HEINKE	H010				N024	R042	
HEINMILLER	H286			HIGGENBOTTOM	P038	R083	
HELDERBRIDLE	E012			HIGGINS	B133	B142	C151
HELFRECH	C123	C124			C152 D025	D154	F001

Surname		Bibles			Surname		Bibles		
HIGH		W049			HOLLOWAY		B213	F006	G007
HIGHBARGER		C161					K058	S008	
HILL		B147	C042	C120	HOLLYDAY		W128		
C221	D108	G039	H024	H279	HOLMES		C181		
H281	K026	M053	P079	R012	HOLMES		M172		
S112	S144	W131			HOLTZ		H261		
HILLAND		V014			HOMEWOOD		G102	S029	
HILLEARY		B216			HONEYWELL		M030		
HILLIS		D056			HONNOLD		M063		
HILLSINGER		A071			HOOD		C151	G119	H271
HILLSON		D171					J017		
HINDES		G088			HOOE		D072		
HINDMAN		H245			HOOK		G008	R033	W035
HINEBAUGH		K051					W169		
HINES		R079			HOOPER		G084	H312	M045
HINKLE		W022			M100	M144	R071	S063	S069
HINSON		C226			HOOPES		W051		
HINTON		G018			HOOPMAN		H240		
HIPP		B211	H213		HOOVER		B001	B176	F085
HIRLINGS		W142					S055		
HIRONS		U008					W169		
HIRSCH		K004			HOPE		D019	F012	
HITCH		G093	S178		HOPKINS		B033	B034	B134
HITCHCOCK		D158			B245	B271	C211	F036	G004
HITCHENS		H260			H044	H053	H079	H110	H293
HOBBS		B006	C151	C152	N006	P075	S039	S095	S119
		H216			S153	T061	W031		
HOBRON		H270			HOPKINSON		C117	S088	
HOBSON		R030	U006		HOPLINS		H220		
HOCH		B064			HOPPER		T017		
HOCKIN		H173			HORACE		H092		
HODGE		B060			HORATH		C142		
HODGEN		T030			HORBIS		H103		
HODGES		H118	M143		HOREN		B105		
HODGKISS		H185			HORN		C181	D099	D105
HOFF		D171	F084				K053	W053	
HOFFMAN		A031	C055	C088	HORNER		Y011		
H113	H180	K041	M089	M180	HORSEY		R092		
W035	W093				HORSLEY		B134		
HOGG		G063			HORTON		B105	B241	
HOGUE		S047			HOSKINS		H173		
HOLBERT		G022			HOSTLER		L073		
HOLCOMB		S021			HOUCK		B035	N003	R066
HOLDEN		R069	R078		HOUSE		G099		
HOLDING		P035			HOUSEHOLDER		S077		
HOLLADAY		M039			HOUSER		P037		
HOLLAND		B150	C073	F070	HOUSTON		C014	C059	
		H216	K013	S052	HOWARD		B276	B355	C090
HOLLAWAY		B217	R079	S095	C098	C113	C149	D119	G119
HOLLEY		H090	H091		G124	H057	H129	H218	H220
HOLLIDAY		W152			H286	K031	L027	L032	M079
HOLLINGSWORTH		D031	K008	M002	W080				
		M040	S039	T025	HOWE		D162		
HOLLIS		G100	J023		HOWELL		C132	L043	T081

Surname	Bibles			
HOWELL, contd.	T086	W134	W169	W177
HOWERTON	L090			
HOWETH	H008			
HOWEY	D139			
HOWLAND	M090			
HOWLETT	B076	W014		
HOYT	H064			
HUBBARD	A059	F074		
HUBEL	W143			
HUBER	L015			
HUBLEY	A084			
HUBNER	M049			
HUDSON	B181	M067	M082	
	V014			
HUFF	B021	R028	S008	
	S162	T035		
HUFFER	F044			
HUFFINGTON	B217			
HUFFMAN	S170			
HUFFORD	S063			
HUGG	F068	L009		
HUGGINS	N024a			
HUGHES	B051	B278	B357	
C018	E065	F089	G038	H255
K058	L071	S185	T015	
HUGUELET	L029			
HULL	E010	G085		
HULSE	H156			
HULTS	H196			
HUMBER	G029			
HUMBERT	L040			
HUMMER	A065			
HUMPHREY	L014	P015		
HUNGERFORD	S100			
HUNT	K012	K058	M173	
	T076			
HUNTER	B269	H279	K047	
	S115			
HUNTSBERRY	W103			
HURDLE	D079			
HURLEY	W188			
HURLOCK	B355			
HURST	D160			
HURT	H108			
HURTT	W111			
HUSH	H290			
HUSTON	B355			
HUTCHESON	S186			
HUTCHINS	M079	W185		
HUTCHISON	B037	W111		
HUTT	G140			
HUTTON	C210	T081	W048	
	W074	W075		
HYATT	S058			

Surname	Bibles			
HYDE	S083			
HYLAND	M047			
HYLTON	A028			
HYMES	H171			
HYMILLER	M038			
HYNSON	J017			
HYRONS	L031			
HYSON	P075			
IGLEHART	R093			
IJARIES	H076			
ILEY	W053			
INGERSOLL	J016			
INGLE	A019			
INGLEHART	D088	E032	M052	
INGLES	H106			
INGRAHAM	H173	H245		
INGRAM	K063	M147		
INGRAMS	G102			
INGTON	W151			
INSHIP	F048			
INSLEY	B231	G068	H003	
	H029	P083		
IRBY	G031			
IRELAND	H148	L033	S114	
IRONMENGER	C133			
IRVIN	M113	M116		
IRVING	H065	K017		
IRWIN	T057			
ISAACS	P040			
ISLER	C119			
IVEY	T043			
IZER	E012			
JACKSON	A051	B041	B134	
C070	C163	C181	C193	C195
E026	F032	H068	H103	H127
H181	L065	L077	M081	O007
P018	P034	P079	S176	S182
JACOB	F071	G008	G123	
	M109	W175		
JACOBS	B309	E047		
JACOBUS	G004			
JAMES	A077	C114	D019	
	D183	W159	W163	
JAMESON	C097	C182	F023	
	J015	W105		
JAMISON	B024			
JARDIN	B068			
JARRELL	B181	L044		
JARRETT	J020			
JARVIS	T035			
JEAN	M121			
JEFFERSON	A053	M036	V013	

Surname	Bibles				
JEFFREES	J048				
JEFFREYS	W202				
JEFFRIES	D181				
JENKINS	D144	E025	J060		
	K027	M026	S105		
JENNINGS	H218	M004			
JERMAN	G027				
JESSOP	B185	D025	O018		
JESSUP	P004				
JESTER	B181	M084			
JEWELL	B296	S058			
JITE	G134				
JOHNS	B042	B043	B091		
C211	F024	G033	P017		
JOHNSON	A043	B036	B043	B158	
B268	C009	C022	C042	C144	
D006	D053	D054	D072	D118	
D124	D125	F070	F087	G062	
G117	H010	H069	H084	H149	
H289	J019	J026	M034	M052	
M053	M088	M092	R045	R094	
S047	S049	S134	W086	W107	
W113	W143	W190			
JOHNSTON	B349	B363	F012		
JOHNY	R034				
JOINER	C016	W122			
JONES	A060	A078	A082		
B060	B190	B195	B233	B334	
B355	B357	C018	C086	C089	
C089	C119	C137	C195	D005	
D021	D022	D103	D177	F010	
F084	G043	G090	G099	G109	
G128	G136	H118	H274	H085	
J028	K015	K025	K052	L038	
L073	M036	M045	M054	M054	
M110	M159	P018	P074	P081	
R021	R061	R068	R075	S042	
S161	T029	T035	T044	T054	
T063	T073	T079	V015	W072	
W105	W106	W122	W169		
JORDAN	B079	S106			
JORDEN	W143				
JORDON	B260				
JOURDAN	M028				
JOY	B257				
JOYCE	M142				
JOYNER	D072				
JULIANO	B355				
JUMP	B155				
JUNKINS	H118				
JUPENLATZ	G119				
JUSTICE	H101				
KABLE	M039				

Surname	Bibles		
KADILAC	D056		
KAHLER	B002		
KAHM	K057		
KAIGHN	M144		
KAISER	H118	Z004	
KALBFUS	G084		
KALKMAN	M004	M005	
KANTNER	S015		
KAPLAN	A028		
KAPTAIN	S112		
KARG	H053		
KARNES	P064	P064	
KAUFFETT	W118		
KAUFFMAN	F085	P057	
KAUFFMANN	B288		
KEAN	H053		
KEANE	H253		
KEARNE	W014		
KEARNEY	M014		
KEECH	E063	W117	
KEEN	A051	B041	B362
KEENE	C194		
KEENER	G084		
KEIRL	D160		
KEIRN	B010		
KEITH	D108	H256	H256
KELLAM	G016		
KELLER	H301	N014	
KELLEY	H093	P004	
KELLY	B129	B359	D018
D020	D078	D136	G060 L003
M113	T063	W097	W105
KEMP	D066	D180	H010
J039	R001	W122	
KENADY	W018		
KENDALL	H009	S021	
KENDRICK	D019	W061	Y012
KENLY	T057		
KENNARD	C014	D029	G037
N036	N037		
KENNEDY	B035	B105	M095
R010	W107		
KENSEY	W141		
KENT	F074	I008	
KEPHART	D114		
KEPNER	M088		
KERFORT	P035		
KERLEN	M181		
KERN	B151		
KERNAN	H125	J014	J015
KERNER	B036		
KERNS	D158		
KERR	B271	B335	D111
	F004		

Surname	Bibles			Surname	Bibles		
KERSHNER	B102	B145	L032	KLOMAN	A029		
KERSPERGER	P052			KLUTS	H043		
KERSTATER	R031			KNACHEL	F029		
KERWAN	M115			KNAPP	F068	L009	
KESSLER	S015			KNAUFF	C209	G006	
KESTER	S164			KNIGHT	A018	B127	H293
KEY	B297	H267	H275	J060 P010	R073	V010	V011
	H276	H277	W027	KNIGHTLY	L092		
KEYS	H221	M146		KNIGHTON	B034	D182	
KEYSER	K002			KNIPPLE	O013		
KIDD	R037			KNOLL	B169	S012	
KIDDER	D115	T073		KNOTT	W192		
KIDSON	O020			KNOW	B147		
KIELEY	H026			KNOWLES	B357		
KIER	B339			KNOX	B160	D112	
KIGER	S184			KOECHLIN	D064		
KIGHT	P057			KOENIG	B089		
KILBOURNE	L073			KOHR	D171	Z002	
KILGORE	B190	W159	W163	KOINER	C183	H105	
KILLAM	J005	S015		KOLB	H054	R043	
KILLEN	F076			KOLLER	B120	B251	
KILLOUGH	H228	H229		KONE	A031		
KILLPATRICK	B060			KOONS	H053		
KILPATRICK	C119			KOONTZ	B001	L040	L047
KILTRY	K023				O013		
KINDER	E015	W004		KOPP	G094		
KINDLE	P077			KORB	R043		
KINDLER	M063			KORNDORFFEIN	W066		
KINDRED	S178			KOSKA	M173		
KING	B047	B105	B134	KOSTNER	S115		
D095 D139	H310	L040	L081	KOWEL	J031		
N014 R001	R064	S077	S118	KRAMER	D055		
S127 S128	W015			KRANTZ	J016		
KINNAMONT	M148			KRAUK	F029		
KINNEMON	S179			KRAUS	P078		
KINNEY	C126	S178		KREH	W131		
KINSLOWE	A043			KREIDER	J062		
KINTZ	H189			KREINER	D142		
KIRBY	M177			KRENSON	K045		
KIRK	D149	R029	W086	KREUTZER	E030		
KIRKER	K014			KRIEL	P035		
KIRKMAN	C045			KRISE	B357	S047	
KIRKPATRICK	M063			KROTZER	N014A		
KITTERWWILL	W118			KRUZE	N024		
KITY	H188			KUHNS	L071		
KIVET	T034			KULLMER	H053		
KIZER	L057			KURTZ	G085		
KLARE	S043			KYLE	D112		
KLAUENBERG	R043			KYNER	C183		
KLAUSMAN	H160						
KLINE	F021	S081		LABRITT	D027		
KLING	S047	T017		LACEY	H286	W093	
KLINGERDER	K027			LACHMAN	AO84		
KLINGHORN	G006			LACKLAND	D032		

Surname	Bibles			Surname	Bibles		
LACY	B264			LAYNOR	E006		
LADD	G065			LAYTON	A034	D186	
LADSON	G041			LEA	B236	W114	
LAFFERTY	B271			LEACH	B276	B333	
LAIRD	G136			LEACHMAN	N025		
LAKIN	A034			LEAGUE	H081		
LAMB	H039	R012	S146	LEAK	W011		
LAMBDEN	D085	K017		LEAKE	M061		
LAMBDON	W089			LEAVERTON	D077		
LAMBER	H189			LEAVETT	C231		
LAMBERT	E035	H188	S059	LeCOMPTE	H250	P020	
LAMBORN	H226			LEDNUM	C004		
LAMPLEY	B254			LEE	A044	B062	B186
LANCASTER	F068	H053	H108	B220 D183	F053	G113	H093
LANDELL	T057			H283 J028	J030	K007	K052
LANDER	S171			M041 M145	S112	S181	W046
LANDES	G011			LEEDS	L043		
LANDING	B217			LEFEVRE	K064		
LANDIS	H179			LeFEVRE	B002		
LANDON	F019	P064		LEFINBY	W183		
LANE	D089	G029	H209	LEGESTER	H261		
	M043	S171		LEGGETT	B171		
LANGDON	G128			LEINBACH	S106		
LANGE	G137			LEIPER	C042	T028	
LANKFORD	A015	H295	L016	LEITCH	H085	W018	
	W185			LEITER	H100		
LANN	S134			LEITHAUSER	L015		
LANTERMAN	G097			LEMANS	B064		
LANTZ	E036	S173		LEMDIN	F068		
LARGART	A085			LEMMON	G006	T001	
LARKIN	D161			LENGAN	C079		
LARMOUR	F047			LENK	G136		
LARRABEE	C007			LENOX	R014		
LARRIMORE	S053			LEONARD	C052	M141	S091
LARSON	M136			LEONHARDT	H250		
LASWS	L076			LERNARD	B001		
LATIMER	I008			LESHER	B145		
LAUB	G033			LESTER	H092		
LAUBLE	D076			LETTON	J035		
LAUDERBACH	M118			LEURS	S059		
LAUDERBACK	M050			LEVENGOOD	H251		
LAUGHLIN	E027	T044	T044	LEWIN	B043	T035	
LAURENCE	B064	H076		LEWIS	B062	B105	B134
LAURENSON	F032			B157 B276	C155	D128	F073
LAVEILLE	I005			G004 H039	H063	H108	K051
LAW	C139	H271		P049B P081	P083	S181	T008
LAWRANCE	H218			W032 Y004			
LAWRENCE	A084	C089	D183	LEY	G022	G022	
	0026	0027	W182	LIDEN	S151		
LAWS	B279	G136	H260 S155	LIEBLING	S012		
LAWSON	A036			LIGHTFOOT	C132	H094	T001
LAYCOCK	R002			LIGON	M062		
LAYCROFT	B153			LILLESON	G032		
LAYNE	L057			LILLY	E034	H072	J015

Surname	Bibles		
LIN	M123		
LINDELL	M036		
LINDSAY	B050	B050	B143
D012 H127	L085	P030	P031
T056			
LINDSTROM	W143		
LINE	F044	H290	J016
LINEBURG	H289		
LINGERFELT	B089		
LINGMAN	S066		
LINKENHOKER	L057		
LINN	S152		
LINNA	L059		
LINSTED	C157		
LINTHICUM	B276	D114	
LINTON	M053		
LIPPOLD	B282		
LIPPY	B321		
LIPSCOMB	H170	M053	
LIRNER	E070		
LIRT	W185		
LISK	M140		
LISTER	M157		
LITCHFIELD	T073		
LITTIG	B151	B185	
LITTLE	F031	F085	G004
	G099	H306	J002
LITTLEFORD	B162		
LITTON	L009		
LIVESAY	B333		
LIWES	A023		
LLEWELLYN	M039		
LLOYD	C078	C103	D085
H010 H203	H245	H275	H276
H277 S039	W089	W170	W171
LOCKARD	A071	H176	K037
LOCKHART	J056		
LOCOM	B227		
LOGAN	B349		
LOGSDON	B288		
LOGUE	H299		
LOKEY	C052		
LOMAX	L025		
LOND	B123		
LONEY	Y004		
LONG	B096	B125	B217
C046 H216	L061	R064	S115
W158			
LONGBREY	H282		
LONTOR	B061		
LOOCKERMAN	C230		
LOOKERMAN	B031	B032	
LOOMIS	H184		
LOTZ	J053		

Surname	Bibles		
LOUD	M158		
LOUDENSLAGER	H216		
LOUGH	L071		
LOUNSBERRY	D143		
LOVE	K064		
LOWDENSLAGER	H155		
LOWE	B004	E049	B231
	D175	J015	
LOWES	G093		
LOWMAN	F044		
LOWNDES	A045	L067	
LOWRY	C020	G130	R039
LOYD	B147		
LUCKEY	R045		
LUCUS	B006	E065	
LUCY	B333	N003	
LUFFBOROUGH	T076		
LUKENS	C104	C105	C165
LUMMER	D122		
LUNETTE	L092		
LUPTON	W191		
LURTZ	R039		
LUSBY	H091	J059	W172
LUSTER	B037		
LYETH	E032		
LYLES	F079	H019	
LYLTE	L084		
LYMAN	B030	W192	
LYNCH	G084	H206	H218
J052 J054	L029	L031	M037
M037 T015	T019		
LYNE	A074		
LYNN	D124	D125	R084
	T008		
LYON	J015	M045	
LYONS	C089	D134	G050
LYSINGER	P035		
LYTLE	L092		
MABEN	H216		
MAC	S159		
MACARTNEY	C158		
MACCUBBIN	H019		
MACE	B132		
MacGILL	G119		
MACHETT	V014		
MACHUHN	F071	F072	
MACK	S015		
MACKALL	L029		
MACKENHEIMER	B035		
MACKENZIE	C231		
MACKEY	B160	C140	D129
	H026	J057	T054
MACKUBIN	B302		

Surname		Bibles			Surname		Bibles		
MacLEAN		W086			MARSH		C059	F053	G114
MACOMBER		W143					H093		
MACTIER		J022			MARSHALL		B111	B187	C084
MACY		S134				C125	C160	C225	F070	G126
MADDOCKS		S112				G138	G139	H306	K056	L018
MADDUX		M127				L052	P037	P040	T010	W031
MADEN		D108			MARTEN		A013	B362	C142
MAFEN		P036					G117		
MAGILL		G120			MARTIN		B030	B108	B147
MAGNESS		W086				B192	C069	D054	G007	H051
MAGRUDER		B091	B216	B264		L020	M088	P085	S099	S141
C063	C140	M033	O002	S019		S158	U006	W053	W109
S158	V016	W149	Y003		MARTINDELL		B158		
MAGUIRE		C138			MARVEL		J013		
MAHAN		B343	S063		MARVIN		E010		
MAHON		B065			MASLIN		D111		
MAHONE		G031			MASON		A005	B148	C093
MAINES		G108				C195	D011	D181	E073	F076
MAISEL		Z001				G084	G126	H263	K056	R048
MAJOR		L081			MASSEY		G050	H247	H247
MAJORS		B231			MASSY		H020		
MAKAN		W143			MATHER		W019		
MALONE		B284	M061		MATHEWS		J035	P068	
MALONEY		M121			MATHIAS		W032		
MALTUS		S173			MATHIESON		B333		
MANGUM		S013			MATTHEWS		H107	J004	J036
MANIFOLD		W159	W159A				P074	S050	W086
MANN		F047	L029	L092	MATTINGLY		H173		
		L092	M062		MATTON		C223		
MANNER		G132			MAULDEN		F049		
MANNING		D101	H112A	J033	MAUPIN		W040		
		Y003			MAUSE		H297	H298	
MANSEN		D181			MAXWELL		H189	M089	W018
MANSFIELD		B294			MAY		F044	R059	W134
MAPES		G004			MAYDWELL		G027		
MAPHIS		N025			MAYER		H120		
MAR		K052			MAYHEW		B272	E009	
MARBURY		B340	C210	G033	MAYHUE		W169		
		W048			MAYLER		E009		
MARCELLUS		H032			MAYNARD		G002	J037	P058
MARCOW		S085					S029	W113	
MARINER		B096			MAYS		E055	G096	
MARKS		G126	H107		MAYSE		D021		
MARLE		W156			McALLISTER		L061		
MARLOW		S158			McATEE		A023	A024	A025
MARQUETTE		E038			McCABE		B355		
MARR		M175	W083		McCAIN		R057		
MARRAST		J017			McCANN		B219		
MARRETEN		G115			McCARTY		M144		
MARRINER		P008			McCARY		G011		
MARRIOT		G102			McCAULEY		C076		
MARROLDT		G050			McCAUSLAND		A085		
MARROW		G077			McCENEY		B216		
MARRY		D040			McCLAIN		W180		

Surname	Bibles			Surname	Bibles		
McCLAUD	T072			McINTURFF	G062		
McCLEAN	B056			McINTYRE	S100		
McCLELLEN	G136			McJILTON	B036		
McCLEMMING	W154			McKAIN	Ro54		
McCLOONEY	S039			McKAY	B224		
McCLUNG	H108	M172		McKECHNIE	G115		
McCLURE	C162	U008		McKEE	B007	R064	
McCOLLISTER	H247	O001		McKEEL	D101	P021	
McCOMES	R094			McKELVEY	S153		
McCONKEY	W118			McKENLEY	A028		
McCONNIER	C014			McKENZIE	L025	R057	
McCORD	C065	J004		McKOWN	H300		
McCORMICK	A042			McLANE	B147		
McCORILL	H148	H148		McLAUGHLEN	F036		
McCOTTER	W198			McLAUGHLIN	H250	L027	R002
McCOWAN	S171			McLELLEN	C045		
McCOY	B227	J036	M080	McLIN	D095		
McCUBBIN	P072	R034		McLINTOCH	D158		
McCULLOH	F026			McMANUS	W113		
McCULLOUGH	K064			McMASTER	H190		
McCURLEY	L062			McMILLAN	S171	S172	
McDANIEL	B021	H170	S114	McMILLIN	S063		
	T079			McMULLIN	K043		
McDANIELS	C167	D025	R082	McNAB	C142		
McDONALD	H115	L012	L014	McNAIR	L067		
McDONOUGH	B089			McNAMEE	D099		
McDORMAN	D020			McNEAL	S005		
McDOW	B300			McNEIL	W117		
McDOWELL	M084			McNEY	C002		
McELDERY	H239			McNISH	D057		
McELFRESH	D114			McNULTY	B097	D064	
McEWEN	C014			McNUTT	B190		
McFADDEN	T035			McPHERSON	W192		
McFADON	W135			McSHERRY	K056		
McFATHON	W169			McVEIGH	B027		
McFEELEY	W130			McVEY	C001	M060	
McGARRY	D167			MEALY	S015		
McGEE	B075	B353		MEARNS	F049	R029	
McGHEE	D053			MEARS	G126		
McGINNES	B226			MECHEM	H053		
McGLATHERY	S181			MEDFORD	A053	A054	D038
McGOWEN	R057				L020		
McGRATH	B284	H124		MEDLEY	D146		
McGRAW	B074	W015		MEDLIN	T081		
McGREEVY	P017			MEEDS	H220		
McGREGOR	F006			MEEK	A045		
McGREW	P019			MEEKENS	C199	H002	
McGUFFIN	B037			MEEKINS	H008	H127	L056
McGUIRE	C015			MEEKS	C016		
McHARRY	M070			MEGEE	B229		
McHENRY	G098	H266	H267	MEGREDY	W152		
	S047			MEHRING	D076	P054	
McILVAIN	G006	S022		MEIER	M182		
McILVANE	L059			MELCHOIR	E028		

Surname	Bibles		
MELVIN	H092	H149	
MENAFEE	M081		
MENDENHALL	B117	C125	R029
MENEFEE	C142		
MERCER	B298	G117	K054
MERCERONI	H222		
MEREDITH	J054	W019	
MERIWEATHER	G120		
MERKUS	D064		
MERRICK	C142		
MERRIFIELD	N024		
MERRIKEN	W184		
MERRILL	D085	M092	S016
MERRITT	C096	G089	G089
	S055	W111	
MERRIWEATHER	D119	G119	H218
MERRIWETHER	B351	S164	
MERSON	B235		
MERYDITH	H170		
MESSICK	M015	W089	
METCALF	B045		
METCALFE	P034		
MEYERS	B348	P065	
MEYRICK	L017		
MICHAEL	B174	H059	J026
	M065	M135	
MICHEL	B224		
MICHENER	T075		
MICHURN	R029		
MICKEL	W014		
MICKLE	B038		
MIDDLEKAUF	S141		
MIDDLETON	S110		
MILBOURN	B008	B010	
MILBOURNE	A013		
MILES	H127	H173	H281
J015 K008	L018	S183	T031
MILLARD	S161		
MILLENS	D138		
MILLER	A030	A051	A070
B028 B041	B061	B099	B107
B333 C031	C046	D094	E030
G020 G100	H087	H260	H290
H310 J062	L062	M003	M044
M054 M181	P018	P035	R038
S017 S074	S085	S121	S125
W025 W032	W169		
MILLIGAN	H283		
MILLINGTON	M021		
MILLS	B019	B263	G008
	H194	I008	N035
MILNER	K045		
MILSOS	D100		
MILTON	K020	M061	

Surname	Bibles		
MINEAR	M063		
MINK	O011		
MINKER	H299		
MINNER	M129		
MINNERT	H102		
MINNICK	H216		
MISTER	B244		
MITCHELL	B030	B051	B051
B219 B344	B355	C014	E030
E073 F074	F075	F088	G047
H064 H081	H131	H283	H293
H085 M022	M065	M115	S118
S169 W192			
MITTEN	U003		
MOCK	C074		
MOFFETT	D104	S058	
MOFFOTT	F047		
MOHLERS	M045		
MOLER	A047	D167	
MOLL	H261		
MONAGHAN	M172		
MONETT	S024		
MONEY	R054		
MONKS	Y004		
MONROE	B019	B217	D114
	J060		
MONTGOMERY	P073	W145	
MOODY	W188		
MOONEY	T029		
MOORE	A059	A060	B140
B217 B352	C024	C160	C163
D072 G009	H068	H228	H233
K052 L057	M051	P084	R033
S008 S162	T006	T031	T032
T043			
MORAN	M136		
MOREHEAD	G018		
MOREHOUSE	M162		
MORGAN	B344	B355	C005
H275 H276	R068	S001	S015
S079			
MORGENSTERN	H261		
MORNINGSTAR	H261		
MORRELL	W117		
MORRIS	B028	B108	B217
B237 B245	C017	C042	C109
C231 F069	G035	G086	G116
G136 H051	H275	H276	J034
M036 N006	N035	T010	W006
W150 W151	W191		
MORRISON	A038	B329	B330
D025 K060	L039	W015	
MORROW	B320	D011	P036
	R020		

Surname	Bibles					Surname	Bibles		
MORSBERGER	T015					MYRES	B121		
MORSE	C195	M172	W006			MYRESS	G009		
MORSELL	D166					MYRICH	J054		
MORTON	B326	D111	J015						
MOSER	Y008					NABB	J025		
MOSHER	C215					NACE	U001		
MOSS	M061					NACH	W039		
MOTTER	M178	M180				NAGLE	B165	C115	
MOTZ	V016					NAGY	G139		
MOULTON	S008	S162				NAIL	M088		
MOWELS	M050	M051				NAILL	B013		
MULDOON	T040					NALL	S173		
MULLAGAN	N024A					NALLS	D099		
MULLAN	W145					NANCE	W127		
MULLER	O014					NAVE	B212		
MULLICAN	H066					NAYLOR	B121	C156	H063
MULLIKEN	D077					NEADELS	W109		
MULLIN	H301					NEAL	E017	G026	K051
MULLINS	R048						V014		
MUMFORD	D004	D005	E030			NEALE	M045		
	T015					NEALSON	M174		
MUMMA	C088	R081				NEELY	C074		
MUMMAUGH	B287					NEFF	D095		
MUMMONERT	J007					NEIDHARDT	H054		
MUNCH	G062					NEILL	C020	F089	
MUNDELL	K010					NEILSON	B228	C144	W135
MUNK	T056					NEIRNS	C174		
MUNROE	W073					NEIRTT	C189		
MUNSON	L012	L014				NELSON	A029	B052	B283
MURDEN	A074						C022	G007	G081	H196	H197
MURDLE	P036						M126	S050	
MURDOCH	S076					NESSLE	M070		
MURDOCK	A017	A018	D072			NETH	M052	M095	
	H271	L078	W086			NEUSEL	M090		
MURDOUGH	F072					NEUSSINGER	W090		
MURIELL	B320					NEVIT	C073		
MURPHY	B239	B302	B344			NEVITT	H094		
D009	G100	H180	M111	M133		NEWBERRY	H270		
P083	W032					NEWBOLD	B340	B341	
MURRAY	C142	F072	G046			NEWCOMBE	D108		
	H164	L067	M174			NEWCOMER	E035	H290	
MURRELL	B170	D103	N018			NEWCOMMER	D171		
MURTS	H258					NEWELL	C186	H036	
MUSE	F027	S175				NEWLEET	W105		
MUSGRAVE	B258	B257B	G018			NEWMAN	C096	G098	H010
MUSSELMAN	E039						J022		
MYER	T030	W037				NEWNAM	F010		
MYERLY	H225					NEWSON	A074		
MYERS	A073	B152	B236			NEWTON	B237	W183	
B321	C128	C161	D079	D099		NICHOLAS	B137		
D136	E046	G108	H189	H193		NICHOLS	B235	G135	H129
H263	H287	H299	K058	L020			J047	L062	W111
L078	N027	R039	R049	S181		NICHOLSON	D048	F036	H181
W050	W086	W172					H245	L092	S164

SURNAMES

Surname	Bibles			Surname	Bibles		
NICODEMUS	B013	E042	L078	OGIER	B033		
NICOL	G006			OGLE	C210	G143	T085
NICOLS	H245			OGLIVIE	C014		
NIGHTENGALE	W143			OLD	M150		
NISBIT	B017			OLDHAM	E051		
NISER	H014			OLDNER	D089		
NISWANDER	M181			OLFIELD	W143		
NIXON	M133			OLIPHANT	B108		
NOBLE	D023	D024	G136	OLIVER	C117	E073	T009
	K007				V001		
NOEL	H245	K016	M039	OLSON	S112		
	M055	N022		ONDERDINK	L024		
NOEY	T017			ONDERDONK	H110		
NOGGLE	C116			ONION	F048		
NOLL	G094			ONRON	G037		
NORMAN	B142	R012	R039	OREM	B068	F074	
NORMEN	C221			ORME	B242		
NORRIS	B236	E044	E047	ORR	B160	C103	M004
	G048	J023	W051		M005	R007	
NORTH	F075	H250	W109	ORREL	A053		
NORTHAM	H310			ORRELL	D077	H061	
NORTHAMER	H163			ORRICK	H021		
NORTHERN	P015			ORT	E064		
NORTON	P038	W143		ORVALE	P039		
NORWOOD	M144			ORWIG	M099		
NOTE	K025			OSBORN	B048	C076	E026
NOTTINGHAM	C103			G103 M070	M111	M112	M116
NOULD	H181			M152 S157			
NOVAK	H286			OSBORNE	H056	M135	
NOVINGTON	B337			OSCER	P039		
NOWLAND	L031			OSGOOD	A004		
NOYES	B255			OSLER	B014		
NROHAUN	N008			OTIS	L023		
NULL	H216			OTTO	L020		
NUNN	G135			OULD	H168		
NUSBAUM	D082			OURSLER	C065	C066	
NUSBAUM	E043	G108		OUSELEY	G014		
NUTWELL	G016			OVERHOLSSERN	S165		
				OVERHOLTZER	B175		
O'BREIN	M055			OVERTHUM	N019		
O'BRYON	S036			OVERTON	H134		
O'DONNELL	J015			OWEN	B300	D063	R057
O'LAUGHLIN	B335	G115	K024	OWENS	B004	B345	C030
OAKLEY	E003			C143 D078	D108	D134	H118
OAS	S039			L062 L065	T065		
OATIS	S152			OWINGS	B178	C120	D117
OBER	G120	G122		D160 G120	H076	H221	J017
OBERHOLZER	B176			OYSTER	O012		
OBERKANDER	B116						
OBERWEISER	C210			PACE	R043		
OCHELTREE	E015			PADDOCK	C125		
ODELL	H312			PADGETT	M061	M090	
OFFUTT	B299	B300	H076	PAGE	B350	F009	H185
OGDEN	K020	M143		PAIN	H186	L020	

Surname	Bibles			Surname	Bibles		
PAINE	J020			PEATROSS	S186		
PAIRA	M076			PECHIN	I004		
PALMER	B353	C195	F010	PECK	B247	C142	S052
	H281	P006	T076	PEEBLES	W177		
	W018			PEERCE	H167		
PALTISON	D097			PEGRAM	A040	H218	
PANTIER	S058			PEIFER	F081		
PARADEE	H124			PEIRPONT	E033		
PARADISE	J045			PEMBER	G128		
PARHAM	T049			PENDLETON	B349	H277	L077
PARK	B166	T084			T008	T058	
PARKE	B260			PENLAND	W032		
PARKER	A053	B035	B058	PENN	C155	M050	M051
E030	J059	M101	R082	S015	R071	T008	
S068	S088	S175	T016	PENNEMAN	D177		
PARKINSON	W186			PENNINGTON	E035	H227	P073
PARKS	G064	K013	M098	S107	W086	W163	W170	W171
	M100			PENTICO	H141		
PARLEE	D058			PENTZ	R014		
PARLETT	G009			PEOPLES	F040	J038	
PARMED	J038			PEPPER	A086		
PARNS	N032			PERACE	L005		
PARR	L092			PERDUE	M127	T063	
PARRAN	S114			PEREGOY	M169		
PARRISH	H148			PERINE	B305		
PARROTT	H108	L013	R037	PERKINS	B106	E056	G137
PARRY	H201				H247	J015	
PARSLOW	C210			PERKIPELE	N029		
PARSLY	A046			PERMAR	B074		
PARSONS	C052	H206	M125	PERRIGOR	P004		
	W046			PERRY	D032	D144	F074
PARTRIDGE	B035				G031	S023	W130
PARVIN	A054				W149		
PASCAULT	G057			PERSON	H069		
PASCO	B037			PETERS	B167	F022	M028
PASQUEL	D079			PETERSON	I008	R069	
PASSANO	B151	M030		PETFORD	M133		
PATTERSON	A042	C022	C183	PETLETT	B258		
D064	D112	E016	G011	H245	PETLETTE	B257B		
H250	R053	S095		PETRE	F044		
PATTISON	B195	D101		PETTIBONE	M142		
PATTON	C132	M070		PETTIGREW	P064		
PAUL	G064			PETTY	A020		
PAULDING	T057			PFOUTY	R073		
PAULING	C093			PFOUTZ	R020		
PAULUS	L008			PHELPS	H291	H294	W049
PAVARD	T029			PHILIPE	G084		
PAYNE	C132	D148	H270	PHILIPS	H008		
J038	J045	P040	S021	PHILLIPS	A027	A059	B119
PAYTON	H173			B231	B278	D142	H002	H005
PEABODY	A055	H112A	H161	H006	H029	H049	M025	M039
PEAK	B024	W004		O001	P015	P019	P037	T015
PEARCE	L085	M079		W018			
PEARSON	P042			PHIPPS	E030	G016	

Surname	Bibles			
PICKERSGILL	Y008			
PICKETT	C084	C137	D063	
	F017	F018	W158	
PIERCE	D114	G109	H286	
	M050	S010		
PIERPONT	R036			
PIERSON	H069	J002		
PIKE	C088			
PILCHARD	J045			
PILCHER	B117	M081		
PILES	C002			
PILKEY	L071			
PIMM	0013			
PINKERTON	C231			
PIPER	B162			
PIQUETT	C043			
PITCHENGER	B063			
PITCHER	C231	H280		
PITT	F004			
PITTEMGER	T082			
PITTS	D072	P008		
PLATER	F009			
PLATT	J015			
PLATTE	T077			
PLOWDEN	J015			
PLOWMAN	F061			
PLUMER	L005			
PLUMMER	B040	G123	G124	
	M109			
POHL	B240			
POLK	B047	B244	C139	
	H126	W154		
POLLARD	B147	J052	T008	
POLLITT	B217			
POOL	A071	H225	W029	
POOLE	C099	G126	H129	
	J037			
POOLEY	G125			
POOR	M145			
POPE	S158	T073		
PORTER	B244	C029	C030	
C059 C164	D085	F053	L018	
S064				
PORTERFIELD	T057			
PORTTICK	W142			
POSEY	M080	T045		
POTEET	S119			
POTTENGER	M008			
POTTER	C153	H061		
POTTENGER	M014			
POTTINGER	L003			
POTTS	A042	H019	H071	
POULTNEY	H058			
POWELL	C181	D005	D019	

Surname	Bibles				
POWELL, contd.	D024	D095	E057	E05	
F085	G026	G091	G125	H237	L01
N007	N012	P072	T039	T063	T07
POWELSON	H113				
POWERS	B252	G106			
POWLEY	C201				
POYSER	B061				
PRATHER	N022				
PRATT	E015	H101	L035		
PRESBURY	D053				
PRESCOTT	R043	T086			
PRESTON	A021	A023	A025		
	H288	W099			
PRICE	A073	B006	B011		
B290	B360	C093	C151	C181	
C185	D062	E008	G052	G078	
H087	H095	H199	H308	K047	
N003	P065	S008	S050	S170	
T057	T061				
PRICHETT	A031				
PRIM	G022				
PRIMROSE	D085				
PRINCKARD	L018				
PRITCHARD	B276	H011	R033		
PRITCHETT	A052	M167	R061		
PROCTOR	J015				
PRUETT	R047				
PRUGH	B120	B143			
PRUVIANCE	R055				
PRYOR	P035				
PTENGER	M014				
PUE	D120				
PULLEN	C158	S119			
PUMPHREY	C002	H118			
PURCELL	M162	Y006			
PURDOM	H188				
PURDUE	S085				
PURDUM	H189				
PURDY	T086				
PURNELL	B209				
PURVES	B260				
PURVIANCE	R054				
PUTNAM	R064				
PYLE	H289	S008			
QUARLES	M174				
QUARRIE	S159				
QUIGG	L033				
QUINN	H053				
QUINTON	B096	B279			
QUIRE	B339				
RADECKE	S163				
RAILEY	D159				

Surname	Bibles			Surname	Bibles		
RAINY	E018			REIGLE	L059		
RAISIN	C102			REILLY	F002		
RALEIGH	S019			REINECKER	F028	G046	
RALEY	K058			REINHOLD	S007		
RALSTON	S176			REINS	J048		
RAMAGE	B213			REINSWALD	D076		
RAMES	B028			REISTER	O027		
RAMEY	D048			REITER	L081		
RANDALL	B120	D158	R033	REMINGTON	W137		
RANDLE	A074			REMMELL	K001		
RANDOLPH	B350	P068	T076	REMSBURG	M179		
RANKEN	M090			REMSEN	W032		
RANKIN	K056	S029		REMSEYER	M084		
RANSDELL	CO83	T024		RENCHER	H252		
RANSON	B278			RENDALL	J005		
RASBERRY	C212			RENDER	T064		
RASCOE	R078			RENSHAW	Y009		
RASH	H026			REPP	B013	P039	
RASIN	B106	C194	W018	RESAU	M022		
RATHELL	H231			RESOR	L062		
RATLEDGE	T039	T042		REVELL	B217		
RAUGHLEY	E015			REVEN	G006		
RAVER	L040			REVES	KO36		
RAWHOUSER	P080			REYNOLDS	B279A	D179	M105
RAWLEIGH	S040	S052	S053		S008	S010	S162 S182
RAWLINGS	F079	G078	GO79	REW	T031		
H129 H155	M060	S024	T053	RHETT	K016		
W052				RHINEHART	B247		
RAY	B160	B257A	G104	RHODES	A028	H231	P079
	H171			RHOE	D142		
RAYER	M180			RHULE	M054		
REA	C199			RICARDS	S155		
READ	H266	H267		RICE	S146	S173	T053
REAMER	M177			RICH	H026	H226	P034
REAVER	B247				W129		
REDD	T010	W015		RICHARDS	B057	J035	M004
REDDEN	H124	W067			N012	T027	
REDDIN	E073			RICHARDSON	B028	B072	B150
REDDISH	B231			D175 E047	E056	M079	M113
REED	B061	M091	P035	M116 R058	R094	T010	W086
REESE	D025	D056	D056	W177			
	L062	L086	R057	RICHFORD	J048		
REEVE	B064	T081		RICKETTS	B230		
REEVES	B360			RICKNER	M144		
REGESTER	C123	C124		RIDDLE	D053	G075	
REHMEYER	D135			RIDGELY	B006	B035	
REICHE	B151			B133	B259	C182	G027
REICHERT	M105			G119	H057		
REID	B153	D101	H087	RIDGERS	B107		
	M172	T068		RIDGEWAY	A088	K017	
REIDENBACH	F010			RIDGLEY	H266	H267	
REIFSNIDER	T051	H197		RIDLEY	J048		
REIGHARDT	E030			RIGDON	F057		
REIGHLER	U003			RIGGIN	B029	L018	

Surname	Bibles				Surname	Bibles			
RIGGINS	G064				ROLKEY	M022			
RIGGS	B274	D014	G119		ROLLINS	B105	M061		
	K016	M011			RONEY	M061	S026		
RIGIN	G086				ROOP	D082	E044	P039	R020
RIGNEY	B052				ROOTES	T044			
RIGS	K033				RORER	H106			
RILENGER	M091				ROSE	F060	H221	J004	
RILEY	B269	C228	G104			W115			
	H273				ROSEBERRY	C090			
RINE	B086				ROSS	B160	B300	C153	
RINEDOLLAR	L010					D027	L039		
RINEHART	A073	K056			ROSSE	C140	D146		
RINGGOLD	B035	H009	S170		ROSZELL	D186			
RISTEAU	R045	W166			ROTH	A065			
RITCHIE	H036				ROTHROCK	D110			
RITTENHOUSE	N012				ROUT	G113			
RITTER	K037				ROUTYON	H248			
RIXDELL	A038				ROUTZAHN	C046			
ROACH	M052				ROUZER	B355	E046		
ROBART	W006				ROWAN	M062			
ROBBINS	A058	J038			ROWBLE	H256			
ROBERTS	B134	B355	D072		ROWE	A031			
D073	D160	J048	L076	L089	ROWELL	D158			
M015	R064				ROWINS	M106			
ROBERTSON	A039	A074	B003		ROWLAND	F044			
B004	B031	B032	D034	D072	ROWLES	D007			
K026	L041	M119	W157		ROY	S021			
ROBEY	H090	H091			ROYALTY	T024			
ROBINS	C130	G054	G055		ROYER	E041			
	H133	W032			ROYSTON	G006			
ROBINSON	A033	B042	B043		RUARK	M102			
B061	B124	B195	C040	D001	RUCKMAN	S008	S162		
E073	F048	G040	H030	H058	RUDDELL	B300	W155		
H138	L024	M040	M182	N004	RUDISELL	R049			
O006	O007	P037	R078	U006	RUDY	W092			
W185					RUE	A086			
ROBISON	A021	A022	T056		RUEHL	G016			
ROBSON	N009				RUFF	D040			
ROBY	K017				RUFFNER	A003			
ROCHESTER	G051				RUHL	S012			
ROCKWELL	M133				RULE	W066			
RODEWALD	V016				RUMBOLD	H207			
RODGERS	F021	P052			RUSH	C072			
RODRICK	D048				RUSSELL	B181	B209	D181	
ROE	B008	B155				H216	S164		
ROELKE	P052				RUSSUM	A079			
ROGAN	B121	B122			RUTH	G052	H001	M070	
ROGER	S111				RUTLEDGE	H107	H112A	H161	
ROGERS	A074	B307	B309			H257	S010		
D087	D105	F076	H164	H186	RUTMAN	S008			
H281	S152	T049	W111		RUTTER	C193	D014	E038	
ROHDE	S028				RYAN	B086			
ROHNER	B058				RYCHER	S187			
ROHRER	B211								

Surname	Bibles		
SACKETT	G128		
SAFFARENS	P037		
SAGASER	B036		
SAGE	B024	S048	
ST. GERMAIN	R071		
SAKERS	W074	W075	
SALISBURY	H122		
SALTREEE	B153		
SAMES	D154		
SAMPSON	T061	U003	
SANDERS	B282	G027	G104
	H033	J015	M105
SANDFORD	M063		
SANDLEN	D019		
SANDS	F005	H010	
SANFORD	H153	R004	S147
SANGER	Y006		
SANGSTON	G143		
SANNER	F024		
SAPPINGTON	S019	S111	W150
SARGENS	M124		
SARGENT	G122		
SATTERFIELD	C016	H053	
SAULSBERY	D077		
SAUNDERS	C008	N036	N037
SAUNER	R022		
SAVAGE	A032	D085	D153
	F030	P007	
SAVIN	H053		
SAWYER	M133		
SAYLES	L092		
SAYLOR	H225	K061	L020
SCANLAND	W131		
SCARBOROUGH	B042	B043	D040
D041 D047	L031	M004	M005
S116 S162	T034	T035	W014
W143 W163			
SCARFF	G142		
SCHAADT	B219		
SCHAFFER	F079	S066	
SCHALL	E021	E022	
SCHEIHING	S041		
SCHERT	S173		
SCHEILD	C089		
SCHILDT	P039		
SCHIPPER	B169		
SCHLERCH	H134		
SCHLERF	M038		
SCHLEY	G059		
SCHLIER	B002		
SCHLOER	S008		
SCHMIDT	W086		
SCHNAUFFER	D084A		
SCHNEBLEY	M163		

Surname	Bibles		
SCHOENLEBER	C215		
SCHOOLEY	H090	H091	
SCHREINER	S163		
SCHROYER	D065		
SCHULTZ	Z005		
SCHUTT	W018		
SCHWARTZ	H142		
SCHWERGART	S111		
SCOLEY	A069		
SCOTT	B134	B185	B271
C128 E025	G143	H216	H268
L031 M070	P037	P078	S116
SCRIMGER	P001		
SCRIVENOR	H296		
SCULL	W177		
SEABREASE	B231		
SEARS	A097		
SEAWARD	S025		
SEBACK	B116		
SEDGEWICK	J022		
SEDURCH	S114		
SEDWICK	H118	I008	L025
SEEKAMP	W145		
SEIBERS	W143		
SEIBERT	N014		
SEIBOLD	H216		
SEIDEL	M108		
SEIDENSTRICKER	A069		
SEIP	B057		
SELBY	T056	T063	
SELDEN	J052		
SELIMAN	G049	M052	
SELMON	R048		
SEMMES	G134		
SENSENEY	E044	H179	
SENTMAN	A069		
SEPNCER	H240		
SERFOS	R075		
SESSA	G104		
SETTLE	D181		
SEWALL	K027		
SEWARD	F075	H227	
SEWELL	H286	M058	P073
	S114	T061	W086
SEYMER	S041		
SEYMOUR	G115	W074	W075
SHACKLEFORD	B351		
SHAFER	M163		
SHAFFER	L081	S012	
SHAGGS	W107		
SHAMBERGER	W091		
SHAMER	A071		
SHANABARGER	C046		
SHANBERGER	C173		

SURNAMES

Surname	Bibles			Surname	Bibles		
SHANK	D115			SHUNICK	E042		
SHANKS	B276			SHUNK	G107		
SHANNON	B309	M108		SHUTE	D103		
SHARGREEN	R022			SIBLEY	G094		
SHARP	F089	M028	M133	SIDAWAY	B257		
	S053			SIEGLER	A070		
SHARROCK	B061			SILL	H301		
SHAVER	E010			SILVAS	B089		
SHAW	B151	D014	H002	SIMMONDS	M102		
	H008	H148	N002	SIMMONS	A053	D099	H105
SHAWN	B030				H129		
SHAY	B230			SIMMS	J015		
SHECKELL	K049	L001		SIMON	C168		
SHEHIE	H003			SIMPERS	J057	L031	U005
SHEILD	C089				W120	W123	
SHELBURNE	H106	H108		SIMPSON	B250	C113	C138
SHELDON	B026				S183		
SHELLER	S120			SIMS	W143		
SHELLY	P053			SINCLAIR	M128	T077	
SHELTON	M136			SINCLARE	F068		
SHEPARD	T010			SINCLEAR	K020		
SHEPHEARD	B024			SINN	K012		
SHEPHERD	S047	T010	W136	SINYARD	F070		
SHEPPARD	S098			SIONS	M145		
SHERER	S187			SKATT	B252		
SHERIDAN	B189			SKIDMORE	B315		
SHERLOCK	G041			SKILES	B107	B108	
SHERMAN	B257	D054		SKINNER	B147	H252	R037
SHERRICK	N015				S040		
SHERRILL	S164			SLACH	M145		
SHERTSER	B140			SLACK	V002		
SHERWOOD	A086			SLADE	G044	M079	
SHIELD	J039			SLAGLE	B185	R075	
SHIELDS	K015	R002	R011	SLARLUCK	C125		
	W122			SLASMAN	F047		
SHIN	B260			SLASS	M092		
SHINGLEDECKER	B175	B176		SLATER	E003	M157	
SHIPLEY	B166	G039	H225	SLAUGHTER	B134	B248	C136
	W092			SLEE	W156		
SHIPPEY	C201			SLEETH	C186		
SHIRK	B166			SLICER	M066		
SHOCKEY	S063			SLINGLUFF	A082	L020	
SHOEMAKER	H299	K062		SLINGLUFT	J037		
SHOPE	R043			SLINKMAN	B283		
SHORT	B137	E028		SLOCUM	D068	L056	
SHREFF	M154			SLOTHOVER	P039		
SHREVE	G003			SLOVIS	S179		
SHREVES	A035			SLUBEY	H174		
SHRINER	B176	G108	L028	SLURMAN	M174		
	L085	L086		SLUSER	K062		
SHRUM	L001			SLUYTER	S001		
SHUEY	D081			SMALL	B160		
SHUGARS	L008			SMARR	D019		
SHUMWAY	M125			SMEDBURG	B259		

Surname	Bibles				
SMICK	L059				
SMICKLE	L059				
SMICKLEY	L059				
SMILEY	P037				
SMITH	A017	A036	A059		
	A064	A076	B001	B013	B033
	B092	B216	B217	B219	B263
	B304	C195	C210	C083	D001
	D114	D144	D180	E045	F032
	G004	G006	G016	G035	G041
	G074	G092	G098	H039	H043
	H098	H106	H118	H144	H281
	H287	J004	J030	J036	K026
	K030	K063	M014	M030	M039
	M043	M053	M150	N017	O010
	P020	P034	P035	P039	P040
	R041	R048	S010	S059	S083
	S085	S091	S152	S181	T030
	T031	T057	W018	W048	W053
	W118	Y009			
SMITHSON	C173	F057	W060		
SMOOT	D141	H004	M028		
	T084	T085			
SMULLING	L017				
SMYTH	N026				
SNADER	B013	D081	E043		
SNAVELY	F044				
SNEDEN	G078				
SNEED	B135				
SNELLING	M142				
SNIDER	B133				
SNIVELY	B145				
SNODGRASS	S008				
SNOOK	D076				
SNOWDEN	E025	H024	H092		
	W035				
SNYDER	B033	L071	M089		
	W180				
SOFSR	P039				
SOLLARS	H222				
SOLLERS	G063				
SOLLERZ	O026				
SOMERS	L041				
SOMERVELL	D166	G093			
SOMERVILLE	W192				
SOMMERVILLE	B166				
SORBOUGH	W086				
SOUDER	S043				
SOUDERS	K058				
SOUTH	M130	W076			
SPAIHT	K023				
SPALDING	J015	L043			
SPARHAWK	Z001				
SPARK	D089				

Surname	Bibles					
SPARKS	B297	G096	N017			
SPATH	M038					
SPAULDEN	F019					
SPAULDING	H173					
SPEAR	C059	R034	S094			
SPEDDEN	A059	C160	R069			
SPEDDIN	B119					
SPENCE	B209	B245	D030			
	H121	H133	K064	L031		
SPENCER	B245	D099	E057			
	H053	P085	W111	W145		
SPERRY	P004					
SPICER	D045	D046				
SPICKNALL	H085					
SPIED	H102					
SPIELMAN	H012					
SPILLMAN	P039					
SPIVEY	C181					
SPRAGENS	T030	W037				
SPRY	B219					
SPURRIER	A030	B086	M122			
SQUIRES	M080					
STACKS	S162					
STAFFORD	N006					
STAGG	B217	M092				
STALEY	S075	W136				
STALLING	M091					
STALLINGS	S019					
STANDEFORD	J020					
STANDIFORD	A023	A024	A025			
	S131					
STANFORD	A079	H227				
STANLEY	T044	T046	U003			
STANSBURY	A082	B307	B310	G038		
		G084	G089	G119	J037	M166
STANSFIELD	M175					
STANTON	A050					
STAPLES	W015					
STARKEY	B011					
STARMER	H193					
STARNER	C169					
STARNES	F061					
STARNS	B298					
STARR	N009					
START	C056					
STATON	G108					
STAUB	M137					
STAUFER	S120					
STAUFFER	T030					
STAUP	D115					
STAVEN	N022					
STEBBING	B097					
STEEL	L031	W099				
STEELE	A040	D108	H116			

Surname	Bibles			Surname	Bibles		
STEELE, contd.	H277	R042		STRAUFF	S119		
STEEN	B240			STRAUGHN	D118	N032	
STEIGER	C210	W048		STRAYER	J007		
STEINMENTS	A064			STREET	D047	F060	H181
STEPHENS	B181	B186	T021	MO15 M135	P068	S010	
STEPHENSON	M177	T049		STREETT	B355	D040	F011
STEPHESON	S095				H288		
STERLING	E038			STRIBLE	W115		
STERN	D082	M044	W111	STRICKLER	J062		
STERRETT	B097			STRIDER	M146	P052	
STERTT	R094			STRINE	H225		
STEUART	T053			STROBEL	L009		
STEVENS	A054	C014	D084	STROBLE	F068		
	D084A	G007	H032	STRODE	B271		
	L039			STROEHLER	H187		
STEVENSON	C040	G033	G126	STRONG	R038		
H076 H259	H272	K060	M092	STROTHER	A035	W040	
STEWARD	G006			STRUTHOFF	E028		
STEWART	B006	B047	C137	STRYKER	D104		
D111 G027	H221	J019	M033	STUART	C065	H168	
P062 R093	S085			STUBBINS	B121		
STILLINGS	M078			STUBBLEFIELD	D186		
STILLWELL	B087			STUDYBAKER	H142		
STIMPSON	G102			STULL	C170		
STIMSON	D118			STUMP	A061	J055	W135
STINCHCOMB	B226	M121	T019		W171		
STINSON	M063			STURGISH	N011		
STITCHER	H291	H294		SUARDE	P020		
STITELY	S017			SUDLOW	S072		
STOAKES	G115			SULLIVAN	B129		
STOCKETT	B235	D182	H016	SULSER	K041		
STOCKMAN	S015			SUMMER	B213	S141	
STOCKSDALE	U003			SUMMERFORD	D019		
STOCKTON	J019			SUMMERS	B211	B359	C092
STODDART	H019				G136		
STOHLER	W093			SUMMIT	W201		
STOKES	B042	B043	S008	SUMPTER	M053		
STOLL	H053			SUNBRUIN	P039		
STOLTZ	N002			SUNDERLAND	C007	H310	
STONE	B301	B351	D078	SUTER	A004	B216	P014
	H045	H185	H209		P014		
STONEBRAKER	B101			SUTHERLAND	S182		
STONER	D069	H179		SUTTON	H273	H279	P001
STONESIFER	M038			SWACKER	R011		
STONESTREET	T037			SWAINE	H231		
STOOKY	B297			SWAM	B052		
STOOPTS	N017			SWAN	C151	C152	E065
STOREY	W141				H277	K016	
STORK	A084			SWANN	G041		
STORM	S171	W172		SWANSON	S077		
STORY	J053			SWARTZ	B236		
STOVER	D114	K061		SWEENE	D095		
STOWELL	F019			SWEENY	W192		
STRATT	D041			SWEET	H026		

125

Surname	Bibles				Surname	Bibles			
SWENDNER	E011				THOMAS, contd.	M042	M047	M053	O013
SWINTON	D160					P035	R022	S007	S039	S100	T032
SWOOPE	G063					W014	W018	W035	W037	W106	W143
SWOPE	A082					W152	W161	Y002	
SYAER	W111				THOMPSON	A019	A085	A097
						B004	B005	B124	B135	B158
TAGGART	B160					B266	C048	C076	C130	C132
TALBOT	B052	H170				C151	C152	F053	G008	G090
TALBOTT	A051	B041	C153			H056	H059	H162	M020	M043
	H085	W148				M054	M066	P036	P062	P079
TALIAFERRO	E017	G143	T044			R009	R052	S119	S145	W040
TALL	A010	G064				W054	W086	Y009	
TALLMAN	S009				THOMSON	C093	J036
TANEYHILL	L063				THORLEY	B075
TANKARD	H300	S015			THORNTON	A074	C226	C227
TAPP	B096					K027	P068
TARBELL	F019				THOROUGHGOOD	H260
TARBUTTON	B072				THRAP	B359
TARLTON	C020				THRELKELD	T024
TARR	D105	W008			THRUSTON	G143
TARVER	B260				THURMAN	R010
TASKER	A017				TIBBETTS	T040
TAVELL	C042				TICE	N014	W108
TAVENER	S161				TIFFANY	A038
TAYLER	W192				TILDON	C007
TAYLOR	AO84	B057	B187		TILESON	G032
B235	B244	B337	B362	C017	TILGHMAN	F001	S120	W112
C062	D105	D136	D143	F009	TILLARD	H129
G098	G140	H002	H008	H053	TILLINGHAST	M061
H065	H272	J015	J026	K035	TILLOTSON	C164
K047	KO36	L071	M066	M067	TILLOW	P004
M132	M172	P006	R046	S001	TILLSON	M162
S153	T076				TILTON	G119	G120
TEACH	S115				TIMMIUS	R053
TEACKLE	S015	S088			TINDLE	M036
TEANY	S181				TINSDALE	W117
TEEL	C060				TINTENS	M133
TELSON	B302				TIPPY	D179
TENECH	B063				TISCHER	S187
TERRELL	B351				TITTLE	R090
TERRILL	R087				TITTON	F068
TERRY	C153	R057	S106		TOADVINE	B284	C180	H044
	T086					T015
TEVIS	T017				TOBIN	W188
TEW	B096				TODD	H053	J047	M138
THARP	S145					S074	S098
THECKELL	K048				TOLLEY	G142
THIELA	J055				TOMLENSON	B021
THILLIPS	B119				TOMLINSON	C181
THOBURN	W170	W171			TOMPKINS	H010	T010	W192
THOMAS	A053	B035	B036		TONGE	G085
B096	B106	B158	B248	B321	TONGUE	F072
C160	C221	D143	F027	G030	TONHBAUGH	E023
H153	J022	L039	L043	M039	TORRENCE	M084

SURNAMES

Surname	Bibles					Surname	Bibles				
TORREY	T041					TURBUT	G056				
TORSCH	P052					TURFORD	A012	D015			
TOWN	D167					TURNBAUGH	M054				
TOWNSAND	L017					TURNER	B260	C082	C089	D183	
TOWNSEND	C073	D004	D005			HO90	HO91	H160	H173	H277	R064
D035	H009	H279	L056	M044		S059	T009	U003			
M092	P065	T079	W040	W139		TURPIN	B030	D141	V014		
W140							W199				
TOWNSHEND	C156					TURRELL	C125				
TRACEY	A068	G062	H069			TUTTLE	B162				
TRACY	B333	T034				TUXWORTH	W120	W123			
TRADER	B118					TWIFORD	A012				
TRAIL	H129					TWILLEY	D161				
TRANSUE	R075					TYDINGS	C063	J060			
TRAUTMAN	H261					TYLER	B115				
TRAVERS	K007	M101	M102			TYSON	B287	H138	H138		
TRAVERSE	B363					S010	S039				
TREADWELL	R021										
TREFFENBERG	S039					UHLER	F084				
TREGE	S055					UHTER	S127	S128			
TREGOE	W173					UNDERWOOD	C036	C055	P074		
TRENT	S106					UPHOUSE	H251				
TREW	W120	W123				UPPERCO	B140				
TRIMBLE	M097	O003	W177			UPSHUR	C230	D071			
TRIMMER	B321					URQUART	L003				
TRIPPE	G046					USILTON	B355	U005			
TRISLER	D027					UTZ	L046				
TROLINGER	H106										
TROLLINGER	G022					VADEN	M034				
TROTH	H227					VALE	B107				
TROUP	W145					VALIENT	C028				
TROUT	L062					VAN BIBBER	C059	U003			
TROWBRIDGE	B269	H179	L001			VAN BUREN	J055				
TROXELL	D076					VAN CAMP	B359				
TRUCHART	T073					VAN DYKE	C221	E010			
TRUETT	O017					VAN HOOK	F089				
TRUIT	H206					VAN METER	S179				
TRUITT	B345	M036	T015			VAN VALEN	D048				
TRUMP	B056					VAN VALKENBERG	D011				
TRUNDLE	H129					VANCE	F089				
TRUSLOW	E039					VANDERFORD	G006				
TUBMAN	T028					VANDERSTILL	B057				
TUCHER	T001					VANLOUVENEIGH	B338				
TUCK	D182	P078				VANMETER	P079				
TUCKER	B089	C042	C131			VARDEN	C113				
D053	D169	H066	H068			VAWTER	K002				
TUCKERMAN	F032					VEAL	D158				
TULL	H004	H006	H006			VEASEY	B074				
HO77	H272	T032	W102			VENABLE	B326				
TULLEY	N014					VERES	HO98				
TUMLESTON	B107					VERGEN	C006				
TUNANUS	E032					VERMILLION	C143				
TUNSTALL	C133					VERNAY	H196				
TUPPER	N032					VERNON	R034	R034			

127

INVENTORY OF MARYLAND BIBLE RECORDS

Surname	Bibles			
VICKARS	D038			
VICKERS	A015	D015	H004	
	H079	J013		
VICTOR	H044	L033		
VINCENT	M109			
VIVIAN	R064			
VOIGHT	C103			
VOLK	H301			
VOLKERS	S173			
VON FOSSEN	M129			
VON GUNTER	E014			
VOORHIES	C174			
VOSS	S151			
VOTAW	S132	S134		
WADDELL	Z001			
WADDLETON	G082			
WADDY	N036	N037		
WADE	W168			
WAESCHE	S047			
WAFFORD	W018			
WAGEMAN	W094			
WAGNER	C143	N035	S019	
WAINWRIGHT	D021	J040		
WAIT	A042			
WALBERT	H009			
WALES	T021			
WALKER	C070	C138	C187	E046
H166 H240	L065	N008	P001	P035
P037 T008	W080	Y003		
WALKING	R074			
WALKINS	H286			
WALL	E061			
WALLACE	D040	D041	D047	
G064 G068	M147	S029	W159	
W159A				
WALLEN	J058			
WALLER	B270	C052	D085	
	D085	G029	G031	
WALLERS	H067			
WALLICE	C182			
WALLING	D122			
WALLIS	B248	H209	W120	W123
WALLS	H284			
WALMSLEY	H274			
WALRAVEN	N017			
WALSH	G037			
WALTER	K050	M166		
WALTERMEYER	W053			
WALTERS	A028	B360	C135	
	G037	S170	T047	
WALTHAM	G103			
WALTON	B181	H216	P075	
WAMPLER	H151			

Surname	Bibles			
WANKOP	M081			
WANN	H195			
WANTZ	R049			
WAPELS	W140	V013		
WAPLES	J013			
WARD	B147	C058	D134	
H129 H310	L038	L077	M164	
P052 R094	T034	T063		
WARDON	M150			
WARDWELL	G050			
WARE	K058	R082		
WAREHIME	M178	M180		
WAREHIME	A073	L040		
WARFIELD	A045	B331	C123	
C124 C197	D122	G122	H218	
O026 T030				
WARING	H209			
WARNACK	G082			
WARNER	B037	D011	H107	
H112A H188	H189	K059	R069	
S039 T030	W109			
WARREN	D005	H112A	W164	
WARRING	D119			
WARRINGTON	M028			
WART	M025			
WASBORN	W083			
WASDEN	M157			
WASE	S076			
WASHBURN	S182			
WASHINGTON	C119	P068		
WASSER	R075			
WATERFIELD	R002			
WATERMAN	S001			
WATERS	A078	B031	C230	D111
D114 F028	F071	H133	H168	M011
R045 V003	V004	W072		
WATHEM	D168			
WATKINS	B102	B250	G018	
	M161			
WATSON	B132	H127	M158	
	M177	S039		
WATTERS	F058	H205	W086	
WATTS	A074	G067	H148	
H222 J011	M142	U001	W191	
WAY	H228	H229		
WAYLAND	W113			
WAYMAN	H218			
WAYMEN	S029			
WEANT	E024			
WEAVER	H142	S043		
WEBB	B004	B296	C065	
G122 H216	J004	M028	M132	
O010 P038	S008	S053	T027	
T036 T081	W027			

Surname	Bibles					Surname	Bibles				
WEBBER	W086					WHEELOCK	C063				
WEBLEY	B270					WHELAM	M145				
WEBNAM	F062					WHERRETT	T041				
WEBSTER	B137	B150	B151			WHETHERILL	S181				
C140	J001	J056	R034			WHETSON	K047				
WEDMORE	B235					WHETTLE	B240				
WEEAT	D091					WHIBELBY	M055				
WEEDMAN	H010					WHILLDIN	L062				
WEEKLY	B171					WHIPP	A070	R003	R025		
WEEMS	N030	S114				WHIPPLE	F019				
WEIL	H160					WHITAKER	C198				
WEIMER	G115					WHITE	A013	B108	C085	C086	
WEISBECKER	L015					C089	C137	D020	G137	G138	H168
WEITZEL	S039					H169	H216	H228	H233	J008	0003
WELCH	B035	D158	S039	W088		P008	T033	W071	W118	W140	
WELD	E009					WHITEFORD	B355				
WELH	W090					WHITEHALL	C114				
WELK	H146					WHITEHOUSE	H110				
WELLFORD	T001					WHITENECK	M083				
WELLHAM	H118					WHITFIELD	C119				
WELLING	C210					WHITLOCK	S185				
WELLS	B019	B179	B353			WHITMAN	H110				
C029	C104	C105	H212	M055		WHITNEY	F074	T040			
M166	S005	S176				WHITSON	K046				
WELLSLAGER	B156					WHITTINGTON	A031	B186	B217		
WELSCH	R094					B244	G078	G079	H227		
WELSH	E020	H072	L012			WHITTLE	C132				
S173	W090	W112				WICKERT	H218				
WELSTER	S053					WICKES	P003	W088	W151		
WENTZ	K050	R064				WICKLEIN	J047				
WERL	M103					WIDGEON	H118				
WERNENGER	S184					WIFORD	W093				
WERNER	A085	B064				WIGET	C045				
WERTH	C123	C124				WIGG	B059				
WESLEY	H118					WIKERT	E059				
WESSELL	S173					WIKES	W150				
WEST	A019	A074	E047			WILAN	H051				
F006	H002	H008	L028	V001		WILBER	B356				
WESTCOTT	W111					WILBORN	H079				
WESTON	D053	L024	Y004			WILBOURN	H149				
WETHERED	W111					WILBOURNE	G074				
WETHERILL	W163					WILCOX	M136				
WETZLER	R064					WILD	H160				
WHALEY	D005	P057	W161			WILDES	G114				
WHANN	M002					WILEY	C231	E063	H125		
WHARTON	H260	P072				0003	R048	W159	W159A		
WHATLEY	G068					WILFORD	R053				
WHAYLAND	K029					WILHEIM	S010				
WHEAT	U003					WILKES	B252	Z002			
WHEATLEY	E001	E002	E061	H004		WILKINS	C137	D154	G074		
H007	H173	L019	L070	R076	W010	H300	J039	J057	K015	M056	
WHEATON	B323	P052				R037	W121				
WHEELER	B211	F061	H068			WILKINSON	B150	C096	D019		
H095	H227	S016	W046	Y008		D077	G093	H047			

Surname	Bibles		
WILLARD	D084A	E1012	
WILLES	E064		
WILLEY	C017	F069	H026
	H255		
WILLHIDE	H301		
WILLIAM	D087		
WILLIAMS	A039	B004	B059
B129 B147	B248	C006	C146
C181 C182	D134	E065	F004
G117 H118	H227	H281	L077
M034 M053	M143	M151	N025
P006 P008	P042	R052	S009
S020 S183	T053	W172	W192
WILLIAMSON	B142	P066	
WILLIARD	H060		
WILLINGHAM	J048	R048	
WILLIS	A007	A051	A053
B041 B236	D142	H043	H045
H169 H198	H231	H265	L017
L092 M039	S185	T018	
WILLISON	T084		
WILLISS	H094		
WILLOUGHBY	J008		
WILLS	T037		
WILLSON	D032	D033	D171
	H009	H129	M158
WILMA	Z005		
WILMER	B178	F049	S019
WILMOT	G033		
WILSOMON	C035		
WILSON	A015	A023	A025
A097 B150	B355	C004	C074
C099 C158	D012	D040	D047
D061 D066	D077	D134	D177
F019 G063	G130	H002	H008
H045 H125	H196	H295	I005
KO36 M014	M090	M110	M147
M162 R037	R094	S010	S039
S059 S095	S171	W013	W135
W143 W152	W190		
WILTBANK	A088		
WIMBROW	D005		
WIMSATT	S079		
WINANT	L029		
WINCHESTER	E025		
WINDER	H050	H275	H276
	L067	M055	
WINDSOR	B047	E001	H286
	M098	R076	
WINEBERGER	F038		
WINFRED	R001		
WINGATE	C160		
WINGERT	E035		
WINGFIELD	B351	P078	R083

Surname	Bibles			
WINKLER	H081			
WINN	C028			
WINSTON	B062	C132	E017	T010
WINTER	D173			
WINTERODE	G067			
WISE	B004	G098	H252	
	M067	N036	N037	
WISSMAN	H025			
WISTER	E064			
WITBECK	B024			
WITHEROW	K056			
WITHERS	M145			
WITT	S152			
WITTS	C099			
WOLCOTT	H186			
WOLF	B285	H146	H236	
WOLFE	B355	L061		
WOLFENSBARGER	S120			
WOLFONBARGER	A042			
WOLLFORD	A079			
WOLSON	A021			
WOLTZ	W017	W058		
WOOD	A065	B071	B088	
B278 G047	G082	H085	H309	
K064 L062	P085	R055	S063	
S069 T038	W027	W097	W109	
WOODELL	J011			
WOODLAND	B252			
WOODS	C143	D108		
WOODWARD	A045	A047	A048	B030
F004 H094	H118	S185	Y010	
WOODYEAR	H271			
WOOLFORD	Y008			
WOOLLEY	F010			
WOOLSEY	B158	H038		
WOOLTON	P006			
WOOLVERTON	D085			
WOOTEN	D032	D033	S178	
WORDEN	E032			
WORKMAN	H142			
WORMLEY	P035			
WORRELL	B353			
WORTHINGTON	A082	B178	B211	C120
C155 D008	D119	G002	G059	G063
G117 H180	H218	H220		
WOSTER	B089			
WRAY	E073			
WREN	M034			
WRIGHT	A054	B260	B297	
C004 D090	D118	E012	E046	
F049 H004	H008	H207	H228	
H230 H233	H286	M063	M113	
M116 N007	T084	T085	V014	
W176 W181				

Surname		Bibles		
WRIGHTSON		A086	D025	H049
		H286		
WROTH		N026	P003	
WRUGHT		H041		
WYATT		B355	C134	M070
		R057	S152	S185
WYCHE		D061		
WYMAN		C045	H112A	
WYNKOOP		K045		
YARLEY		A021	A022	
YASTE		D179		
YATES		B040	B323	D009
		E003	G097	W113
YEADHALL		H118		
YEAGERLINE		Z003		
YEANEY		H283		
YEATES		L024		
YELLOTT		H198		
YERBURY		G057		
YETTER		K058		
YEWELL		C102	W050	
YINGLING		B092	B321	H053
YOCUM		G130		
YONGE		M061		
YOUNG		A070	B260	B271
F067	F085	G135	H067	H164
H209	H286	I005	L063	M070
P034	S110	T041	T075	W145
YOUNGER		B353		
YOUNT		C183		
YOUTZEY		M103		
ZARBAUGH		H162		
ZEALER		B227		
ZEIGLER		G104		
ZELLER		A065		
ZELLINGER		H157		
ZEPP		C128	H169	S054
ZIEGLER		P056		
ZILE		W050		
ZIMMERMAN		B172	E032	F044
F070	G138	G139	H188	O014
P052	S054			
ZIMMERSON		P052		
ZIRKLE		D095	D099